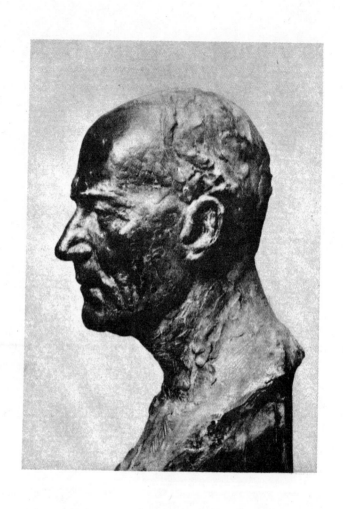

COLLECTED ESSAYS

OF

W. P. KER

EDITED WITH AN INTRODUCTION BY

CHARLES WHIBLEY

IN TWO VOLUMES

VOLUME I

Essay Index Reprint Series

BOOKS FOR LIBRARIES PRESS, INC.

FREEPORT, NEW YORK

First Published 1925
Reprinted 1967

LIBRARY OF CONGRESS CATALOG CARD NUMBER:
67-28736

PRINTED IN THE UNITED STATES OF AMERICA

CUSTODI · ET · COLLEGIO ·
ANIMARUM · OMNIUM · FIDELIUM ·
DEFUNCTORUM · IN · UNIVERSITATE ·
OXONIENSI · AD HONOREM ·
WILLELMI · PATON · KER · ET ·
AD · PROFECTUM · BONARUM ·
ARTIUM · HOC · FLORILEGIUM ·
D.D. · CAROLUS · WHIBLEY.

WILLIAM PATON KER, b. 30th Aug., 1855, son of William Ker, merchant, Glasgow. Educated, Glasgow Academy and University; Balliol, 1874-8. Tutors: Francis de Paravicini and Thomas Hill Green. Snell Exhibitioner, 1st Classical Mods., 1876; 2nd Lit. Hum.; Taylorian Scholar (Italian) and B.A., 1878; Fellow of All Souls, 1879; M.A., 1881. Rowed in the Torpid; won the Morrison Fours, 1875. Devorguilla Soc. Assistant to W. Y. Sellar, Professor of Humanity, Edinburgh, 1879-80; Professor of English Literature and History, University College of South Wales, Cardiff, 1883-9; Examiner in English Literature, Oxford, 1897- and 1900; Professor of English Literature, University College, London, 1889; Professor of Poetry, Oxford. Trustee of the Jowett Memorial Fund. Hon. Fellow of the Icelandic Literary Society; Hon. member of the National Forfatterforening (Denmark) and Scandinavian Society of America. Romanes Lecturer, 1906; Hon. LL.D., Glasgow; Hon. D.Litt., Victoria University; F.B.A.; member of the Oxford Dante Society; member of the Academic Committee of the Royal Society of Literature. Epic and Romance, 1897; The Dark Ages, 1904; Essays on Mediaeval Literature, 1905; Sturla the Historian, 1906; Tennyson (Leslie Stephen Lecture, Cambridge), 1909; The Art of Poetry, 1923, etc. Died climbing at Macagnaga on 17th July, 1923.

CONTENTS OF VOLUME I

CONTENTS

W. P. KER. From a Bust by John Tweed.   *Frontispiece.*

INTRODUCTION

WILLIAM PATON KER belonged to the true race of travelling Scots. At once scholar and wanderer, he was sib to Thomas Dempster, Francis Sinclair, George Buchanan, and the other Scots who fought and taught their way across Europe. For him, as for them, learning was a dangerous enterprise, which might end in victory or defeat. The word " adventure " was always on his tongue or at the point of his pen. " The spirit of adventure," said he, " is the same in Warton as in Scott." It is not among the pedants, but among the *conquistadores*, that he places Ritson, in Lockhart's despite, with Percy, Warton, Tyrwhitt, Scott, Ellis, and Leyden. And when he discoursed on the philosophy of history, he found history's justification, if it needed any, " in the journey to the Western Isles, and in the last voyage of Ulysses. . . . Adventure is the motive." And it was his motive, as it was the motive of Johnson and Ulysses. Nor did the field of his adventure differ from theirs. He took a gay and wide view of his profession. " You have imposed a pleasant duty," said he once upon a time to the members of a learned association. " I do not mean the obligation to make a speech, but the charge that will remain with me when this compulsory sermon is ended : the thought that I have been chosen one of the captains

of a band of adventurers, whose province is the ocean
of stories, the Fortunate Isles of romance, kingdoms
of wonders beyond the farthest part of the voyage of
Argo." In the same spirit he likened himself to
Francis Drake, taking his men to the treasure-house
of the world, and thus he turned to romance that
which for many is darkened by the gloom of drudgery
and fatigue.

His quiet enthusiasm changed every quest to gold.
He was possessed by the true passion of the adventurer
—curiosity. He must always be exploring, finding out
new things, and his voyage was none the less hazardous
because it was shaped among unknown literatures, not
among unknown islands. He never lost the zest of
discovery and of risk. "It would be less difficult," said
he, as professor of poetry in his inaugural lecture, "to
find words for the danger of the task ; this is the
Siege Perilous." Easily he overcame the peril of this
last adventure but one, and he brought back with
him a rich and fortunate spoil.

Thus happily did he interpret the business of his life,
which was to think, to talk, and to write about literature.
And as for the earlier voyagers there were no seas which
in their ships they thought they might not safely pass, so
W. P. Ker acquired, safely also, language after language
until there was scarce a country in Europe which he had
not made his own in speech and understanding. " In
the other arts," said he, speaking of poetry, "there is
nothing like the curse of Babel." That is a truth, " so
obvious that it escapes notice in many panegyrics of
the Muses." And if ever a man were born into the
world to mitigate that curse, to batter the walls of that
tower, it was W. P. Ker. It was, as I have said, part
of his adventure to conquer familiarly the tongues of

others. The journeys which he took in the untiring
quest were many and long.   You heard of him travelling
north and south and east—never west, and you knew
that he was adding always to the vast knowledge which
he won easily and carried lightly. As he travelled
widely, so he read assiduously ; yet he was never
surprised at work, he never gave up to an imagined
necessity of toil the hours which he might dedicate to
talk and to his friends.

Deploring that the light of poetry was broken up
among the various languages, he complained in a
characteristic passage that " you are required to spend
on the tongues the time that might be given to bear-
baiting (as Sir Andrew discovered, ancestor of so many
old gentlemen whose education has been neglected, so
many seekers of culture)." For himself, he never
missed a bear-baiting, and he loved them, or their
equivalents, with a constant heart, and no less because
he was mastering the grammar and dictionary of a
foreign speech.   Somehow or another he acquired what
he wanted as he went along, and he acquired it all with
so fine a precision, so exact a scholarship, that he
easily overcame the barriers set up about us at the first
diffusion of tongues. You cannot read a book or a
lecture of his composing without being struck by the
ease wherewith he illustrates one literature by another.
He will call in Horace, as quoted by Corneille, to
summarise the writings of Sir Walter. He will trace
you a measure through the French psalter of Marot
and Beza to " the time of the gude and godlie ballads "
of the Scot who translated the Psalms, and back again
for a thousand years to the Greek and Latin—and
then astonish you by asserting that the tune of Dr.
Johnson's "Long-expected one-and-twenty" made its

first appearance in the poetry of William of Poitiers, to whom also shall be ascribed the authorship of Burns's favourite stanza.

The natural result of this wide and constant study was a catholicity of mind unequalled in our time. W. P. Ker was like the scholars of old, who took all knowledge for their province. He would put nothing and nobody under the ban. Quiet as he commonly was in statement, the limits set in a certain report compelled him " to draw a line." " I draw the line," said he in his lecture on Ritson, " at the report addressed to the President of the Board of Education on the teaching of English. It is useful as a statement of most things which our Association does not want. It prescribes for our Universities a study of language which must not go too far, and particularly not too far back ; it is suspicious of Anglo-Saxon and Middle English. . . . No hope for Burke and Johnson, Words-worth and Shelley, if students, studying English, are asked to study English ! The poor victim of Sweet's *Reader* is cut off from *Rasselas* and the *Present Discontents*. That is the assumption ; his head is unanointed with oil ; he has no time for more than his masters allow him. His pitiable case resembles that of an older day as rhymed in an Oxford poem :

 ' Say, shall our authors, from Morris to Malory,
 Languish, untaught, on their several shelves ?
 Say, shall, for want of a reader (with salary),
 Students be forced to read Keats for themselves ? '

The law of our Association was not made for pupil-teachers : ' I hate a pupil-teacher,' the noble words of Milton in *Areopagitica*, might be taken for one of our impresses." Never was W. P. Ker, always happy in quotation, more happily inspired than when he came upon the unexpected words in *Areopagitica*, "I hate a pupil-teacher." How much rejoiced was he to find a worthy application for it! Thereon he proceeds to discourse upon Ritson, who was not limited to this period or that, who did not allow anything to be "easier of approach" than another, or too difficult to be crowded out, and who snatched leisure from a solicitor's office to bring forward, as Scott said, "such a work on national antiquities as in other countries has been thought worthy of the labour of Universities and the countenance of princes."

So widely catholic, indeed, were W. P. Ker's mind and erudition that he never fell under the reproach of specialism. To think of him, perhaps, is to think of those dark ages upon which he turned the light of his learning, and proved to be not dark after all. But if we think of him and the dark ages together that is not because he was more intimately at home in them than in other times, but because he alone had the key which unlocked the door of their mysteries. As he had mastered many languages and had wandered in many lands, so few periods of the world's history were strange to him. It is characteristic of him that when he was President of the English Association he chose the eighteenth century to discourse about. He saw clearly that the eighteenth century was coming into favour again, and he delighted at its recovery. He had no more sympathy with the American critic who chattered of "the poor little eighteenth century" than he had with Mark Twain, who once complained that "the South had not yet recovered from the debilitating influence" of Sir Walter Scott. He disliked Matthew Arnold's phrase, "our excellent and indispensable eighteenth century," which he thought expressed a very common nineteenth-century opinion : " We can't do without the eighteenth century, but we don't want to think of it more than we can help." Still more deeply did he dislike Matthew Arnold's description of Dryden and Pope as " classics of our prose," a description which has influenced falsely the judgment of a generation. It is " a double sin in criticism," said W. P. Ker, " because it confuses the kinds in two ways, ignoring their poetry and their prose alike. For, of course, they are classics of our prose when they write prose."

For him the eighteenth century was an age of enlightenment, of enlightenment which was sorely needed. It was an age of criticism also, and it was far more and better than that. In his own words, " it is one of the greatest ages of the world in artistic imagination. It is also the great heroic age of England." He celebrates in his tranquil prose " the wonderful year " of which Chatham was the hero ; the year in which Burns was born and which Burns understood ; the year of Minden and Quebec, which no true Englishman, and no true Scot neither, will ever forget. Nor is this all. With pride in the century he reminds us that when we want music for the death of a king or hero, we get it from *Saul,* and that the lyric, the song for singing, old-fashioned and not antiquated, the song that still lingers in our ears, is Pope's " Where'er you walk, cool gales shall fan the glade."

Architecture, too, he calls to his aid, and tells " literary persons " that they may learn something of the meaning of the eighteenth century from the library of Trinity College, Cambridge, the work of Wren, and the library designed in the tradition of Wren for Wren's own college of All Souls. " They might see there for themselves," says he, " how far different is restraint from restriction and moderation from meanness ; what thrilling life there may be in simple harmonies of spaces. It is not negation or privation to be content with the right lines, to refuse the wrong ornamentation." Restraint, moderation, space—these are the true lessons of the eighteenth century, lessons which none taught with greater clarity than W. P. Ker, even when he wrote about the contrasted qualities of Epic and Romance. From this it follows that he refused to separate classical and romantic in times or places. He detects a classical quality in the lyrics of Germany and Provence ages before Dante and Petrarch, and admitting that romantic or classical may denote " fashions of the reading public or of pedantic criticism," he sees the sole hope of poetry " in new minds free to choose their own way." The fairy way of writing, in Dryden's phrase, Hurd's world of fine fabling, were made possible again " by the birth of two or three infants in the early 'seventies—Wordsworth, Scott, and Coleridge, and a few more a little later—Byron, Shelley, and Keats." And that is all that need be said of romance, except that it is, like happiness, " there where thou art not."

He had a dislike, in general, for catchwords or labels, and there are others yet more easily misleading than classical and romantic. " The spirit of the age," said he, " is a dangerous demon " ; " march of intellect " he hated more profoundly than Peacock himself ; and he points out with a sly irony that Shelley was the first to use the one phrase, Keats the other. Moreover, there was one text to which he was never tired of preaching, that happy was the artist who inherited a strong tradition, who belonged to a school. School and tradition, indeed, those things which alone will save a disaffected world, never found a more zealous champion than he. Nor was he of those who could keep letters and life in water-tight compartments. He was a Tory in politics, as he was a Tory in literature. He preferred to walk firmly in the ancient ways. He knew well that new heavens and new earths were not to be had for the asking. What has been and what was contented him because he had no faith in the illusion of progress, and saw plainly that whatever else marched, intellect did not. Thus he avoided the pitfalls into which the most of critics are pleased to tumble. The difference of opinion about Diderot's *Le Neveu de Rameau* pointed his moral more than once. For W. P. Ker, " the god of the old Comedy had few more glorious triumphs in modern times " ; it was the miracle of Dionysus with a new application. And Lord Morley of Blackburn sees in Diderot's masterpiece no more than " the rotten material which the purifying flame of Jacobinism was soon to consume out of the land with fiery swiftness." Thus may a false view of politics and history darken the understanding of wit and humour.

W. P. Ker, then, did not exclude from his judgment of letters the gathered results of his own experience. He was a patriot, not in Dr. Johnson's sense, but in the true sense. He loved his country with a generous ardour, and since he was incapable of a narrow nationalism, he included England, as well as Scotland, in the Britain of his reverence and his love. If Burns was his compatriot so also was Shakespeare, and when he came to discuss the politics of Burns, he showed plainly that he and the poet of his own land were on the same

side.   Complaining that ever since 1786 Burns has been
taken as "a representative man," speaking for his
nation, or for the rank he belonged to, or for some
reviving spirit of liberty, or for the old traditional
Scottish loyalty, or for these two together, as Jacobin-
Jacobite, he insists that loyalty to the house of Stuart
and the French Revolution did not influence the politics
of Burns.   "The French Revolution," he says, counted
for very little in the poetry of Burns, for the good
reason that in 1786 the French Revolution was not yet
in sight, at any rate from the horizon of Mauchline."
Wisely he confutes Matthew Arnold's argument that
if Gray, like Burns, had been just thirty when the
French Revolution broke out, he would have shown
perhaps productiveness and animation in plenty.
Here is our old friend, "the spirit of the age," asserting
itself in the wrong place.   Burns lived in a time of
expansion, and therefore he was himself expansive!
True, Burns was thirty years of age in 1789, and
understood something of the explosion when the news
reached him.   But, as W. P. Ker pertinently asks,
what had it to do with the Kilmarnock edition of 1786,
or the Edinburgh of 1787?   The truth is that the
politics of Burns in 1786 were not affected by that
which happened some years afterwards, but by what
happened in the year of his birth, by the high political
spirit of 1759, the true year of England's expansion,
when Pitt was adding dominion to dominion, and when
Gray, living in London at the midst of it all, showed
neither productiveness nor animation.

As W. P. Ker says, 1759 was the wonderful year of
Minden and Quebec and Quiberon and of *Hearts of Oak*.
"Burns," he writes, "knew well enough what that
year meant, and his hero is William Pitt, Earl of

Chatham, and also, for the father's sake chiefly, William
Pitt, the son :

> ' An' Will's a true guid fallow's get,
> A name not envy spairges.' "

In other words, Burns's politics were the politics of
W. P. Ker and other patriots. For a time he was a
Pittite, who proved a clear talent for history, and
attended to British history in preference to Scottish,
despite his Jacobite sentiment. So in the same spirit,
a far better spirit than " the spirit of the age," whatever
that intoxicant may be, W. P. Ker insists that Burns's
poetry, " for all its rustic character and language, has
the distinctive mark of aristocratic literature. It is
self-possessed, at ease and sure of itself, classical."
That is to say that it is in all respects the reverse of
Jacobinism. It was the fine flower of a great tradition,
not an untidy weed of new and sudden growth. And
W. P. Ker was well fitted by temper and training to
understand the close accord that exists between poetry
and politics. He did not leave his opinions on the door-
mat when he entered the lecture-room, and he framed
those opinions, as he conducted his life, by the rules of
the past. He hated innovation with a constant hatred.
When the electric light invaded his college, he stayed
its approach outside the door of his rooms. A bath-
room was installed upon his staircase. He never used
it. The tub, appropriate to the place, which had
always been sufficient for his needs, sufficed him still,
and it is impossible to think of him as ever making a
compromise with the noisy ingenuities of modern times.
Of Matthew Arnold's praise of Oxford, he said : " It
is well remembered, and keeps alive an Oxford still
recognisable, in spite of the thin ends of wedges and the

thick of unnecessary suburbs." He looked upon wedges, thin or thick, with a wholesome and a reasonable dread. Yet scholar as he was, he never took refuge in his quiet pursuits from the controversies of the hour. Nothing modern affected him so deeply as did modern politics. He shared the disgrace of what was done by the politicans in the name of the country. Like other righteous men, he felt the shame of our pitiful surrender to the assassins of Ireland. In a letter which he wrote to me, two days before he set out upon his last journey to Italy, he said, " I went to Windsor Castle yesterday. . . . There are the flags of the disbanded Irish regiments, all together, looking very honourable, and each succeeding swarm of tourists is told what they are. I hope they will be remembered." You know at any rate that W. P. Ker would never have forgotten them.

As he disliked rhetoric in others, so he refrained from it himself. His genius was for under-statement and irony. When, in reading a paper to the Royal Philosophical Society of Glasgow, he reminded his fellow-citizens of Saint Kentigern's descent, of Merlin's appearance on the hill beyond the Molendinar burn, of the High Kirk as Osbaldiston saw it, of the crypt on that Sunday, and of the warning of Rob Roy, " it is not all vanity," he said. So in a discourse held in honour of Thomas Warton, he said : " We might be open to some criticism, in these days of University reform, for choosing an idle Fellow, the editor of the *Oxford Sausage*, a lover of ale and tobacco and low company in taverns, to be commemorated in this way as an authority." There is no friend of his who will not, reading these words, hear in them the slow and measured tones of his voice. As he was in writing, so was he in speech—

parsimonious always of words. The deliberate restraint of his style was matched by the periods of silence which marked his talk. It was not the silence of embarrassment, or even of shyness. It meant the enjoyment of what he had said or heard, the cheerful contemplation of what he hoped to say or hear. If it sometimes intimidated those who did not know him well, it was to him a simple harmony of space, not unlike the ample dignified interior of the library of All Souls. And he spoke always to excellent purpose. Who that knew him will ever forget the solemnity with which, when he sat down to dinner, he would say, "We'll begin with a Scots pint." One day a friend, walking with him, espied a bird unknown to him. "What bird is that?" asked the friend. He was told, "A woodcock." "It's not my idea of a woodcock," said the friend. "It's God's idea of a woodcock," replied W. P. Ker. One more example : on the day of the Armistice he sat silent among men who were talking in his club. They said this and that about the war, about the peace, and W. P. Ker said nothing. Then, in a lull, he murmured, "God is not mocked," and went his ways.

He loved all the genialities of life, hospitality, dining with his friends, sitting up and talking late into the night or early into the morning, hard work on road or river. What Leslie Stephen said of Swift is true of him : "He had the characteristic passion of the good and wise for walking." He was at home in London as in Oxford, and most intimately was he at home in All Souls, whose history he reverenced, and whose traditions he guarded with a simple unquestioning loyalty. And though he never fussed about himself, though he did not ask you to take an interest in what he thought or did, you knew all the time that he was there, and that he was a great man. Now that he is gone, you may measure his greatness more easily by the emptiness which he has left behind. Nor will the day ever come, even if the larger world neglect him, when his wisdom is not understood and his sayings are not recalled in the College which he loved.

CHARLES WHIBLEY.

I

THE ELIZABETHAN VOYAGERS

THE English voyages and the glory of Queen Elizabeth are in near relation to the splendours of English poetry in that time, as Mr. Raleigh has fully explained ; and there is a temptation, perhaps, to magnify the literary skill of those ancient mariners, through the association of their exploits with the thoughts and ambitions of Marlowe, Spenser, and Shakespeare. They are very various in their gifts of story-telling, and not all of them are always good. Those that wear best are the plainest ; and these, it will be found, are not peculiarly Elizabethan. Hakluyt did not confine himself to contemporary or to English travellers ; one of the earliest records that he gives is the narrative of the Norwegian captain Ohthere, which he told to his lord King Alfred, and which the King included in his version of the history of Orosius. There is really very little difference in style, apart from differences of vocabulary, between the tale of Ohthere and the simpler kind of ship captain's narrative much later. The man has definite memory and knowledge of what he did, and he tells it in straightforward language, undecorated. Swift, writing as an explorer in the person of Gulliver, uses the very phrase of Ohthere—" On the 17th we came in full view of a great island, or continent, for we knew not whether " ;

the Norwegian rounding the North Cape for the first time describes how the land bent round, or the sea made an inlet into the land, " he knew not whether." Ohthere and Wulfstan, King Alfred's two navigators, are the ancestors of Frobisher, Drake, and Davys—this Elizabethan work, like so much else, had its pattern fixed many hundred years before. The beginnings of sea exploration in the North and West of Europe are, of course, very much older than King Alfred ; and long before Pytheas of Marseilles, even, there were sailors to bring back stories of the Northern coasts and islands and the endless days of summer. But Ohthere's voyage, beyond the desert parts of Norway and Finmark, and round to the White Sea, is one of the earliest attempts at exploration of the modern kind. It is not mere sea roving, it is a beginning of land settlement and of trade which from the first, or nearly from the first, are under the control of a central Government, as Norwegian history declares. And it is reported, not in the form of an adventurous romance or a Viking legend, but in clear, positive, one might say, scientific, terms, with interest of geography as the leading motive. When the Elizabethans take to the same kind of work as Ohthere, they use the same kind of language ; and they are at their best when they keep clear of rhetorical temptations, such as were common in the days of Don Adriano and Osric. One great excellence of these traffics and discoveries is that they bring out a plain sort of Elizabethan prose, which was very much wanted in that showy age as a relief from the more ambitious ornamental kinds, being not too bright or good for the practical business of prose, not striving to compete with poetry. The Renaissance did a great deal of mischief by making people think too much of grammar and the construction of periods. Not all the writers in Hakluyt's collection are free from literary vanity, but the importance and the novelty of their matter seem to prevent any excessive rhetoric ; they cannot afford the time for fancy work. Very often they are rightly and truly eloquent in their choice of words and the rhythm of their cadence ; none more so than Hakluyt himself in his noble preface. But generally speaking, the language of the narratives is simple and matter of fact, doing well the kind of work that was done in earlier times by the medieval chroniclers, and later by the writers of personal memoirs. The Elizabethan narratives are not exceptional. The world is full of good stories, and no nation has a monopoly of the art. Hakluyt's collection is memorable, but there are a thousand such elsewhere scattered up and down the world—chronicles, memoirs, diaries, traditional histories—from the Book of Judges down to the autobiographies of Lord Roberts and Sir Evelyn Wood. Few things, perhaps, are more amazing, when one considers it, or more creditable to the human race, than the fact that the talent for adventure and for tales of adventure should be common everywhere in all nations and languages.

The English, as both Mr. Payne and Mr. Raleigh bring out, were among the last people to take to sea exploring in the sixteenth century. Italians, Spaniards, Portuguese, and French were all before them. And though nowadays the popular history represents Hawkins and Drake as masters of the sea, the Spaniards as clumsy, benighted, and rather pitiable enemies, that is not Hakluyt's view. His devotion to England is unqualified ; but he is not blind to the merits of other people ; he makes the Seville school of navigation a model for the English to follow. The Hakluyt Society

is equally liberal ; and Mr. Beazley, who has translated
for it the Portuguese historian of Guinea, has given in
his *Dawn of Geography* an account of the progress of
discovery in which the English have their proper share
—something very far short of a monopoly.   Mr. Froude
also, strong admirer of Hawkins and Drake as he was,
did something like justice to the Spaniards, not only by
his praise of Oquendo and the other heroes of the Armada,
but by calling attention in England to the remarkable
book of Captain Duro, in which the Spanish documents
of the Armada are collected and printed.   That is the
book which more than any other, more than the Portuguese chroniclers of Africa and of Asia and the Spanish
historians of America, brings out the essential community between the sailors and the sea stories of
different nations, and offers a Spanish counterpart to
much of Hakluyt.   The documents in Duro's *Armada*
are not things prepared by authors for the press ; they
are, many of them, letters giving news at first hand of
adventures which otherwise would have been forgotten
altogether.   Froude gives the substance of one of the
most interesting of them—the adventures of Cuellar in
Ireland, in perils and disgraces of different kinds,
between the Irish and the more malignant " Sassanas"
(which, he records, is the Irish name for Englishmen),
and there is very little indeed to chose, in either point
of style or interest of matter, between this Spanish
memoir and the narratives in Hakluyt of the wanderings
of lost Englishmen on the mainland of America,
unfortunate people cut off from Hawkins's company at
San Juan de Ulloa.

Hawkins, whether he does the writing himself or not,
is always worth reading and remembering.   There are his
orders to his fleet at Ferrol—" Serve God daily ! love

one another ! preserve your victuals ! beware of fire ! and keep good company ! " And so we go down along by Teneriffe to Cape Verde, and find that the people of Cape Verde are of a nature very gentle and loving. We meant to have taken some of them away, but the Minion's men gave them warning. We have better luck with the negroes, Sapies and Samboses, some of them ignorant people who weighed not the danger of harquebusses. They used a marvellous crying in their fight, with leaping and turning their tails, that it was most strange to see and gave us great pleasure to behold them. Hawkins takes account of their religion and has a theory of its origin. " For their belief I can hear of none that they have, but in such as they themselves imagine to see in their dreams ; and so worship the pictures, whereof we saw some like unto devils." It took more than a month in this year of 1564-5 for Hawkins to make up his cargo of Samboses, etc. " The Almighty God (who never suffereth his elect to perish) sent us the 16th February the ordinary breeze, which is the north-west wind." Hawkins had some difficulties in this voyage, finding the Spanish authorities generally unwilling to believe his story—that being in a ship of the Queen's Majesty of England, bound to Guinea, he had been driven to America by wind and weather. But on the whole he was successful, and in one way or another (sometimes with use of his ordnance) obtained a market and sold his negroes. It was on this voyage that he made his way through the islands, with some mistakes of navigation, to Florida, and visited Laudonnière's French settlement on the river of May. This is one of the best voyages in Hakluyt ; very vigorous and sensible and full of good descriptions of people and products—not unlike King Alfred's notes and so on sledges to Moscow, as Antony Jenkinson proved. Hakluyt in his preface makes as much of the North-East voyages as of those to America, and one of the principal exploits of the English, in his eyes, was " to open and unlock the sevenfold mouth of Dwina," the great river of the White Sea.

The north-west passage, however, has always had a more popular reputation, and the names of Frobisher and Davys are more famous than those of Sir Hugh Willoughby, Richard Chancellor, Stephen Burroughs, and Antony Jenkinson. Of all the Elizabethan voyagers, if we had to make a choice, we should take John Davys as the staunchest and readiest, the most capable and most single-minded. His voyages and works on navigation are collected in one of the volumes of the Hakluyt Society ; his life has been written and his career appreciated by Sir Clements Markham, and it cannot be said that his memory is unhonoured. But we are inclined to nurse a grievance against Mr. Beazley for leaving John Davys out of the selections from Hakluyt, of which mention has been made above. Davys was there, in Mr. Payne's original second volume; for Cavendish's last voyage is mostly Davys, as reported by Mr. John Jane, " a man of good observation, employed in the same and many other voyages." Mr. Beazley's reasons seem to us inadequate and even wrong —with a misconception of the value of this story. He omits, he says, " the melancholy, almost disgraceful last voyage and last letter of Thomas Cavendish " ; " here at least the reader will no longer have to wade through the unworthy recriminations of Elizabethan heroes turned by misfortune into scolds, forgetful of dignity and truth." With regard to which judgment it is possible to maintain that, on the contrary, the last voyage of Cavendish exhibits more than any other, and more vividly, the realities of the sea-life of those days, and makes one feel the actual strain and oppression of the old difficulties, the anxieties of the chief captain, the tragedy even (for it is something like that) of misunderstanding between fairly well-intentioned men. Would Mr. Beazley cashier Brutus and Cassius because of their scolding? Cavendish and Davys parted company in stress of weather; Cavendish thought he had been deserted, as Hawkins also thought when he missed Drake after San Juan de Ulloa. Very sad, no doubt, especially as Cavendish died with his low opinion of Davys, "that villain that hath been the death of me, and decay of this whole action." But where is the indignity here, if Cavendish really believed that Davys had left him? " There was no cant about Cavendish," says Mr. Payne. Can there be any doubt that Cavendish honestly thought himself wronged? We prefer Mr. Payne's opinion to Mr. Beazley's—" this unique and pathetic narrative," he calls it—meaning Cavendish's letter to the executor of his will, from which reference to " that villain " has been quoted. And on the side of Davys there is even greater loss in leaving out Mr. John Jane's account of the perils in the Straits of Magellan. The difficulties of navigation were great, and though they were too much, in one way, for Davys, they proved his skill and temper to a degree that can scarcely be matched in any other voyage. The doubling of the Cape at the western mouth of the Straits, on the return from the vain attempt at the Pacific, makes a story as thrilling as Marryat's club-hauling experience in Arcachon Bay, while the hideous discomforts of the voyage, and the risks of rotten tackling, and the devices to make it last, and the captain's patience and resource, are brought to the reader's mind as fully as any such distant things and long past trials can be.

Davys, we are inclined to think, came nearer than any of the other heroes to Hakluyt's ideal of the sailor. He had Hakluyt's own tastes ; he was a skilled navigator and one of the best pilots in the world ("our captain, as we first passed through the Straits, drew such an exquisite plot of the same as I am assured it cannot in any sort be bettered"), and also, like Hakluyt, he thought much of commodities and new openings for trade. He seems to have had a freer mind than most of his fellows ; at any rate, he is always very quick to notice things. He is interested in languages, both in Greenland and at the Cape of Good Hope, and has left a description of the speech of South Africa : "their words are for the most part inarticulate, and, in speaking, they clock with the tongue like a brood hen, which clocking and the word are both pronounced together, very curiously."

II

DRYDEN

I

DRYDEN's critical writings have been less damaged by the lapse of time and have kept their original freshness better than any literary discourses which can be compared with them, even taking the next century into consideration. He has suffered much less from changes of literary fashion than Addison or Dr. Johnson. Although there are many things that are antiquated or conventional in his discussion of literary principles, although he had his share of the literary pedantries of his age, there is an inexhaustible liveliness and spirit in his essays which has given them an advantage over many more laborious and philosophical pieces of criticism. Every one of his essays contains some independent judgment. His love of literature was instinctive ; his mind answered at once to the touch of poetry, and gave in return his estimate of it, in " the other harmony of prose." It is true that his opinions are sometimes encumbered by the respect which he feels himself bound to pay to established authorities, and sometimes he condescends to hackwork and compilation, as, for instance, in much of the essays on *Satire* and on *Epic Poetry*. But even when he is tired of this business he keeps his ease of manner, and it is in the manner of his discourses that he shows his power as a critic. There is nothing in literary criticism more satisfactory, merely as a display of literary strength and skill, than the essays in which Dryden's mind is expatiating freely, as in the *Dramatic Poesy* and the Preface to the *Fables*, where he faces his adversaries, personal and impersonal, with the security of a man who has confidence in his own powers, and in the clearness of his eye. He is at his best when he has set himself to try the value of dogmatic rules and principles; cautious, respectful, seeming to comply with them, till the time comes for the stroke that ends the encounter, and leaves the arena to be cleared for the next antagonist. " Now what, I beseech you, is more easy than to write a regular French play, or more difficult than to write an irregular English one, like those of Fletcher or of Shakespeare ? " The natural grace and the readiness of his style in explanation and controversy have never been surpassed. His language is a creature moving at its own will, in its proper element.

The other great critic of Dryden's time, Saint-Evremond, had found it to be the fault of the English that they dug too deep, and lost themselves in the windings of their own thoughts before they could bring anything to the surface, to be made available for the common sense of mankind ; as, on the other hand, the defect of the French was that they would not follow an argument home, and were too easily contented with the sound of their own voices. It would be good for each nation to learn from the other ; for the English to acquire the art of human conversation ; for the French to go deeper in their studies. This balance of faculties is secured in Dryden more completely than in any other English writer, and there is no better account of the excellences of his prose than is given in these phrases of templations, and from which he might bring down his knowledge for the instruction of modern poetical artificers. The patterns of Epic (commonly called the " Heroic Poem ") and of Tragedy, or the Heroic Play, are those that chiefly concern Dryden. What influence those ideal patterns had, what reverence they evoked, is scarcely conceivable now, and is seldom thought of by historians. The " Heroic Poem " is not commonly mentioned in histories of Europe as a matter of serious interest : yet from the days of Petrarch and Boccaccio to those of Dr. Johnson, and more especially from the sixteenth century onward, it was a subject that engaged some of the strongest intellects in the world (among them, Hobbes, Gibbon, and Hume) ; [1] it was studied and discussed as fully and with as much thought as any of the problems by which the face of the world was changed in those centuries. There might be difference of opinion about the essence of the Heroic Poem or the Tragedy, but there was no doubt about their value. Truth about them was ascertainable, and truth about them was necessary to the intellect of man, for they were the noblest things belonging to him.[2]

About the middle of the seventeenth century there was an increased activity in the business of epic poetry, especially in France and England ; owing, no doubt,

[1] See " The Answer of Mr. Hobbes to Sir William Davenant's Preface before Gondibert," 1650, and " The Iliads and Odysses of Homer, translated out of Greek into English by Thomas Hobbes, of Malmesbury. With a large Preface concerning the virtues of an Heroic Poem, written by the translator," 1676 ; Hume, " Letter to the authors of the *Critical Review* concerning the *Epigoniad* of Wilkie," April 1759 ; Gibbon, " An Inquiry whether a Catalogue of the Armies sent into the Field is an essential part of an Epic Poem," Dec. 23, 1763.

[2] " A Heroic Poem, truly such, is undoubtedly the greatest work which the soul of man is capable to perform " (*Dedication of the Æneis*).

to the accumulation of testimony on the subject by the older generations. It was discussed between Hobbes and Davenant ; it was meditated by the French poets ; and Davenant in England, Chapelain and others in France, undertook to show by their example how the rules and principles of the Heroic Poem might be carried out in practice. *Paradise Lost* is one of those experiments. It is easy to pass by *Gondibert*, and to accept the unanimous judgment which disposes of Chapelain's *Pucelle* ; but Milton's work was begun and carried out under the same critical principles, and no small part of his motive was the same learned ambition to embody the abstract form of Epic in a modern vernacular work. Like Ronsard and Tasso before him, like Davenant, like Chapelaine, Desmarests, Scudéry, and Father Le Moyne, he was under the spell of the phantom Epic, the pure idea of a Virgilian poem. The heroic poem was an unbodied ghost that might choose for the habit of its earthly life either the story of Paradise or that of the Round Table ; just as the tragedy which is *Samson Agonistes* might have been *Samson Hybristes* or *Pursophorus*, or even *Solomon Gynæcocratumenus*, or any other of the inventions noted by Milton in his list of subjects in the Trinity MS. The abstract inspiration of the Virgilian form of Epic, or of the Euripidean form of Tragedy, before the subject was determined at all, must count for more than a little in the history of Milton's poetry ; to realise the importance of these abstract ideas is one of the first requisites in coming to the study of Dryden's critical essays. His freedom cannot be rightly estimated except in relation to the potent authorities with which he had to deal.

Dryden's attitude towards the pure Abstract Forms

of Poetry is not very difficult to understand when once
their character has been appreciated. He had read
and admired the Latin poets. He appreciated clear
reasoning and exposition, such as he found in Rapin
and Bossu, and he was not by nature inclined to dissent
from established opinion without sufficient cause. He
shows respect to the orthodox views wherever he can.
The worship of the pure form and the ambition to
realise it affected him strongly ; for example, in his
theory of Heroic Plays, and in his contemplated Epic
on King Arthur. But he will not make it a point of
honour or of faith to enforce the principles of Heroic
Poetry. His original work is determined by present
conditions of taste (among which of course a respect
for orthodox literary canons must count for something),
and his general criticism, having always a reference to
his own present undertakings, follows his judgment of
what is desirable and feasible for him (or for contemporary English authors) at the moment. The patterns
of literature have to demean themselves accordingly.
Dryden is willing to pay reverence to the Heroic Poem
and to the ideal of Tragedy : it never occurs to him to
hesitate. But he does not " believe what he knows to
be untrue," and nothing is further from his thoughts
than to impose on his fellows a bondage like that of
Trissino in Italy or Gabriel Harvey in England—two
similar spirits in their flat, uncompromising zeal for the
purity of classical example, and in their abhorrence of
anything like modern novelty. The rules of the pedants
are a different thing from the genial influence of the
great ancient poets, and they are treated by Dryden in
a different way. He felt strongly the conventional
obligation to admire the classical poets ; but this
element of convention or duty was corrected by his

Dryden, he had an original love of freedom ; it was his business as a critic to find some compromise between freedom and authority, to explain the laws of Poetry in such a way as to reserve for himself the faculty of doing his own work without undue sacrifices. The great difference between Corneille and Dryden is that Corneille in his criticism was limited to the Drama, to the kind of composition in which he was at home, for which he had a natural gift. It detracts somewhat from the value of Dryden's essays that so many of them are concerned with kinds of work for which he was not suited. Corneille is at the centre ; he has made the province of Tragedy his own before he begins to write about it as an expositor. Dryden began to write as a critic of the Drama while he was still finding his way, and, unhappily, where there was no satisfactory way to be found. The difference in situation between Corneille and Dryden is that Corneille is a master reviewing the work he has already done and explaining it ; Dryden is a master of forms of poetry not dramatic, trying in his dramatic essays to find his way into provinces not his own, to plant a new dramatic colony, by artifice if not by violence, in place of the older kinds of drama which he sees to be exhausted. The fault of his prefaces is that they make one disappointed with his plays, when one comes to them after his criticisms. This is not the case with his nondramatic work ; there the drawback is of another kind, namely, that so much of his Discourses on Satire (the Preface to *Juvenal*) and on Epic (the Dedication of the *Æneis*) is mere unoriginal learning, without the freshness of the earlier essays. For this, however, there is compensation, and something more, in the glorious Preface to the *Fables*, written more than thirty years commentators, there is no general opinion on the subject, or none worth considering : " thought is free " ; and what Dryden thinks about Shakespeare is, like Ben Jonson's estimate, on this side idolatry. But if Dryden speaks about Shakespeare with little anticipation of the vast multitude and the many voices that were to follow him with their praises, his judgment is none the worse for that. The isolation of his point of view, the simplicity of his statement (one mortal man and good writer talking happily about another), the enthusiastic tone, and at the same time the want of reverence, all bring out the individual genius of Dryden as a critic, the directness and truth of his answer when he is appealed to by good poetry. No critic has ever given so convincing an account of his own poetical likings with so little display, so little expense of rhetoric.

IV. ANCIENTS AND MODERNS

In the *Battle of the Books* Dryden is one of the Moderns. His critical work cannot be fully understood without some reference to this long debate, which had several new beginnings and no end during his lifetime. There was more reason in the debate, and it was conducted, at times, with more good sense than might be gathered either from Swift's allegory or from some of the impertinences on either side that preceded it. It was the inevitable result of the Revival of Learning ; it had gone on for centuries ; the splutter of Perrault's fireworks being a minor incident in the contention. What was the right way to think of the Ancients ? What was the right way to make use of their example ? These were questions that were asked long before the time to which the name *Renais-*

sance is generally given. They were questions that
might be made inconvenient by any pedant to any
poet, as by Gabriel Harvey to Spenser. Tasso's *Discourses* are an attempt to make a compromise without
giving up either respect for the Ancients or any rights
of the Moderns. If Aristotle left *Romance* out of his
Poetics he was none the less Aristotle : if Romance had
existed, it would have come into his system. Tasso
in this way tried to reconcile the two sides, and he
is followed by Corneille and by Dryden with similar
attempts at a compromise. But in Dryden's time the
debate between Ancients and Moderns was not merely
between classical precedent and modern liberty : there
was a cross-debate, with a different motive. In the
Battle of the Books the Moderns are not on the side of
liberty ; they are not for romance against classical
authority. The superstition of classical authority
brought its own Nemesis in the most singular way,
almost as soon as the French Academy was founded to
provide an audience for the new views. The champion
of the Moderns claims a hearing, like Boisrobert in the
French Academy in 1635,[1] and Perrault later, not
because the Moderns want more freedom, but because
they are more correct than the Ancients, more classical
than Homer. This new claim for the Moderns is quite
unlike Tasso's gentle plea for the realm of the Fairy
Queen, for the elements of chivalry. These new Moderns
are really more ancient and more pedantic than Gabriel
Harvey. The Revival of ancient Learning has succeeded so well that the ancient poets are disqualified
and treated with disrespect.

Dryden's attitude in this *Battle of the Books* is

[1] See Rigault, *Histoire de la querelle des Anciens et des Modernes*,
1856.

throughout consistent and honourable. As, with Corneille and even beyond Corneille, he vindicates the freedom of modern art against the positive laws derived from the Classics, so against the more furious and ultra-classical Moderns he stands up for the honour of Greek and Latin poetry. He was one man at any rate in the seventeenth century to whom the shocks of literary conflict brought advantage. Between the classically-minded, who would have imposed the Ancients on the world as infallible lawgivers, and the modern precisians, in whose sight the *Iliad* itself was a shocking example of licence, Dryden kept his head and his own opinions. The soundness of his judgment saved him from the classical vanity, as is sufficiently proved in his comparison of Ovid and Chaucer ; the sensitive appreciation and the unfailing *gusto* with which he applauded the good things of poetry secured him from all risks of doing injustice to either side. Out of all the contradictions and paradoxes of the *Battle of the Books* Dryden seems to have taken nothing but a further strengthening of his natural habit of criticism, which led him instinctively to recognise what was good, and to praise it. Between the ancient and the modern pedants Dryden found it natural to see things with his own eyes, and the effect of the charges and counter-charges in the literary tumult was if anything to make him all the more resolved that neither Ovid nor Chaucer should suffer wrong, either from ignorance on the one hand or pedantry on the other.

V. " NATURE."

There is one idea common to Dryden and all his contemporaries which, in spite of its ambiguity, is

seldom misleading ; that is the idea of Nature : " At
once the source, and end, and test of Art." Pope could
not help himself in the *Essay on Criticism* ; he had to
say " first follow Nature," because all the critics and
poets had been saying the same thing for generations
past, and it was not his business to disagree with them.
Nor was it Dryden's wish in this respect to avoid con-
forming with the rest of the guild. " Nature " means
whatever the author thinks right ; sometimes it is the
reality that is copied by the artist ; sometimes, and
much more commonly, it is the principles of sound
reason in poetry ; and sometimes it is the Ideal. Thus
Dryden refers to Nature to justify heroic couplets in
serious drama ; " heroic rhyme is nearest Nature, as
being the noblest kind of modern verse." It might
seem as if there were little value in a conception so
vague, so mutable, so easily turned to sophistry and
fallacy. Yet it would be a mistake to think so.
" Nature " made many writers say good things by way
of criticism who were unsuccessful in their original
works. The French heroic romances have long been
fair game for satirists, but Scudéry's preface to *Ibrahim
ou l'Illustre Bassa* (1641) is by no means ridiculous :
" Pour moy je tiens que plus les avantures sont natur-
elles, plus elles donnent de satisfaction : et le cours
ordinaire du soleil me semble plus merveilleux, que les
estranges et funestes rayons des comettes." Chapelain's epic poem has been a byword since it was printed,
but his motives were good : " Je me suis plus attaché
aux sentimens de la Nature, qu'aux subtilités de la
Déclamation." These are commonplaces, no doubt,
and they would not carry one very far in the composition of the Epic Poem or the Heroic Play. But as commonplaces they had their value ; they discouraged the

invention of conceits, they made young authors think of the arrangement of their work, of that *ordonnance* which the critics of those days picked up from the schools of painting. Dryden by his adoption of these commonplaces did much to strengthen the hold of " Nature " on English criticism without doing much to explain it. One correction indeed he made. When he found " Nature " turned into an excuse for dulness he spoke out, in the *Apology for Heroic Poetry*. For though he grew out of the " Metaphysical " School, and repented of *Maximin* and *Almanzor*, he would make no terms with correct insipidity.

In the *Parallel of Poetry and Painting* he gives a clear statement of the current idealist theory of Art and Nature, which was taken up afterwards and taught more fully, not without reference to Dryden, in the *Discourses* of Sir Joshua Reynolds.

VI. STYLE

Dryden's prose has been described by Dr. Johnson in one of the pleasantest passages in the *Lives* : " Criticism, either didactic or defensive, occupies almost all his prose, except those pages which he has devoted to his patrons ; but none of his prefaces were ever thought tedious. They have not the formality of a settled style, in which the first half of the sentence betrays the other. The clauses are never balanced, nor the periods modelled : every word seems to drop by chance, though it falls into its proper place. Nothing is cold or languid ; the whole is airy, animated, and vigorous ; what is little, is gay ; what is great, is splendid. He may be thought to mention himself too frequently ; but while he forces himself upon our esteem, we cannot refuse him to stand high in his own. Every thing is excused by the play of images and the spriteliness of expression. Though all is easy, nothing is feeble ; though all seems careless, there is nothing harsh ; and though since his earlier works more than a century has passed, they have nothing yet uncouth or obsolete."

To this account of Dryden's style there is little to be added except in the way of illustration. It is a paragraph in which the great master of formal periods has taken occasion to salute the master of the other sort of prose, and in so doing to pay honour to both styles. Nowhere has the grace of Dryden's free elocution been better described. Dryden's sentences are like sentences of good conversation, in which it is not necessary that every point should be deliberated. They run on easily, clauses are added to qualify the chief proposition, and in one case at least there is so much freedom and exuberance in the dependent clauses that the grammar of the sentence is left helpless in the tangle and thicket of relative pronouns.[1]

In his revision of the *Essay of Dramatic Poesy*, Dryden came to believe that he ought to put some restraint on his tendency to leave hanging phrases at the end of his sentences. As he tells us himself, he noted as a fault the preposition left at the end of a clause and belonging to a relative understood ; and in the revised version of his Essay he carefully corrected " the end he aimed at " into " the end at which he aimed," and " the age I live in " to " the age in which I live," and so on. But this correction and restriction, though it was a move towards greater propriety of language, was very far short of conversion to the

[1] Preface to *Juvenal*.

periodic structure of sentences, and Dryden's prose remains in the Preface to the *Fables* in 1700 essentially what it was in the Essay of 1668 ; no less " airy and animated," and no more stately and dignified.

Dryden's prose, which is intended for the greatest number, which is meant to be popular, loses nothing of its value by being compared with his contemporaries, though it may be found to be not altogether exceptional nor new in character. Dryden himself, according to Congreve's well-known evidence, acknowledged Tillotson as his master in the art of familiar discourse ; [1] and there were others ; before all, there was Cowley, whose style obtains from Dr. Johnson little less than the praise given to the *Essays* of Dryden for their lightness, grace, and ease. There were also the French authors. However much the influence of France may have been abused by historians as an explanation of the new fashions of literature at the accession of Charles II., there is no reason why it should be disallowed or refused its due in accounting for the changes of taste. French criticism, French talk about literature, had already found the right kind of expression thirty years and more before the *Essay of Dramatic Poesy*. The ancestors of Dryden's prose are to be traced in Chapelain's Preface to the *Adone* of Marino, in Mesnardière's *Poëtique*, in the Dialogues and Essays of Sarrasin, in the Prefaces of Scudéry, in the Discourses and *Examens* of Corneille. In all these different authors, and in others, there was to be found, with different faculties, the same common quality of clearness in exposition and argument, which even without genius may be

---

[1] " I have heard him frequently own with pleasure that if he had any talent for English prose, it was owing to his having often read the writings of the great Archbishop Tillotson." Congreve, Dedication of *Dryden's Dramatic Works*.

pleasing, and with genius is the most valuable auxiliary, as in the essays of Dryden and Corneille. What criticism might be without the example of the French is shown in the Preface to *Samson Agonistes*. In date it is some years later than Dryden's *Essay* ; in temper it belongs to the Italy of a hundred years before ; it is like one of the solemn sermons before an Italian learned society, in which the doctrine of Poetry used to be expounded more gravely than any text of St. Thomas. The difference between an Italian and a French education in their influence on prose may be seen by comparing Milton and Chapelain, authors much alike in ambition, self-respect, and solemnity of mind ; in everything but poetical genius and the circumstances of their lives. Milton writing his opinions about Tragic Poetry writes like an Italian contemporary of Tasso, with grave magnificence ; Chapelain, by nature no less grave, and as much inclined as Milton to walk with the gait of " the magnanimous man," is obliged by his associates to let his dignity go and to speak like other people. Between the scholar who was also a wit— Ménage—and the man of the world who was also a student—Sarrasin—there was no more room for declamation than there is in a reading party in summer. Chapelain the pedant has written a dialogue with Ménage and Sarrasin the wits taking part in it, and it is as easy and pleasant as the writing of the wits themselves, as fresh as anything of Dryden's ; a defence of Lancelot and the library of Don Quixote, a delightful apology for Romance, by the great champion of literary authority, the patron if not the inventor of the Unities. It is no small part of the attraction of Dryden's *Essays* that they bring their readers into acquaintance with that new world of France in the age of Louis XIII.,

when all the world and the Dramatic Unities were
young, when Corneille at the Hôtel de Bourgogne
scarcely knew himself as yet for anything different from
Hardy, when Scaramouche and Jodelet were getting
things ready for Molière, and when the cloak and sword
of Madrid, and the Castilian Point of Honour, were
mingled in the visions of the dramatic poet with an
idea of some unattained perfection, a sort of inaudible
dramatic music, a harmony partly moral, partly imaginative, which should constitute the absolutely faultless play. It is from this world, so adventurous yet so
decorous, so strangely mixed of " Gothic " traditions
and pedantic authority, Spanish comedies and classical
learning, and through all of it the zest and interest of a
society which sees a long day before it and much to be
won, that the spirit of Dryden's Essays is in great
measure derived.

Much also is native to them in England ; they inherit from Ben Jonson's *Discoveries* as well as from the
Discourses of Corneille. But it is from the language
and the manners of Corneille and his fellows that the
Essays of Dryden have caught their style and accent.

There is little that is peculiarly French in the details
of Dryden's prose. In a well-known passage of *Marriage à la Mode*, Act iii. sc. 1, there is a satire on the
importation of French phrases and their use in the
warfare of conversation. " They begin at *sottises* and
ended *en ridicule* " ; they include *foible, chagrin,
grimace, embarrasse, double entendre, equivoque, eclair-
cissement, suitte, béveue, façon, penchant, coup d'etourdy,
languissant.* Dryden does not allow himself to be led
very far on this way in his own practice. In the
Dedication of the Rival Ladies (p. 5) he protests against
the abuse of foreign terms, and in the Preface to the

Second Miscellany (p. 266) he even seems to note the word *diction* as not completely naturalised. But Dryden was not the man to make any fanatical opposition to a prevailing fashion, and he uses French words as they come convenient.

If there is anything old-fashioned in his style it is perhaps that liking for conceits which fortunately never disappears from his verse nor from his prose. He is indeed more temperate than the men *moribus antiquis*, such as Butler must be reckoned in spite of Butler's affection for lucidity and good sense. But there are many places where Dryden seems to be writing for a sentence or two in the manner of Butler or Cleveland. So in the Dedication of *Love in a Nunnery* :

" For this reason I have often laughed at the ignorant and ridiculous descriptions which some Pedants have given of the Wits, as they are pleased to call them, which are a generation of men as unknown to them as the people of Tartary or the *Terra Australis* are to us. And therefore as we draw giants and anthropophagi in those vacancies of our maps, where we have not travelled to draw better, so these wretches paint lewdness, atheism, folly, ill-reasoning, and all manner of extravagancies amongst us, from want of understanding what we are."

Other aspects of Dryden's criticism may be noted under the separate headings that follow.

DEDICATION OF THE RIVAL LADIES (1664)

At the end of his answer to Sir Robert Howard (*Defence of the Essay*) Dryden explains how the argument about dramatic verse began in the dedication of the *Rival Ladies*, and led to the *Essay of Dramatic*

Poesy, and further. Lord Orrery had written rhyming plays before Dryden took up the fashion (" yet I must remember it is your Lordship to whom I speak, who have much better commended this way by your writing in it, than I can do by writing for it," p. 9). The example followed by Lord Orrery is found by Dryden in D'Avenant's *Siege of Rhodes*. More important, however, than the dramatic criticism in this preface is the acknowledgement of the authority of Waller as the founder of the new school of English verse, and the coupling of his name with that of Sir John Denham. That " the excellence and dignity of rhyme were never fully known till Mr. Waller taught it," and that Waller in this reform was seconded by Denham, became a dogma in the schools of criticism. Though opinions have changed about the value of Waller's verse, his influence as the master of Dryden and Pope is still recognised in the history of English poetry. Dryden's early reference to him here is the expression of an opinion from which he never altered, and he repeats his homage at the end of his life, in the Preface to the *Fables*.

None of Lord Orrery's plays seem as yet to have been published in 1664. Dryden perhaps had seen *Henry the Fifth*, which was acted in this year. His praise of Lord Orrery's dramatic genius may be compared with Pepys's estimate (Dec. 8, 1668) : " and so went home to dinner, where my wife tells me of my Lord Orrery's new play *Tryphon* at the Duke of York's house, which, however, I would see, and therefore put a bit of meat in our mouths, and went thither, where with much ado, at half-past one, we got into a blind hole, in the 18*d*. place, above stairs, where we could not hear well, but the house infinite full, but the prologue

most silly, and the play, though admirable, yet no
pleasure almost in it, because just the very same design,
and words, and sense, and plot, as every one of his plays
have, any one of which alone would be held admirable,
whereas so many of the same design and fancy do but
dull one another ; and this, I perceive, is the sense of
everybody else, as well as myself, who therefore showed
but little pleasure in it."

PREFACE TO *ANNUS MIRABILIS* (1667)

The " Account of the ensuing Poem " breaks the
sequence of dramatic criticism, but more in form than
in substance. Dryden's interest in the theatre was
always connected with a stronger interest in nondramatic forms of poetry : his " Heroic Drama " is
professedly founded on the " Heroic Poem." Here, for
once, he has an opportunity of speaking about the
Heroic Poem apart from the distractions of the stage.
If this essay is compared with the *Dedication of the
Æneis* it will be found to display the same literary
tastes, with some differences of judgment. In *Annus
Mirabilis* Dryden had not yet fully appropriated the
lessons of Waller. The poem is a series of fragments,
with no more than an accidental unity : it is not
organic, it is not, like the poems of 1681 and 1682, an
argument secure of itself and directing its own progress
from beginning to end ; it has to keep to the events of
the year, under a constraint which Dryden, later, would
have refused to submit to. In another respect *Annus
Mirabilis* shows clearly its comparatively old-fashioned
character, namely in the use of technical details. The
Preface states the principal without hesitation : " We
hear indeed among our poets of the thundering of guns,

the smoke, the disorder, and the slaughter, but all these are common notions. And certainly, as those who, in a logical dispute, keep in general terms, would hide a fallacy, so those who do it in any poetical description would veil their ignorance." The *Dedication of the Æneis* contradicts this : " I will not give the reasons why I writ not always in the proper terms of navigation, land-service, as in the cant of any profession. I will only say that Virgil has avoided these proprieties, because he writ not to mariners, soldiers, astronomers, gardeners, peasants, &c., but to all in general, and in particular to men and ladies of the first quality, who have been better bred than to be too nicely knowing in the terms." In *Annus Mirabilis* Dryden agrees with Ronsard : " Tu practiqueras bien souvent les artisans de tous mestiers, comme de *Marine, Venerie, Fauconnerie,* et principalement les artisans de feu, *Orfèvres, Fondeurs, Marechaux, Minerailliers* ; et de là tireras maintes belles et vives comparaisons avecques les noms propres des mestiers, pour enrichir ton œuvre et le rendre plus agreable et parfait " (*Abrégé de l'Art Poëtique François*). In 1697 Dryden has given up the technical dictionary and gone over to the school of general terms, whose principles were formulated by Buffon in his *Discourse on Style* ; [1] he has become more " classical." Nevertheless the preface to *Annus Mirabilis* takes up a position which, with all its concessions to the older fashions, is definitely opposed to the vanities, the " trimmings slight," of the poetical art : " 'Tis not the jerk or sting of an epigram, nor the seeming contradiction of a poor antithesis " : it is " lively

---

[1] " A cette première règle, dictée par le génie, si l'on joint de la délicatesse et du goût, du scrupule sur le choix des expressions, *de l'attention à ne nommer les choses que par les termes les plus généraux,* le style aura de la noblesse " (Buffon, *Discours sur le Style,* 1753).

and apt description " with one's eye upon the object, in which the proper " wit " of an Heroic Poem consists. Dryden never wrote anything so definite, in his critical works, as the account of the three functions of the poetical imagination in this preface. He never again committed himself to anything so nearly resembling philosophical analysis as his distinction between *Invention*, *Fancy*, and *Elocution*, the three modes of *Imagination*. " Fancy," which might be thought to have more than its due share in the " ensuing poem," is in this critical preface duly restrained, by the authority of Nature and Virgil. It is true that Virgil here is chiefly admired for separate passages of description, and that not enough consideration is given to the *unities* of the Heroic Poem. This is characteristic of Dryden's earlier point of view, and of the older fashion of richly figurative details which he was following in the *Annus Mirabilis*. At the same time the preface, as criticism, goes beyond the poem in recognising more kinds of poetical work than the poem itself contains. The praise of the dramatic imagination of Ovid leads naturally on to the essays immediately following, in which the Drama is the principal theme, and the Historical and Heroic Poem is brought in only for purposes of illustration.

AN ESSAY OF DRAMATIC POESY (1668)

The argument for rhyme in the Dedication of the *Rival Ladies* (1664) was answered by Sir Robert Howard in the preface to his Plays (1665) ; " that," says Dryden, " occasioned my reply in my *Essay*." The *Essay* is, however, much more than an argument on behalf of rhyming plays : the four friends in their dialogue are led to discuss the question of Ancients against Moderns, of French against English, the Three Unities, the *liaison des scènes*, the plots of Terence, the art of Ben Jonson, and many other things besides the original problem of rhyme. It is Dryden's most elaborate piece of criticism, and the most careful of his prose works, while at the same time it is the liveliest and freshest till the incomparable Preface to the *Fables*, in the last year of his life.

The Dialogue was a favourite form of composition in all the languages after the revival of learning, through the examples of Plato and Cicero. It was common in French among authors whom Dryden had probably read. Sometimes the persons appeared under their own names, like Ménage, Chapelain, and Sarrasin in Sarrasin's Dialogue, *S'il faut qu'un jeune homme soit amoureux* (*Œuvres*, ed. G. Ménage, Paris, 1656).[1] Sometimes the names were allegorical, like Eusèbe and Philédon in Desmarests' *Délices de l'Esprit* (1658). It is not impossible that Dryden may have known, though he does not mention, the *Cigarreles de Toledo* (Madrid, 1624) of Tirso de Molina, the author of the original *Don Juan*, who reports conversations about the nature of Comedy, the Unities, the authority of the Ancients, and other subjects in which Dryden was interested, in something like Dryden's liberal manner. " Dryden has assured me that he got more from the Spanish critics alone than from the Italian and French and all other critics put together " is the evidence of Bolingbroke in Spence's *Anecdotes*, and the Spanish conversations of Tirso de Molina may claim to be considered among the possible sources of the *Essay*—

[1] The same persons take part in Chapelain's remarkable Dialogue, *De la Lecture des Vieux Romans*, which, however, seems to have remained in manuscript till 1870 (ed. A. Feillet).

" a little discourse in dialogue, for the most part
borrowed from the observations of others ". (*Defence
of the Essay*). The principal source, however, as
Dryden plainly indicates, is not a dialogue, but the
series of Discourses prefixed by Corneille to the
three volumes of his collected Dramas in 1660, with
the *Examens* attached, in the same edition, to each of
his plays.

Martin Clifford accused Dryden of pilfering from
" Monsieur Hédelin, Mesnardière, and Corneille."
Dryden had not professed to be original, and made no
secret of his obligations to Corneille. It does not
appear that he owed much to the others, but he had
probably read them. " Monsieur Hédelin," the Abbé
d'Aubignac, whose *Pratique du Théâtre* appeared in
1657, though it was written long before, is one of the
most wearisome of all the righteous critics. Saint-Evremond has disposed of him : " On n'a jamais vu tant
de règles pour faire des belles tragédies ; et on en fait
si peu, qu'on est obligé de représenter les vieilles. Il
me souvient que l'abbé d'Aubignac en composa une,
selon toutes les lois qu'il avait impérieusement données
pour le théâtre. Elle ne réussit point ; et comme il se
vantait partout d'être le seul de nos auteurs qui eût
bien suivi les préceptes d'Aristote : ' Je sais bon gré
à M. d'Aubignac,' dit M. le Prince, ' d'avoir si bien
suivi les règles d'Aristote ; mais je ne pardonne point
aux règles d'Aristote d'avoir fait faire une si méchante
tragédie à M. d'Aubignac.' " His book was translated
into English (*The whole Art of the Stage*, 1684) and had
some reputation in England.

Mesnardière is much livelier in his *Poetique* (1640),
and by no means scrupulous. Dryden probably also
knew Sarrasin's *Discours sur l'Amour Tyrannique*, a

Preface written in 1639 for G. de Scudéry's drama of that name, printed in 1640.

The persons of Dryden's dialogue are EUGENIUS, that is, Charles, Lord Buckhurst (Earl of Dorset, 1677) ; CRITES, Sir Robert Howard ; LISIDEIUS, Sir Charles Sedley ; and NEANDER, who is Dryden.

The Dialogue is Socratic, or Platonic, in its arrangement ; [1] beginning by an account of the circumstances, and leading gradually, and by easy and natural stages, to a restriction of the talk with a view to the definition and description of one *species*, the Drama. The polemic motives, as they might be called, the rallying cries which lead to the debate, are those of *Ancients* against *Moderns* ; the *last generation* against the *present*, and *French* against *English*. The issue of the debate, to which it is guided by Neander, is a compromise. The conventional admiration of the classical dramatists (Crites) and the superstition of the French stage (Lisideius) are challenged by Eugenius and Neander and shown not to bear examination. The dramatists of the last generation, Shakespeare, Jonson, and Fletcher (*theirs was the giant age before the Flood*), are vindicated by Dryden against the " mechanic " view of dramatic art ; while by means of a detailed *Examen* of one of his plays, the *Silent Woman*, it is shown that Jonson had little to learn from the French in the way of exact construction. On the other hand, the Ancients and the French are not treated with any disrespect. Dryden's mind is working on lines of its own, but not so as to cut across the lines of the Ancients

---

[1] Cf. *Defence of Essay* : " My whole discourse was sceptical, according to that way of reasoning which was used by Socrates, Plato, and all the Academics of old, which Tully and the best of the Ancients followed, and which is imitated by the modest inquisitions of the Royal Society."

or of Corneille. The Unities, which give him a good deal of anxiety, are not adopted by him because they are ancient, or because they are French, but still they are adopted, because to a great extent they seem to agree with his own judgment of what is requisite in a play.

Corneille was a great help to him in getting through his perplexities. Although Dryden saw that a good deal of the French " correct " drama was pretence, and that the French symmetry and neatness were obtained by throwing away some of the most essential elements of a play, still he could not help admiring their protest against slovenly and ill-braced Drama, and he was attracted by sympathy with Corneille's frank and unaffected confession of his difficulties in his *Discours* and *Examens*. The Unities had been, and were still for some pedants, authoritative principles, positive laws. Corneille had begun his dramatic work in years of freedom, when the French popular stage was scarcely more restrained than the English stage when Sir Philip Sidney criticised it. He had gradually come under the influence of formal criticism, but the formal principles had to prove themselves reasonable before they were accepted : they were not to be accepted under the authority of Aristotle or Horace. Dryden was going through a similar progress in his own views about his work, and Corneille's discussion of principles must have seemed to him in many places the echo of his own thoughts.

THE UNITIES. 1. *Action*

The Unity of Action was interpreted in different ways by different dramatists. As a decree excluding disconnected episodes and separate secondary plots, it was not the peculiar property of any classical school : as a strict rule, requiring no more than one single theme of interest in a play, " single and separate, not composed of parts," [1] it was generally too severe for even very correct authors, and Jonson had rejected it with a solemnity more impressive than the curses of Ernulphus or of Milton. " Which thing out of antiquity itself hath deceived many, and more this day it doth deceive." Corneille does not refuse to allow subordinate actions, working into the main plot, and Dryden accepts this as sufficient : " Eugenius has already shown us, from the confession of the French poets, that the Unity of Action is sufficiently preserved, if all the imperfect actions of the play are conducing to the main design."

It is in the *liaison des scènes* that Corneille exhibits the efficient working of this Unity of Action, and it is here that Dryden follows him with least reserve. The Unity of Action is proved to be valid when the exits and entrances explain and justify themselves, when each successive grouping of the *dramatis personæ* is seen to follow naturally out of what went before, when there is no sudden break in the middle of the act to introduce new actors and a change of interest. That the action should be continuous is a rule for the practical dramatist ; with the " scenes unbroken " the play gets hold upon the attention of the audience, and the art of the playwright has its reward. By calling attention to this rule of the working dramatist (which he had been rather late in discovering, as he confesses), Corneille not only gave practical and much needed help to beginners, but saved the stage from some of the afflictions of pedantry, especially from some of the

[1] Ben Jonson, *Discoveries.*

exhaustion and depletion which were sure to follow from too pertinacious observance of the Unity of Action. Dryden, and the English generally, felt that the French plays were apt to be rather thin and abstract. Dryden must have felt that Corneille's accounts of his plots allowed too little room for movement and variety :

" Il faut donc qu'une action, pour être d'une juste grandeur, ait un commencement, un milieu et une fin. Cinna conspire contre Auguste, et rend compte de sa conspiration à Emilie, voilà le commencement ; Maxime en fait avertir Auguste, voilà le milieu ; Auguste lui pardonne, voilà la fin. Ainsi, dans les comédies, j'ai presque toujours établi deux amans en bonne intelligence, je les ai brouillés ensemble par quelque fourbe, et les ai réunis par l'éclaircissement de cette même fourbe qui les séparait."—*Premier Discours*.

Simplicity of this sort appeared to an English observer and to St. Evremond in England rather dearly purchased. But the *liaison des scènes* was some compensation, for if there was not the variety and substance of the English romantic drama or of Jonson's Comedy of Humours, there might at any rate be the life and speed of a well constructed play, and the want of body might be made up by neatness, elegance of design, and a clear and reasonable sequence in the action and the dialogue. In England, with all the difference between French and English taste in drama, there was no reason why the *liaison des scènes* should be neglected, why, with greater weight of argument, the dramatists should be slovenly about the arrangement of the exits and entrances. The English Drama was fuller of body and more substantial than the French ; but there was no reason why it should not be improved, and it might be improved by not trusting wholly to its weight. The French device of skilfully mortised scenes—*Ce nouvel usage qui passe en précepte*, as Corneille calls it—was available for dramatists of different schools. This is what Dryden points out, and this is the most important part of his dealings with the Unity of Action.

THE UNITIES. 2. *Time*

Everywhere in the sixteenth and seventeenth centuries there was to be heard the protest of scholars against the loose ways of the popular drama in regard to the time supposed to be covered by the action. Sir Philip Sidney's well-known description in the *Apology for Poetry* is to be found, with very little difference, in Spanish and French, in Cervantes and Boileau.

Boileau (*L'Art Poëtique*, iii. 39 sq.) refers to the licence of the Spanish stage almost in the same terms as Sidney speaking of the English :

> Un rimeur, sans péril, delà des Pyrénées,
> Sur la scène en un jour renferme des années :
> Là souvent le héros d'un spectacle grossier,
> Enfant au premier acte, est barbon au dernier.
> Mais nous, que la raison à ses règles engage,
> Nous voulons qu'avec art l'action se ménage ;
> Qu'en un lieu, qu'en un jour, un seul fait accompli
> Tienne jusqu'à la fin le théâtre rempli.

Boileau did not think it necessary to say that the French popular drama had been within a generation as rude in this respect as the Spanish, and that the audiences of the Hôtel de Bourgogne about 1630 might have deserved what Lope in his apology for his comedies said of his spectators in Madrid : that they thought

themselves ill provided for unless they were shown in
two hours from Genesis to the Day of Judgment :

> la cólera
> De un Español sentado no se templa
> Si no le representen en dos horas
> Hasta el final juicio desde el Genesis.[1]

The Unities which had been exemplified (though not
always strictly) by the authors of correct Tragedy, such
as Jodelle, Garnier, and Montchrestien, were neglected
in the popular drama of the Hôtel de Bourgogne, in the
tragicomedies of Alexandre Hardy and his contemporaries.   For tragedy they were still requisite ; for
the popular drama they were unnecessary.   The correct
tragedies were for the popular dramatist in France what
Gorboduc was to Marlowe and his companions ; something to be taken into consideration by the practical
playwright, not something to be followed religiously as
an authority, unless he chose for his own purposes to
commit himself to the stricter and more learned kind
of composition.   But the same thing happened with
the Unity of Time as with the Unity of Action.   The
popular practice came to approximate to the learned
ideal : practice in dramatic writing taught the playwright to work for concentration, and without pedantry
his natural instincts led him to restrict the time of his
story.   This spontaneous concentration and compres-
sion led to increased respect for the critical theory of
the Unities.   The success of Mairet's *Sophonisbe* does
not seem to have been due to pedantry, but to the
genuine satisfaction of the audience in neat workman-
ship.   The process of approximation may be partly
traced in the *Examens* of Corneille's early comedies,

---

[1] *El Nuevo Arte de hacer Comedias.*

which show how the French dramatist about 1635, like the English forty years before, had shortened the time of the action, because it was convenient and effective to have it so. Corneille goes further than the English, and comes under the influence of the revival of the learned rules, but his treatment of the Unity of Time in his *Discourses* is generally free enough. It helps the effect of the Drama to have the imaginary action taking up no more than the two hours required to play it. But more time may be taken, if necessary.

Dryden follows in Corneille's spirit, and goes further. He was evidently touched with sympathy for Corneille's struggles against the pedants; he quotes with approval as a full expression of his own opinion the concluding words of Corneille in his *Discourse of the Unities* : " 'Tis easy for speculative persons to judge severely ; but if they would produce to public view ten or twelve pieces of this nature, they would perhaps give more latitude to the rules than I have done, when by experience they had known how much we are bound up and constrained by them, and how many beauties of the stage they banished from it." Dryden thought of the Unity of Time in the same general way as Corneille, and in the same way as he thought of the Unity of Action : both of them were good negative or corrective rules, prohibiting waste of time, prohibiting incoherent plots ; but they were not to be allowed to fix any positive limit for the dramatic poet ; and the English poet (this is Dryden's main contention) will take more liberty than the French. He will require more time for his story, as he puts more into it than the French authors, and embraces more subordinate actions under the control of his *primum mobile*, his principal dramatic theme.

The Unities. 3. *Place*

Dryden found comfort in Corneille's explicit refusal to accept the Unity of Place as one of the ancient rules. Crites had spoken, in the usual manner, of the Unity of Place as one of the rules derived from Aristotle. Eugenius, following Corneille, will not accept this conventional pedigree : " in the first place give me leave to tell you that the Unity of Place, however it might be practised by them, was never any of their rules ; we neither find it in Aristotle, Horace, or any who have written of it, till in our age the French poets first made it a precept of the stage."

The Unity of Place is in a different class from the other two. Action and Time were to be considered by the dramatist in shaping and proportioning his story ; Place was naturally restricted along with Time and Action, and did not need special consideration until it came to be a question of the decoration of the stage, a matter for the scene-painter. Here came in an organic difference between French and English customs which led to a great deal of confusion when the French critics were studied in England.

The Elizabethan stage, not being hampered with scenery, made no unnecessary difficulty or absurdity for the audience in changing the scene. It all depended on the story ; if the story required it, the change was all right ; if the change was wrong, it was not on account of any absurdity in pretending to move from Venice to Cyprus, or from Sicily to Bohemia ; it was as easy to make the scene in one place as in another ; the change must be criticised, and approved or condemned, by reference to the standards of Time and of Action, not of Place ; *Place* was not an independent category but a subordinate species dependent on the other two. The introduction of painted scenery made no difference in this respect. Whether and how often the scene should be changed, must be determined by the structure of the play, by the manner in which the plot was developed.

In France things were different, and the Unity of Place meant a different thing, something scarcely intelligible to an untravelled Englishman. Considerations of Place were forced upon the French dramatists not only by the arrangement of their stories but more forcibly by the mechanical conditions of their stage.

The popular stage of the Hôtel de Bourgogne at the beginning of the seventeenth century was more antique in its appliances than anything in London in the time of Marlowe or Shakespeare. The Hôtel de Bourgogne had inherited the goodwill of the Confraternity of the Passion, and the stage devices of the medieval religious drama. The Elizabethan Drama, by a " divine chance," had got rid of the medieval stage management, except for incidental purposes, as in Peter Quince's entertainment. The French stage, when Corneille began to write, was still faithful to the old traditions, in accordance with which all the different scenes required in the play were represented on the stage at once. Some compromises had indeed been made ; a kind of shorthand or symbolic representation. The old *mansions* of the *Mystères* were placed side by side on a long stage which might have seven or eight different places represented on it, as in the Mystery of the Passion described by M. Petit de Julleville, where the *mansions* represent (1) Paradise ; (2) Nazareth ; (3) the Temple ; (4) Jerusalem ; (5) the Palace ; (6) the Golden Gate ; (7) the Sea of Galilee ; and (8) Limbo and

Hell.[1]　In the Hôtel de Bourgogne there was more art :
the decoration was often in the form of a perspective
view, which could give beside the central picture two or
more different places on each side, one behind the
other. The commonly accepted theory of the scenes is
represented in a passage quoted by M. Rigal[2] from *La
Poëtique* of Jules de La Mesnardière (c. xi. *La Disposition du Théâtre*) :

" Si l'Avanture s'est passée moitié dans le Palais d'un
Roy en plusieurs appartemens, et moitié hors de la
Maison en beaucoup d'endroits différens ; il faut que le
grand du Théâtre, le προσκήνιον des Grecs, je veux dire
cette largeur qui limite le parterre, serve pour tous les
dehors où ces choses ont été faites ; et que les Renfon-
dremens soient divisez en plusieurs Chambres, par les
divers Frontispices, Portaux, Colonnes ou Arcades.
Car il faut que les Spectateurs distinguent, par
ces différences, la diversité des endroits où les par-
ticularitez que le Poëte aura démeslées, seront ex-
actement depeintes, et que les Distinctions de Scene
empeschent que l'on ne treuve de la confusion en
ces Lieux, qui embarrasse l'Auditeur, et qui seule

---

[1] Cf. Eugène Rigal, *Alexandre Hardy*, p. 170, and *Histoire de la
Littérature Française*, ed. Petit de Julleville, t. ii., where a reproduction of the original picture of the stage is given.

[2] *Ibid.* p. 173. M. Rigal gives illustrations—pictures as well as
descriptions—from the MS. notebook of Laurent Mahelot, head of
the scenery and properties department at the Hôtel de Bourgogne
about 1630. Perhaps the most interesting of all the notes is that of
the scene required for Hardy's *Pandoste, Première Journée (A Winter's
Tale)* : " Au milieu du théâtre il faut un beau palais ; à un des
côtés, une grande prison où l'on paraît tout entier ; à l'autre côté,
un temple ; au-dessous, une pointe de vaisseau, une mer basse, des
roseaux, et marches de degrés ; un réchaud, une aiguière, un chapeau
de fleurs, une fiole pleine de vins, un cornet d'encens, un tonnerre,
des flammes ; au quatrième acte, il faut un enfant ; il faut aussi
deux chandeliers et des trompettes." Compare also the chapters
on the Drama by M. Rigal and M. Lemaître in Petit de Julleville,
Hist. Litt. Fr. t. iv.

et tantôt c'est le palais du Roi, tantôt l'appartement de l'Infante, tantôt la maison de Chimène, et tantôt une rue ou place publique. On la détermine aisément pour les scènes détachées ; mais pour celles qui ont leur liaison ensemble, comme les quatre dernières du premier acte, il est malaisé d'en choisir une qui convienne à toutes. Le Comte et Don Diegue se querellent au sortir du palais, cela se peut passer dans une rue ; mais, après le soufflet reçu, Don Diegue ne peut pas demeurer dans cette rue à faire ses plaintes en attendant que son fils survienne, qu'il ne soit aussitôt environné de peuple et ne reçoive l'offre de quelques amis. Ainsi il seroit plus à propos qu'il se plaignît dans sa maison où le met l'Espagnol, pour laisser aller ses sentimens en liberté ; mais en ce cas il faudroit délier les scènes comme il a fait. En l'état où elles sont ici, on peut dire qu'il faut quelquefois aider au théâtre, et suppléer favorablement ce qui ne s'y peut représenter. Deux personnes s'y arrêtent pour parler, et quelquefois il faut présumer qu'ils marchent, ce qu'on ne peut exposer sensiblement à la vue, parce qu'ils échapperoient aux yeux avant que d'avoir pu dire ce qu'il est nécessaire qu'ils fassent savoir à l'auditeur. Ainsi, par une fiction de théâtre, on peut s'imaginer que Don Diegue et le Comte, sortant du palais du roi, avancent toujours en se querellant, et sont arrivés devant la maison de ce premier lorsqu'il reçoit le soufflet qui l'oblige à y entrer pour y chercher du recours. Si cette fiction poëtique ne vous satisfait point, laissons-le dans la place publique, et disons que le concours du peuple autour de lui, après cette offense et les offres de service que lui font les premiers amis qui s'y rencontrent, sont des circonstances que le roman ne doit pas oublier, mais que, ces mêmes actions ne servant de rien à la principale, il n'est pas besoin que le poëte s'en embarrasse sur la scène." Remembering that this was written in 1660, when Corneille had long given up his early freedom, one may be surprised at the leniency with which he speaks of his licentious ways of 1636 ; especially in comparison with his careful apology for a much smaller irregularity in *Cinna*.

The Unity of Place offered few temptations to the English dramatist. When Addison in *Cato* went out of his way to copy the French pattern, Dennis waited upon him and showed up his contradictions in the passage of criticism preserved by Dr. Johnson (*Life of Addison*) ; Dennis's method and point of view are those of Neander in the *Essay of Dramatic Poesy*.[1]

The first Prologue to the *Maiden Queen* is an epilogue to the *Essay*, and a summing up of the whole matter. Dryden's aim is to make as much as possible out of the teaching and example of his predecessors ; he takes what he can :

> The Unities of Action, Place, and Time,
> The Scenes unbroken, and a mingled chime
> Of *Jonson's* humour and *Corneille's* rhyme.

But he has no fallacious views about the things that may be borrowed or learned from others ; these are mechanical things,[2] " not the living beauties of a play." With that phrase the learning of the critics is assigned to its proper subsidiary place.

---

[1] The history of the Unities is stated with admirable clearness by H. Breitinger, *Les Unités d'Aristote avant le Cid de Corneille*. See also Jules Lemaître, *Corneille et la Poétique d'Aristote*.

[2] " The mechanic beauties of the plot, which are the observation of the three Unities, Time, Place, and Action."—*Preface to Troilus and Cressida*.

A DEFENCE OF AN ESSAY OF DRAMATIC
POESY (1668). RHYMING PLAYS

The argument about rhyme is now the least important part of Dryden's *Essay*; at the time it was more exciting, and led to more debate than anything else in the work. Crites in the *Essay* had proved that rhyme was inconvenient for dramatic composition; shortly after the publication of the *Essay*, Sir Robert Howard, the original of Dryden's *Crites*, continued the argument, and answered Neander in his Preface to his play of *The Great Favourite, or, the Duke of Lerma* (printed for H. Herringman, in the Savoy, 1668, 4°). Dryden replied in a short paper prefixed to the second edition of his *Indian Emperor*—a defence of his *Essay*. It is written with spirit; the phrasing is effective for debate : " the Muses have lost him, but the Commonwealth gains by it; the corruption of a Poet is the generation of a Statesman." Sometimes, too, the phrase is ennobled above the immediate purpose of the dispute : " Rhyme (for I will deal clearly) has something of the usurper in him; but he is brave and generous, and his dominion pleasing." It is for sentences like this that the occasional papers of Dryden are worth reading. This present *Defence* was read by Pepys apparently with some satisfaction at the way Sir Robert Howard was treated in it, but it seemed to Dryden too severe; he was reconciled to his brother-in-law, and the Defence of the Essay was dropped out of later editions of the *Indian Emperor*.

The dispute about rhyming plays was decided as time went on, when Dryden came to discover that what had really attracted him in rhyme was something different from its suitability for dramatic purposes. The *Defence* contains one of his rather sad confessions of the uncongenial nature of some of the dramatic work he had to do. Comedy is not for him : " I want that gaiety of humour which is required to it ; my conversation is slow and dull, my humour saturnine and reserved." For the other kind, for heroic drama in rhyme, he seemed to find more affinity in his genius. It is easy to see now, after *Absalom and Achitophel*, that it was the rhyme itself to which he felt himself drawn, rather than the heroic play.

Among the sayings in the *Defence* that illustrate the general position of Dryden is the remark on the end of poetry as principally *delight*, and only in the second place *instruction* : " Delight is the chief, if not the only end of poetry : instruction can be admitted but in the second place, for poesy only instructs as it delights." The combination of pleasure and instruction in poetry was one of the inherited commonplaces of criticism which every author had to face ; Corneille had met it before, and very much in the same manner. It is touched on in the Preface to the *Mock Astrologer* ; it reappears again, and more formidable, in the *Dedication of the Æneis*.

The *Defence* goes over again some of the ground of the Unities of Time and Place, without adding much to the conclusions of the *Essay*. The Unities are good and useful in so far as they save the spectator from too much distraction and interruption ; that is the upshot of it all. The observance of them may, as Dennis put it, " add grace and clearness and comeliness to the representation," if they can be observed without breach of the probabilities.

PREFACE TO AN EVENING'S LOVE, OR THE MOCK ASTROLOGER

The Mock Astrologer, taken from the *Feint Astrologue* of Thomas Corneille, which was from *El Astrólogo Fingido* of Calderon, was acted in 1668,[1] and published by Herringman in 1671. The Preface begins with an account of Dryden's interests and intentions with regard to literary history ; promises which were not left unfulfilled. For the present, however, he left over a number of subjects : among them Heroic Plays, in which the age had something to boast of as against Fletcher and Shakespeare. The theme of the Preface is Comedy. Dryden declares for a different ideal of Comedy than that of Ben Jonson. He was aiming at something more refined ; whatever his own temperament might be, however he might want that " gaiety of humour " which is the spirit of Comedy, he saw that the old-fashioned English Comedy was played out ; something more elegant must surely be within reach. The preface to the *Mock Astrologer*, like the *Defence of the Epilogue to the Conquest of Granada*, is a cry for a new artist in Comedy ; it places the Siege Perilous for Congreve to occupy later.

OF HEROIC PLAYS : AN ESSAY (1672)

The Conquest of Granada (two parts), published in 1672, was accompanied by two pieces of Dryden's prose : the Essay *Of Heroique Plays* prefixed, and at the end of the volume the *Defence of the Epi-*

---

[1] See Pepys's *Diary*, June 19-21, 1668.

logue, or an Essay on the Dramatique Poetry of the last Age.

The Essay on *Heroic Plays* is an explanation of that part of Dryden's work in which he was most in agreement with contemporary and transient literary modes. The difference from the *Essay of Dramatic Poesy* or the *Preface to the Fables* is felt at once by every reader, and it is easy to point out where the difference lies. Dryden in this present work has submitted himself to the idols of his time much more fully than in most of his essays : although he can never get rid of the accent of freedom in his voice, he has here professed obedience to certain literary conventions which he was quite able, if he had chosen, to treat in his sceptical manner, " according to that way of reasoning which was used by Socrates, Plato, and all the Academics of old." The Essay *Of Heroic Plays* is Dryden's profession of faith in that ideal of the Heroic Poem, whose authority in the seventeenth century was so great and unquestioned. It explains the origin and aim of the English heroic plays. They were attempts to realise upon the stage that superhuman grandeur which was the soul of epic poetry. They were still another of the speculative enterprises of the modern world to rival the divinities of Greece and Rome, and to employ for modern purposes and in a modern language the grand style of which the example had been set by the classical authors— not, in this case, the ancient tragic poets particularly, or even in any considerable measure, but rather the epic poets. Homer and Virgil are the masters of Dryden in his heroic plays ; that is his own account of the matter. *The Conquest of Granada* has its origin, like so much Renaissance work, in a literary apprecia-tion and admiration ; and the origin of the *Conquest of*

Granada is the same as the origin of *Paradise Lost*.
Almanzor belongs in one limb of his pedigree to the
English stage ; his ancestors are among the Elizabethans ; he derives from Tamburlaine. But it was
not that relationship which seemed important to
Dryden, even if he had ever noticed it. Almanzor is
a pattern of heroic virtue, and the ambition which led
Dryden to think of Almanzor is the same as that which
led Spenser to his epic scheme of virtuous and gentle
discipline, and Tasso to his didactic poem of Godfrey
and Rinaldo. " I must therefore avow in the first place
from whence I took the character. The first image I
had of him was from the *Achilles* of Homer ; the next
from Tasso's *Rinaldo* (who was a copy of the former),
and the third from the *Artaban* of Monsieur Calprenède,
who has imitated both."

The mention of *Artaban* brings to view another of
the many effects and manifestations of the idea of the
heroic poem. The French heroic romances of the
seventeenth century, the *Grand Cyrus* and all the rest,
were descended in one line from *Amadis of Gaul*, as
Dryden's *Almanzor* descended in one line from the
Elizabethan Tragedy. On the other side, the French
romances are an emanation of the Abstract Epic Poem ;
like Tasso's and Trissino's poems, like *Gondibert* and
Clovis, like *Paradise Lost* again, they are rivals of the
Aeneid for the crown of pure epic imagination. Even
before *Cyrus* it had been not unusual to think of
romances as epics in prose ; so Sidney seems to think
of Heliodorus (*Theagenes and Chariclea*), and so Tasso
of Heliodorus and of *Amadis of Gaul*. Scudéry in the
preface to his epic poem of *Alaric* (1654) takes the
relationship for granted ; in the preface to his sister's
romance of the *Illustrious Bashaw* he had cited Homer,

Virgil, Tasso, and Heliodorus as the authorities for that
kind of fiction.[1]   Thus there did not appear to Dryden
or his readers to be anything particularly incongruous
or absurd in the combination of Achilles and Artaban.
There was no mixture, no discord, for the heroes of the
French romances were not regarded by their authors
as " Gothic " or unclassical personages ; Artaban, like
the Illustrious Bashaw and the Grand Cyrus, could
boast of belonging to the pure heroic strain of the Greek
Epic.   Dryden, however, it will be observed, does not
make very much of the French romances in his estimate
of his hero : " For my own part I declare myself for
Homer and Tasso, and am more in love with Achilles
and Rinaldo than with Cyrus and Oroondates.   I shall
never subject my characters to the French standard
where love and honour are to be weighed by drachms
and scruples."   The heroic point of honour had been
treated with disrespect in the *Rehearsal* ; and Dryden
wished to safeguard himself as far as possible from
association with the exaggerated virtue of the " faultless
monster."

Among the properties or, at any rate, the almost
inseparable accidents of the heroic poem in Dryden's
time was the interest of the love story ; Love and

---

[1] " Comme le Poëme Epique a beaucoup de raport quant à la
constitution avec ces ingenieuses Fables que nous apellons des
Romans, il est presques superflu que i'en parle icy : puisque i'en ay
traitté assez amplement, dans l'Auant-propos de mon Illustre Bassa :
et que d'ailleurs l'heureux succès de ce Grand Visir, et celuy du
Grand Cyrus qui l'ont suiuy, ont assez fait voir, ce me semble, que ie
n'ignore pas absolument ce genre d'escrire dont ie me mesle quelquefois."—From Preface to *Alaric ou Rome Vaincuĕ, Poëme heroïque,
dedié a la serenissime Reyne de Suede par Monsieur de Scudery,
Gouverneur de Nostre Dame de la Garde,* MDCLIV.

Ibrahim ou l'Illustre Bassa was published in 1641 under the name of
M. de Scudéry.   The preface is briskly written : it takes the Romance
as a kind of Epic : " I'ay creu que pour dresser le plan de cet ouvrage
il faloit consulter les Grecs, qui ont esté nos premiers maistres ;
suivre la route qu'ils ont tenuĕ, etc.

Valour were the two motives. The heroic poem of the
modern authors was not purely classical, for all their
boasts. The tradition, the vogue, of chivalrous sentiment was too strong for all but one or two of the graver
poets, and a few of the extreme classical pedants.
One of Tasso's leading motives in his laboured arguments about epic poetry was to find a satisfactory
compromise between Homer and Amadis of Gaul.
Dryden takes for granted, without any hesitation, that
this is the right kind of theme for an heroic poet; he
has his key from Ariosto. " For the very next re-
flexion which I made was this, that an heroic play
ought to be an imitation, in little, of an heroic poem;
and consequently that love and valour ought to be the
subject of it." Corneille had protested against the
excessive importance of the love story in tragedies, and
had chosen other interests by preference for his own
dramas, but not till he had written the *Cid*, the one
great and unrivalled heroic play of love and valour,
the play that shows how much there was of reason
behind all the confused and tedious formulas of the
poetical theorists. The heroic ideal of love and valour
and honour was not utterly abstract and sterile.

One of the passages in this essay of Dryden's may
appear rather oddly irrelevant : the note upon the
" enthusiastic parts of poetry," by which he means the
magical or supernatural episodes. He instances the
Ghost of Polydorus in Virgil, the Enchanted Wood in
Tasso, and the Bower of Bliss in Spenser. The bearing
of all this is rather difficult to understand in connection
with a play like the *Conquest of Granada*. It is partly
a defence of the astral spirits in the play of *Tyrannic
Love* (1670) which had been burlesqued in the *Rehearsal*. There is a sting in Dryden's language here

(in touching on the " phlegmatic heavy gownman," the adversary of the poet) which is not accounted for by the scientific interest of the problem. At the same time this passage is not merely polemical or meant for the occasion ; it is an outbreak from Dryden's meditations upon the right use of " machines " in an epic poem, such as he afterwards explained more particularly in his *Preface to Juvenal*. He is not really much interested in dramatic form, and though his present theme is Almanzor, it may be suspected that his heart is with the unwritten epic for which the right time never came.

The Defence of the Epilogue to the Second Part of the Conquest of Granada belongs, like the *Epilogue* itself, to a different point of view from the *Essay of Dramatic Poesy*, and is generally in agreement with the Preface to the *Feigned Astrologer*. The difference in eloquence between the present age and the age of Ben Jonson is what Dryden has in his mind. His *Essay on the Dramatic Poetry of the Last Age* is an explanation of the superiority of the present times in *Wit, Language, and Conversation*.

As to Language, Dryden selects a number of examples from the older dramatists, and points out their irregularities. In Wit he finds himself obliged to make distinctions. The definition of Wit engaged Dryden's attention, and he finally arrived at a statement which satisfied him, and by which he was content to abide. In this *Essay* he comes near his later account of Wit as adequacy or propriety of language ; but he distinguishes farther between two senses of the term : Wit in the larger sense is propriety of language ; Wit in the narrower and stricter sense is *sharpness of conceit*.

Jonson's Wit in the larger sense is unquestioned : " he always writ *properly*, and as the character required " ; his fault was that his subjects were too uniformly low. In sharpness of conceit he was not admirable ; Dryden expresses the natural aversion of a later generation for the Elizabethan taste in epigrams. He remarks on the extremes between which the careless genius of Shakespeare has its range, and on the luxuriance of Fletcher ; " he is a true Englishman ; he knows not when to give over." Conversation, the third head of Dryden's discourse, brings him to the summary of his argument. His age is better than Shakespeare's because it has better manners, a more refined society, a more affable monarch. Hence the change in the dramatic ideal, as already explained in the *Mock Astrologer*. It is an ideal of refined comedy ; for though the Epilogue had spoken of the heroic motives of Love and Honour, both the Epilogue and this Essay defending it take Comedy as the form of Drama to be most thought of. The Comedy of Jonson is still an example and a standard as far as concerns the virtues of construction, of arrangement, of coherence. But, " the poets of this age will be more wary than to imitate the meanness of his persons. Gentlemen will now be entertained with the follies of each other ; and though they allow Cobb and Tib to speak properly, yet they are not much pleased with their tankard or with their rags."

THE AUTHOR'S APOLOGY FOR HEROIC POETRY AND POETIC LICENCE (1677)

This Essay was prefixed to *The State of Innocence and Fall of Man, an Opera in Heroic Verse*, Dryden's version

of *Paradise Lost*. The Essay has nothing very particular to do either with the Epic or the Opera. It is
an expansion of one of Dryden's views about poetry
which he had already expressed in the *Essay of Heroic
Plays* ; it defends the magnificent language proper to
the noblest kind of poetry, and is to some extent
reactionary. Dryden had acknowledged the reforms
of Waller and Denham, but he was not prepared to go
all lengths with the new order of things. There was
too much of the Elizabethan in him, and he could not
accept the common sense of his contemporaries as an
adequate test of good and bad poetry. " What
fustian, as they call it, have I heard these gentlemen
find out in Mr. Cowley's *Odes* ! " " All that is dull,
insipid, languishing, and without sinews in a poem, they
call an imitation of Nature." Dryden, like Tasso
before him, is compelled to stand up against the
scholars who have learned their lesson too well ; it
is as if he foresaw the sterilising influence of the
prose understanding, and the harm that might be done
by correctness if the principles of correctness were
vulgarised.

Imitation of Nature was no new catchword of art
criticism. It came from Aristotle, and was one of the
chief formulas in the endless talk about Poetry which
grew out of the rhetorical and grammatical studies of
the Revival of Learning. It was made the guiding
principle in all sorts of literary undertakings : even the
French Heroic Romances professed to be imitations of
Nature, if we may trust the preface to the *Illustrious
Bashaw*. Butler, in his *Character of a Small Poet*, puts
the same formula in his mouth—" a nasty, flat description he calls *great Nature*." Pope, in the *Essay on
Criticism*, made this his text, and found an easy way

out of it by recommending the Ancients as an equivalent. *To follow Nature is to follow them.* Nature in these discussions generally implied, as it did for Aristotle, the right conception of the true character of the subject by the reason of the poet ; hence due subordination of details ; hence abstraction from the manifold details of reality, a selective and logical method of treatment, in opposition both to the realistic accumulation of particulars (" nasty, flat description ") and to the fantastic licence of conceits.

Sir Joshua Reynolds in his *Discourses* expressed the mind of many previous generations when he explained the derivation of the grand style from that ideal beauty which is Nature. The painter must transcend reality ; " and what may seem a paradox, he learns to design naturally by drawing his figures unlike to any one object. The idea of the perfect state of Nature, which the artist calls the ideal beauty, is the great leading principle by which works of genius are conducted. By this Phidias acquired his fame. He wrought upon a sober principle what has so much excited the enthusiasm of the world ; and by this method you, who have courage to tread the same path, may acquire equal reputation."

This lofty ideal was one to which Dryden, like Corneille before him, had given his homage in many passages of his criticism. It was, however, capable of being misunderstood, and the *Apology for Heroic Poetry* is directed against the conventional admiration of reasonable art, the conventional depreciation of everything fantastic and capricious, which, as Dryden saw, was apt to condemn as fustian everything that was not respectable prose. Dryden defends Fantasy in the name of Reason, and concludes his *Apology* with the definition of Wit (which here means the faculty of poetical style), as *a propriety of thoughts and words*. He had already shown that this definition was in his mind, and he repeats it afterwards. Thus his apology, although it is in fact reactionary, and generally in favour of the Elizabethans and the "metaphysical" poets, is not one-sided, like the later romantic rebellion against Pope. It is comprehensive, a claim for poetical freedom, a protest in the name of Reason and Common Sense against a narrow and trivial misuse of Common Sense to the detriment of Imagination.

As in the *Essay of Heroic Plays*, so also here the question of supernatural "machinery" is important, and Dryden repeats his dissent from the critics who objected to the agency of gods or fairies. Boileau and Rapin are referred to as among the chief of modern critics, and Dryden had probably attentively studied the deliverances on the subject of "machinery" in Boileau's *Art Poétique*. The critical authorities to which he attaches himself in this *Apology for Poetic Licence* are not specially romantic or extravagant. It is not a factious or partisan composition, though it moves in the thick of the most dangerous matters of debate.

About this time Dryden was growing tired of his heroic plays ; the last of them, *Aureng-zeb*, was published in 1676, and contained in its *Prologue* the author's farewell to that kind of drama.

PREFACE TO ALL FOR LOVE (1678)

Aureng-zeb, the last of the rhyming heroic plays, was published in 1676. The tragedy of *All for Love* (written to please himself, as Dryden afterwards tells us) was meant to follow both Shakespeare and the classical rules. " I have endeavoured in this play to follow the practice of the Ancients, who, as Mr. Rymer has judiciously observed, are and ought to be our masters." But the Ancients are not to be followed to the disparagement of the English genius : " though their models are regular they are too little for English Tragedy, which requires to be built in a larger compass." Shakespeare is acknowledged by Dryden as his master in dramatic style ; the play is in blank verse, rhyme is abandoned ; " not that I condemn my former way, but that this is more proper to my present purpose."

The Preface further touches upon those themes of ignorant and malicious criticism which were provided for Dryden in his feuds with Settle and others, and most recently in Rochester's imitation of Horace (*An Allusion to the Tenth Satire of his First Book*).

THE GROUNDS OF CRITICISM IN TRAGEDY

(Preface to *Troilus and Cressida*, 1679)

Dryden was still interested by the problems of regularity which had been discussed in the *Essay of Dramatic Poesy* ; he had since been reading some of the more recent critics, and they had some influence on his ideas. None of them are equal to Corneille, his master in the *Dramatic Essay*, and it is with some depression of spirits that one finds oneself obliged to listen instead to Rapin, Bossu " the best of modern critics," and " my friend Mr. Rymer." Among the changes of view is the greater tolerance shown to the moral formula : " to lay down to yourself what that precept of morality shall be which you would insinuate into the people " is the first rule of the heroic and not less of the dramatic poet :

in his earlier essays Dryden had followed Corneille in taking the instructive part of poetry more lightly. The "fable is the example built upon the moral, which confirms the truth of it to our experience," and so on. There are few things more wonderful in history than the way in which this allegorical theory of poetry survived through all the most enlightened modern ages, and was not only accepted but cherished and honoured as a vital truth by authors who prided themselves on nothing so much as their modern taste and their freedom from Gothic darkness. "The allegorical fable" is not merely a necessary part of the seventeenth-century professional epic (Chapelain's *Pucelle*, Scudéry's *Alaric*, etc.), it is one of the headings in Pope's Preface to his *Iliad* (1715), and there is no limit to the range of its worship in the age of Dryden. It survived all the humanist attacks on the medieval allegorising method ; the "Renaissance" left the allegorical theory of Poetry to be honoured by philosophers who kept no other relic of the Middle Ages.

There is rather more constraint in this essay, more obsequious respect for authorities, than is common with Dryden ; the tone of it recalls the *Essay of Heroic Plays*. He goes further than usual in submitting Shakespeare and Fletcher to the authority of the Ancients : the plots of Shakespeare and Fletcher are to be followed "so far only as they have copied the excellencies of those who invented and brought to perfection dramatic poetry." Yet in this case again as in so many others, after he has made concessions to his friend Mr. Rymer, and to the standards of correct writing, he saves himself by speaking out before the end, and lets it be seen that all his apparent depreciation of Shakespeare is only on the surface. "I cannot leave this subject before I do

justice to that divine poet." There is some resemblance
in details between Dryden and Voltaire in their criticism of Shakespeare ; they condemn and praise the
same things. The difference is that the praise always
appears to be extorted from Voltaire, while Dryden
has difficulty in keeping back his admiration long
enough to put in his censures upon the faults of
Shakespeare.

PREFACE TO OVID'S EPISTLES (1680)

There are many passages in which Dryden speaks of
Ovid between the *Essay of Dramatic Poesy* and the
Preface to the Fables. There was an affinity between
the two poets in the inexhaustible readiness of their
elocution ; and, further, Dryden was able to detect
and half admire in Ovid some of the rhetorical excesses
which he recognised in his own work. The account
of Ovid in this Preface is, however, subordinate to the
discussion of the principles of translation, a subject of
much importance then, as it was also in the succeeding
generation. Dryden's references to Cowley and Denham explain sufficiently the current opinions and
tastes.

DEDICATION OF THE SPANISH FRIAR, OR
THE DOUBLE DISCOVERY (1681)

The *Spanish Friar* was a return, on Dryden's part,
from different attempts at dramatic correctness to the
old English irregularity ; it is an Elizabethan play,
with its double plot, and its blending of tragedy and
comedy. The Dedication is one of the liveliest of
Dryden's Prefaces, especially in its confessions of his

changes of taste, his early admiration for Du Bartas, his repentance for some of the rhetoric of his heroic plays, the sublimities of Maximin and Almanzor, " those Delilahs of the theatre." In none of Dryden's prose is the language more vigorous, or less affected by the superstitions of polite literature. It was written when Dryden was warming to his work in his best year ; it has some of the glow of his great satirical poems, and all their self-possession and security of tone.

PREFACE TO SYLVAE (1685)

The Preface to the *Second Miscellany* is a good deal like that to Ovid's *Epistles* ; it discusses the problems of translation, and contains some of Dryden's opinions about the classical poets, chiefly Virgil, Ovid, Lucretius, Theocritus, Horace, and about other matters. Among the rest it states, what ought to have been in those days a commonplace, but was pretty generally neglected, the rule of " Pindaric " verse in English. It was generally written in those days as if the object were merely to make irregular patterns of lines different in length ; it was a variation on the old game of writing poems in the shape of altars, wings, and diamonds. Dryden knows better, and takes the opportunity of pointing out that in English free verse each line must be justified by its relation to the line preceding, " the cadency of one line must be a rule to that of the next." What he meant he demonstrated in the *Ode on Mrs. Anne Killigrew*, one of the few poems of its order which it is not absurd to compare with the free verse of Milton. Pindarics were at their height in that year, as may be seen in Hearne's collection of the poems on the death of King Charles, preserved in the Bodleian.

PREFACE TO ALBION AND ALBANIUS:
AN OPERA (1685)

Dryden, like Corneille and Molière, was led to try his hand at the new form of entertainment which was brought from Italy to Paris by Mazarin, and which came to take the place of the older Masques. The difference between the seventeenth-century Opera and the Masques and Pastoral Plays of the previous generation is not very great, and Dryden in this Preface refers to the *Pastor Fido* of Guarini as one of the ancestors of Opera. These matters, however, belong rather to the history of Dryden's poetry than of his criticism, and he does not go very deeply into the nature and origin of this kind of Drama. It was first introduced into England by Sir William D'Avenant, and the Preface to *Albion and Albanius* described the relation of that Opera to the adaptation of the *Tempest*, in which D'Avenant had been Dryden's helper. The old conception of Opera, as properly a mythological pageant, with music, dancing, and tableaux, is affirmed by Dryden, in agreement with Corneille, whose *Andromède* and *Toison d'Or* were among the most famous examples of Opera in their day. The *Machines* were as essential to Opera as the music and the poetry, and the artist of the scenery and dresses was at least the equal of the poet and the musical composer, like Inigo Jones in his rivalry with Ben Jonson. Dryden leaves these topics in his Preface, and discusses questions of prosody, or rather the general subject of melody of language, a subject to which he afterwards returned, though his treatise on English Prosody was never completed.

At the opening of the Preface he repeats his
account of poetical Wit—" a propriety of thoughts
and words."

King Charles died before the Opera was published,
and the Postscript records this change for the worse
in Dryden's fortunes.

PREFACE TO THIRD MISCELLANY
(EXAMEN POETICUM, 1693)

This Preface opens with one of the most vigorous of
Dryden's assaults on his critical adversaries, for whose
benefit an old epigram, used long before in the controversy with Sir Robert Howard, is revived and sharpened
into the final and perfect form : *thus the corruption of a
poet is the generation of a critic.* This is meant for
Rymer, by whom Dryden had been " seemingly courted
and secretly undermined " in the *Short View of Tragedy*
then recently published.

The Preface goes on to defend the English Drama
against those who would depreciate it by comparison
with the Ancients ; and it also makes a stand for the
honour of Dryden's own generation against those who
use the names of Shakespeare and Ben Jonson to vilify
their own contemporaries. It is in this way a supple-
ment to the *Essay of Dramatic Poesy*, and repeats some
of the former positions, *e.g.* as to the thinness of French
dramatic plots, and their too servile following of the
" mechanic rules." The question between Ancients
and Moderns has taken new forms since the *Essay* of
1668, and has been brought to a head by Perrault's
demonstrations in France ; Dryden is careful to guard
himself against misconstruction ; it will not do to be

associated too closely with the French advocates of the Moderns, and he points out that " there is a vast difference betwixt arguing like Perrault on behalf of the French poets against Homer and Virgil, and betwixt giving the English poets their undoubted due of excelling Æschylus, Euripides, and Sophocles." From these controversies Dryden passes to the contents of the present *Miscellany*, and says something about the poets there translated, and about his own principles of versification, a subject on which one would gladly have heard him longer.

A DISCOURSE CONCERNING THE ORIGIN AND PROGRESS OF SATIRE (1693)

The Preface to Juvenal addressed to the Earl of Dorset (Eugenius of the *Essay on Dramatic Poesy*) is not one of the best of Dryden's critical papers, as a great part of it is little more than an adaptation from Dacier's account of Satiric Poetry, in his translation of Horace. But the style, for all Dryden's references to the failings of " an old man's memory," and to " the tattling quality of age," is not much depressed by the amount of learning which has to be packed into the discourse, and made intelligible and palatable to the studious reader. The themes, apart from the main one, are old favourites with Dryden. The nature of Epic is discussed again, and again the problem of " machines " is brought up, in relation to Dryden's own plans for the poem that never was written, either about King Arthur or about the Black Prince ; while the abstract of the history of Satire leads to some less formal passages of literary history in which Dryden is left free from the cumbersome authority of Casaubon, Heinsius, and Dacier.

PARALLEL OF POETRY AND PAINTING (1695)

The Latin poem *De Arte Graphica* of the French painter Charles Alphonse Du Fresnoy (1611-1665) was first published in 1668, with a French translation in prose ; it was dedicated to Colbert.

Dryden's *Parallel of Poetry and Painting* is in the main a statement of the case for Idealism in Art, with the implication that the true following of Nature in Art is to discover the ideal and to neglect the distractions of the manifold particulars of experience. Thus Dryden's *Parallel* is the forerunner of Sir Joshua Reynolds's *Discourses*, and indeed Reynolds associated himself with Du Fresnoy and Dryden in the notes which he contributed to Mason's version of the Latin poem in 1782. " There is an absolute necessity for the Painter to generalise his notions ; to paint particulars is not to paint Nature, it is only to paint circumstances. When the Artist has conceived in his imagination the image of perfect beauty, or the abstract idea of forms, he may be said to be admitted into the great Council of Nature, and to

> Trace Beauty's beam to its eternal spring,
> And pure to Man the fire celestial bring.—v. 19." [1]

Dryden supports himself in the arduous study of the Ideal with the help of a long quotation from Bellori, the Italian critic, in which the commonplaces of the Platonic theory, as accepted by Italian artists, are expounded with an eloquence rather too florid for

[1] Reynolds on Du Fresnoy, Note iii.

Dryden's taste. "But in short, this is the present genius of Italy." The subject was not altogether new to Dryden ; long before this, in his studies for the Heroic Drama, he had pondered on the ideal character of the Hero, and had found that in poetic diction the style which was most noble was at the same time most truly in accordance with Nature. But it had not previously occurred to him to work out a demonstration of the principles that were involved in his earlier dogmas. Hitherto his furthest point in this direction was in the *Apology for Heroic Poetry* (1677). Now when he takes up the subject again, it is not altogether of his own initiative ; it is part of a task required by the booksellers, and there are signs in his *Parallel*, *e.g.* in the quotation from Bellori, that he is compelled to take the same devices for eking out his tale of work as are to be found, more lavishly employed, in the Prefaces to *Juvenal* and to *Virgil*. Nevertheless this Essay, though one of the less lively of Dryden's critical works, is kept from flagging, and from showing signs of fatigue, until something like a fair and consistent exposition of the general principles of composition has been attained, and then, judiciously, Dryden breaks off his theme without labouring it out to the conclusion of Du Fresnoy's argument.

DEDICATION OF THE ÆNEIS (1697)

The *Dedication of the Æneis*, like the *Preface to Juvenal* four years earlier, is one of the less original of Dryden's Essays, a remarkable contrast to such free and spirited passages as the *Dedication of the Spanish Friar*. It repeats the commonplaces of the respectable Fathers of Criticism for whom the Epic Poem was all but a matter of religion. It goes deep into the moral functions of Epic as compared with Tragedy, and into the defence of the character of Æneas. Great part of it is borrowed, to save trouble, from Segrais's Preface to his translation of the *Æneid*, including the question whether Virgil, when he spoke of Orion, meant the heliacal or the achronical rising of the constellation. But the good sense of Dryden is clearly manifest throughout the essay, and there are not wanting passages of his livelier manner, *e.g.* in the account of the modern epic poets, concluding with the note on *Paradise Lost*: " if the giant had not foiled the knight and driven him out of his stronghold, to wander through the world with his lady errant." And the last pages, a series of remarks on prosody and on poetical rhetoric, " the turn on thoughts and words," etc., are completely free from the depressing influence of the French authors.

Dryden's Virgil was published by Tonson in a magnificent folio, with many engravings, by Hollar and Lambert, after Cleyn, which had already appeared in Ogilby's folio Virgil of 1654. Æneas in these " sculptures " was, however, not quite the same personage as in their previous state in Ogilby. His nose in Tonson's impressions is more Roman, and sometimes he bears also something like the wig of King William ; a circumstance which must have given additional point to certain malign allusions in Dryden's preface. " Æneas, though he married the heiress of the crown, yet claimed no title to it during the life of his father-in-law."

In spite of the publisher's magnificence, the book was carelessly printed : " the printer is a beast, and understands nothing I can say to him of correcting the press." One considerable error was allowed to remain in all the editions till Malone's : *Aristotle* as an author of " novels."

Probably the printer's obstinacy showed itself most in the punctuation, which looks capricious, and which seems generally to have been a difficulty. " The printer has enough to answer for in the false pointings," as Dryden puts it in the *Preface to the Second Miscellany*.

PREFACE TO THE FABLES (1700)

The *Preface to the Fables*, addressed to the Duke of Ormond, is a piece of work of which it is hard to speak except in some such terms as those which Dryden himself employs in it when he has to write about Chaucer. There is no need here for any such apologies for the failings of old age as are made by the author in the *Preface to Juvenal*. The *Preface to the Fables* is more full of life than anything else in Dryden's prose ; not inferior even to the *Essay of Dramatic Poesy* ; while nothing, either in prose or verse, brings out more admirably or to better advantage the qualities of Dryden as the great English man of letters. For this is what he was, rather than essentially a poet ; his genius is one that commands both vehicles of expression, it is not one that is specially inclined to verse ; and the free movement of his mind and speech is scarcely less wonderful in a prose tract like this Preface than in the verse of *Absalom and Achitophel*. " *His chariot wheels grow hot with driving*," and this vehemence and speed are of the same kind whatever chariot he may happen to have selected. In this present case, he is absolutely at home in the work he has undertaken, and it brings out all his best qualities both of mind and character, from the generous, unenvying spirit in which he converses with the great masters, to the humorous correction of Milbourne and Blackmore, and the straightforward answer to Collier.

POSTSCRIPT

For the belief in " Nature " (*supra*, p. 41) the following verses of Chapman may be quoted, from the address *To the Reader* prefixed to the *Iliads* ; speaking of Homer—

Whose right not all those great learn'd men have done,
In some main parts, that were his commentars :
But as the illustration of the sun
Should be attempted by the erring stars,
They fail'd to search his deep and treasurous heart ;
The cause was, since they wanted the fit key
Of Nature, in their downright strength of Art
With Poesy to open Poesy.

III

THE EIGHTEENTH CENTURY

LAST year, after Sir Sidney Colvin's address, I was asked by Mr. Henry James what my subject would be when my turn came. I was not able to tell him, but you will understand how I was pleased at the time, and how I still think that his question added something to the importance of my present task, and encouragement in an equal degree to make the best of it. I do not take it upon me now to praise the work of Henry James, but it is worth while to put on the record of the English Association that it had the benevolent sympathy of that most subtle mind ; he knew what the Association was aiming at, and was interested in its conversation. Henry James has amused himself in more than one parable concerning the vanity of literary fame ; the Death of the Lion, the Lion dying among the conventional worshippers who have not read his books, who toss about and lose his manuscript entrusted to them. But I do not believe he would refuse the thanks of this assembly for the profusion of gifts they have received from him, though there cannot be many who have read everything, even in that "definitive" edition which needs so many supplements before it can be complete.

Many of us have often doubted since the war began, and are still doubting, what is the right way to take with the old peaceful studies ; how much time is to be spared for the humanities. Whatever our several decisions and private casuistries may be with regard to this problem, we must all recognise that Henry James took one of the right ways. I put it at the lowest valuation, to begin with ; before we come to the end of our thinking about him most of us will have discovered that there is no end to our admiration, simply because he is now, through his conduct in the last year and a half of his life, part of the great alliance for freedom. He could not think of neutrality or indifference when the human race was challenged ; he called in his imagination from its familiar brooding-places, and gathered the energies of his mind into a concentrated flame of indignation against wrong, of hope and confidence in victory for " that noble France," and for the England to which he devoted himself.

The Eighteenth Century is the subject which I have chosen ; partly, no doubt, in obedience to that stream of tendency which we used to call the *Zeitgeist*. For the eighteenth century is coming again into favour ; and if the English Association should think none the worse of it when this discourse is finished, the result will be due to the influence of which I have spoken ; a growing amiable wish not to be unjust to the eighteenth century, a growing intelligent opinion that some of the common judgments have been wrong.

I had an early opportunity of reading the *Peace of the Augustans* by your former President, Mr. Saintsbury, and that of course set me thinking again about Swift and Pope and Johnson. I believe the thing that really pointed finally to my text and made it inevitable, was an ironical letter from a friend about *The Times* literary reviewer of Mr. Saintsbury, and how the reviewer pitied

Dr. Johnson who was not able to see over the garden wall ; Dr. Johnson, who could not be high-minded and aspiring like us. My correspondent, you see, did not quite agree with the reviewer ; there was room for discussion—" if one had a mind "—with respect to the indispensable eighteenth century. " Our excellent and indispensable eighteenth century," Matthew Arnold called it, and his phrase expresses a very common nine-teenth-century opinion. We can't do without the eighteenth century, but we don't want to think of it more than we can help. Yet the nineteenth century has thought a good deal about the eighteenth ; we do not forget Leslie Stephen, nor Mr. Courthope, nor Mr. Austin Dobson ; we sometimes forget that Carlyle, the chief opponent of the eighteenth century, gave half his time to eighteenth-century history and literature, and that not in order merely to refute and explode, but to explain, even to admire. His essay on Diderot shows up the weakness of the century ; it also brings out the genius of the great man of letters with whom it is dealing, and appraises him not merely as an indispensable stage on the way to something better (namely the nineteenth century and " us "), but as an original genius turning out, *e.g.* in *Le Neveu de Rameau*, a lawless, extravagant, unreasonable, living piece of imagination. In Carlyle's *Diderot* the whole business is explained, as well as is possible in any summary prose—the defects of eighteenth-century philosophy, the genius limited by the fashions of the time but undefeated, finding its own way.

Carlyle's *Diderot*, we may say, does justice to the eighteenth century from the nineteenth-century point of view. It points out the limitations and the prejudices of eighteenth-century " Enlightenment," it shows with great spirit and instinctive sympathy how prejudices and narrow principles may be occasionally transcended by genius. Diderot's originality wins through, in spite of the hindrances put in his way by the fashion of his time.

This is one way of dealing with the eighteenth century, and it seems to be just and fair. That there are common prejudices, fallacies, idols (in Bacon's sense of the term) besetting the intellects of the eighteenth century can hardly be denied. They are not restricted to the French Encyclopedists, to the mechanical materialist philosophy, the object of Carlyle's censure. They are found in Bishop Butler, as may be seen in two remarkable essays, Thomas Hill Green on " Popular Philosophy," and Matthew Arnold on " Bishop Butler and the Zeitgeist." Orthodoxy, Deism, Atheism in the eighteenth century, all alike are subject to certain ruling notions or names—the faculties of the mind, reason a separate thing from passion, self love and social—formulas and modes of thought which have a horrid resemblance to reality—like the dodder, that busy plant, which is related in the vegetable kingdom, though at some distance, to the healthy green flowering whin bush which it strangles in its pale systematic reticulations. Le Neveu de Rameau might be compared to a fresh living outburst—the miracle of Dionysus with a new application—the fresh flaming sap of the vine breaking out and disposing of the philosophical dodder.

The " enlightenment " of the eighteenth century has suffered depreciation in the nineteenth : negative, barren, unspiritual, moderate, tame, respectable—these are words employed to describe it in days that have given a different value to " enthusiasm " from that which it had in the eighteenth century. It is not always recognised what a benefit enlightenment was to the world in general, and how much it was needed. " Philosopher," as we all know, came to be a common term applied to any gentleman who was known not to believe in the Devil. This is a fair caricature of " enlightenment." But really in the seventeenth century it was time to have a serious policy about the Devil. The witch trials of the seventeenth century, raging over the whole of the Protestant North, make up a record of cruelty unequalled in the history of the world—at any rate down to the last year or so—not perhaps for mere human suffering, but for the hideous combination of religion and complacent insensibility. It was time to relieve the Prince of Darkness from the loathsome calumnies of the witch-finders.

Much of the eighteenth-century rationalism, which of course belongs to the seventeenth century in great measure—to Descartes and Spinoza, Hobbes and Locke —much of this is negative, abstersive, clearing away obstructions. But though the negative process of cleansing came to be overvalued, as we know, in many quarters, and made into a receipt for the salvation of the world, yet there was always much more than this in the life of the eighteenth century. It is nothing if not critical, but it is not purely critical and nothing more. It is one of the greatest ages of the world in artistic imagination. It is also the great heroic age of England. The " wonderful year " comes in the middle of it, and Chatham is the hero. Burns understands this. The poet of the lost cause—" It was a' for our rightfu' king " — Burns clearly understands that Chatham, and after him his son, is the right leader of the United Kingdom of Great Britain. This is the true Commonwealth in which the Jacobite poet lives, and for the sake of this Kingdom he does not object to pay heavier taxes, as long as the Navy is kept safe from economical retrenchment. Burns was born at the beginning of the wonderful year (Jan. 25, 1759), and he knew its history. It was Minden and Quebec that taught him what sort of a country he belonged to, and what sort of statesman was desirable to have the guiding of it—one who " could impress his own energy on every branch of the public service," and under whose direction " our chiefs both by land and sea viewed obstacles and dangers as he did—only as a spur to exertion, and as an enhancement of fame " (Stanhope, c. 36). The year of Minden and Quebec, of Lagos and Quiberon, had the luck to find a poet. *Hearts of Oak*, the best war-song in the language, was written by David Garrick and Dr. Boyce—" to add something more to this wonderful year."

The music of the eighteenth century does not come into my discourse, but I think readers of books sometimes forget that when we want music for the death of a king or hero we get it from the eighteenth century, from *Saul ;* and that though Shelley is probably a better lyrical poet than Pope, yet Pope is sung and heard with pleasure much oftener than any of Shelley's words—" to an Indian air," or to any other musical accompaniment. You all know Pope's lyric ; it is better sung than said :

> Where'er you walk, cool gales shall fan the glade,
> Trees where you sit shall crowd into a shade ;
> Where'er you tread, the blushing flowers shall rise,
> And all things flourish where you turn your eyes.

It is not the very finest poetry, but those four lines from Pope's juvenile Pastoral have by good fortune, and we may say by the good genius of the eighteenth century, turned into a lyric, a song for singing.   Might not the life of this song be taken as a kind of symbol of the eighteenth century, an example of its present value ? It is old fashioned, and every one feels that at once, as soon as the tune begins : but it is not antiquated ; it needs no learned curiosity to give it a meaning or flavour ; you do not need to pretend you like it. It is a popular song.

Ought not the architecture and the painting of the eighteenth century, and the seventeenth, to be more frequently remembered by readers of books ? The Library of Trinity College, Cambridge, which is the work of Wren, the Library designed in the tradition of Wren for his own College of All Souls (it was opened with an oration by Dr. Edward Young the poet), those inventions and many others might impress upon the minds of literary persons something of the true meaning of that age. They might see there for themselves how far different is restraint from restriction, and moderation from meanness ; what thrilling life there may be in simple harmonies of spaces. It is not negation or privation to be content with the right lines, to refuse the wrong ornamentation.

As for painting, do not the advocates of the romantic revival, and the return to Nature, sometimes speak as if no one in the eighteenth century had ever looked from a height over open country, as if the daedal earth had been treated for the time somehow like Giotto's portrait of Dante in the Bargello at Florence, its green, white, and red made decent and uncompromising with a coat of chocolate ? The truth is that the eighteenth century had not to wait for the nineteenth to be told about Claude and Poussin and Salvator Rosa ; that both in the careful study of landscape and in the extravagances of scenery hunting it had gone far, before the

date of *Modern Painters*. Also it had painters of its
own. The beauty of Hogarth's painting has suffered
in the general estimate through interest in the story of
his pictures, which can be followed most conveniently
in the engravings. His pictures where they are seen
at all are often glanced at carelessly. The story of
Marriage à la Mode is well enough known already in
black and white ; why waste valuable time looking at
the coloured version ? Reynolds has suffered in
another way by the perishing of his colours. But
surely there is enough of Hogarth, Reynolds, and
Gainsborough—one might add Canaletto, a London
painter—to prove that the eighteenth century in
England was not colour-blind. Reynolds perhaps may
be called to prove some points of rather doubtful value
in the character of the eighteenth century. Did he not
comply too much with " a hypocritical and hackneyed
course of literature," the conventional idealism of the
conventional grand style, in his discourses to the Royal
Academy? But that may be left for another inquiry.
Whatever contradictions may be found between his
painting and his preaching, or even in his painting by
itself, as in the allegorical picture of the triumph of
Truth and Dr. James Beattie in Marischal College,
there can be no question that his painting is painted, or
that it is full of the individual character which he
continually underrated in his presidential lectures. In
the Aberdeen picture, happily better preserved than
some of Reynolds's, the eighteenth century as well as
Truth is vindicated. It is a cheerful thing. *Gusto*, the
term of art which was so frequent in that century
and such a favourite with Hazlitt afterwards, is a word
that sums up much of the spirit of that age. What is
meant by *gusto* is that hilarity of spirit in the artist as

he works, which as it is the direct opposite of one of
the seven deadly sins must be somewhere near one of
the Christian graces. I have not had time to consult
St. Thomas Aquinas on this point ; I hope he will
pardon me if I refer to a more compendious philosopher,
the author whom Gibbon mentions as " the infamous
Spinoza." *Hilaritas excessum habere nequit, sed semper
bona est.* Hilarity is the harmonious efficacy of the
whole being ; you may find it in the portrait of Beattie,
and more easily, for the Marischal College picture visits
this town only at long intervals, in the portrait of Lord
Heathfield in the National Gallery. When you go
there do not forget to look at the floating batteries in
the picture beside it of the relief of Gibraltar, and do
not let any too exclusively painting friend of yours
persuade you that it is wrong to think of the subject
of those two pictures and their historical and literary
associations. They come in to illustrate Burns's *Jolly
Beggars*, and a quotation from Burns's old soldier will
not be irrelevant here. I have spoken of *Hearts of Oak*,
the war-song of 1759 ; Burns's old soldier begins at
Quebec in that year, and goes on to 1782 and the French
floating batteries off Gibraltar :

> My prenticeship I past where my leader breath'd his last,
> When the bloody die was cast on the heights of Abram ;
> And I served out my trade when the gallant game was
>   play'd,
> And the Moro low was laid at the sound of the drum.
>
> I lastly was with Curtis, among the floating batt'ries,
> And there I left for witness an arm and a limb ;
> Yet let my country need me, with Elliot to lead me,
> I'd clatter on my stumps to the sound of the drum.

Hilaritas excessum habere nequit, sed semper bona est.
The painter and the poet, his younger contemporary,

have hit upon the same subject, and both have taken it with hilarity—with that *gusto* which is nothing but life itself, in the soul of the artist. Inspiration is another word for the same sort of life. Neither word is much better than x or y, but you know the meaning of it when it comes upon you in the picture or the song, if you are not yourself too dispirited and dull to see and hear.

The people of the eighteenth century were not always hilarious. Swift and Johnson and Gray and Cowper —these names are present to all our minds, and they imply a great part of the century; their lives cover more than the whole of it. But it should be observed that the gloom of Swift and the melancholy of Johnson, Gray, and Cowper are not dispiriting like the Deadly Sin of Sloth or Accidie, which is *Tristitia*. The dispirited man, the victim of Wanhope, the sluggard, does not write odes to Melancholy. If he turn his melancholy or his despair into verse, to that extent he is not despairing. The misanthropy of Swift, the melancholy of Johnson, the despair of Cowper refute themselves when they are uttered as those famous men know how to utter them.

Has any great man been treated with more injustice than Swift, in the traditional popular estimate of him? This I take to be generally a repetition, in one form or other, of Macaulay's most ludicrous bombast. Macaulay, reviewing the History of the War of Succession in Spain, has to make a passing allusion to the political journalism of the time. There were many ways of touching this off. If he wanted simply to give the facts, he might have said Steele and Swift were the eminent hands who wrote plausibly for the Whigs and Tories respectively. If he wanted particularly to give

the Whig dogs the best of it, there were many decent
rhetorical ways of doing so. The impossible way was
chosen by Macaulay. He vilifies Swift when nothing
is to be gained thereby. He is writing about the Peace
of Utrecht on a scale which leaves him no room for any
discussion of the *Examiner* or the *Whig Examiner*.
But he cannot let Swift go, and his pompous phrasing,
brought in for no reasonable literary purpose except
the familiar flourish of sounding brass, has left its mark
on every mind that has thought about Swift at all.

" In the front of the opposite ranks appeared a
darker and fiercer spirit, the apostate politician, the
ribald priest, the perjured lover, a heart burning with
hatred against the whole human race, a mind richly
stored with images from the dunghill and the lazar-
house." The curse of Ernulphus was nothing to this.
But it serves no purpose, and the writer forgets it at
once. With this loud sentence still in our ears, we hear
Macaulay a minute later observing that it is possible
to discuss the peace of Utrecht without irritation.

I will not trouble to find the right word for the loud
sentence, I think it is as bad as it could be. I may say
also that I know no one who admires Macaulay more
thoroughly than I do ; but I think that his treatment
of Swift is a great wrong. Not every one who reads
Macaulay reads the admirable life of the apostate
politician by Sir Henry Craik, or Mrs Wood's commentary on the perjured lover ; perhaps even fewer
think for themselves, and ask for the proof of Swift's
misanthropy.

Swift has described his sentiments in the well-known
passage of a letter to Pope, Sept. 29, 1725, written at
the time of *Gulliver's Travels* : " I heartily hate and
detest that animal called man, although I heartily

love John, Peter, Thomas, and so forth." Is there any reason to doubt Swift's honesty in this ? And is this misanthropy ? If it be misanthropy, is it a heart burning with hatred against the whole human race ? Is not Swift's misanthropy really just the converse of philanthropy ? The philanthropist, the friend of humanity, combines love of the whole human race with indifference to John, Peter, Thomas, and so forth. From these hustings I ask you to vote for the misanthrope :

> Dean, Drapier, Bickerstaff, or Gulliver,
> Whether he choose Cervantes' serious air,
> Or laugh and shake in Rabelais' easy chair,
> Or praise the court or magnify mankind,
> Or his grieved country's copper chains unbind.

I am told that Swift's account of the Yahoos is madness ; but I am not sure. I think some readers of Swift have been very easily taken in by a very simple imposture. Gulliver, in his fourth voyage, comes to the land of the horse—whose name only innocence will attempt to pronounce, or arrogance to spell. The horses are his Utopia, we are told. Of course they are, and so is the king of Brobdingnag, a benevolent reasonable being. Some people talk as if the fourth voyage was meant to prove that any horse is better than all men. Even Thackeray is deceived : " the meaning is that man is utterly wicked, desperate, and imbecile, and his passions are so monstrous and his boasted powers so mean that he is and deserves to be the slave of brutes, and ignorance is better than his vaunted reason." This closely resembles some of the foolish opinions about Thackeray himself, who has been accused of seeing nothing noble in humanity : " a sneerin' beast."

Thackeray has spoken nobly about Swift : " An immense genius ; an awful downfall and ruin. So great a man he seems to me, that thinking of him is like thinking of an empire falling." But he has left out the essential part of that great genius ; he has left out Swift's Utopia, which is not very different from Sir Thomas More's. Here it is, in the opinions of the king of Brobdingnag :

" For I remember very well in a discourse one day with the king, when I happened to say there were several thousand books among us written upon the art of government, it gave him (directly contrary to my intention) a very mean opinion of our understandings. He professed both to abominate and despise all mystery, refinement, and intrigue, either in a prince or a minister. He could not tell what I meant by secrets of state, where an enemy or some rival nation was not in the case. He confined the knowledge of governing within very narrow bounds, to common sense and reason, to justice and lenity, to the speedy determination of civil and criminal causes ; with some other obvious topics which are not worth considering. And he gave it for his opinion ' that whoever could make two ears of corn, or two blades of grass, to grow upon a spot of ground where only one grew before, would deserve better of mankind, and do more essential service to his country, than the whole race of politicians put together.' "

The likeness to More's ideal is strong in the next paragraph, about education in Brobdingnag :

" The learning of this people is very defective : consisting only in morality, history, poetry, and mathematics, wherein they must be allowed to excel. But the last of these is wholly applied to what may be useful in life, to the improvement of agriculture and all mechanical arts ; so that among us it would be little esteemed. And as to ideas, entities, abstractions, and transcendentals, I could never drive the least conception into their heads."

No one can write like that who has lost interest or belief in humanity. And this is the essential positive part of Swift's argument, which is very often ignored, even by writers whose business it may be to explain Swift. It is not quoted by Leslie Stephen, who however makes some amends to Swift in another place and in a memorable sentence : " He had the characteristic passion of the good and wise for walking."

Johnson has been unjustly depreciated in a different way—as the representative of everything which we of a later age find to be prejudiced and conventional. He saw nothing to admire in *Lycidas*, and he wrote artificial periods containing words like " anfractuosity." He had no eyes for the Western Islands, and did not see in them what every tourist sees, with quotations from the *Lord of the Isles* supplied in his guide-book. Some of those judgements may be met and contravened. Dr. Johnson was taken without acknowledgement by Stendhal as an advocate against the rule of classical French tragedy, in the great days just before *Hernani*. As for the Western Islands, it is true that Dr. Johnson did not write about them in the modern way. He neither compared the Hebridean sunset to a glorified soda-water bottle, nor did he survey and label the gullies and pinnacles of the Coolin. But those who say that he travelled indifferent and insensible through the air of that enchanted ground have forgotten the verses that Johnson wrote at Armadale and Corrichatachin—

where he spoke of the naked rock mixing its stony ruins with the clouds,

> Permeo terras ubi nuda rupes
> Saxeas miscet nebulis ruinas,

and of the soft green soothing welcome of the Land of Skye :

> Quam grata defesso virentem
> Skia sinum nebulosa pandis.

What more does any one want ? The quintessence is there. We remember also the day spent on the West of Mull, between Inch Kenneth and Iona ; Johnson has found the right words for it—without " anfractuosities " :

" The evening was now approaching, and we were yet at a considerable distance from the end of our expedition. We could therefore stop no more to make remarks in the way, but set forward with some degree of eagerness. The day soon failed us, and the moon presented a very solemn and pleasing scene. The sky was clear, so that the eye commanded a wide circle ; the sea was neither still nor turbulent ; the wind neither silent nor loud. We were never far from one coast or another, on which, if the weather had become violent, we could have found shelter, and therefore contemplated at ease the region through which we glided in the tranquillity of the night, and saw now a rock and now an island grow gradually conspicuous and gradually obscure."

Dr. Johnson did not go out to see those reeds shaken in the wind on the shore of mountain waters that to other adventurers have been more worth than all the riches of town. Like the old German *minnesinger*, he had more to do than to shed the tears of sensibility over a flower. *Ich hân mê ze tuonne danne bluomen klagen.* But he was no more indifferent than that other idolatrous Londoner, Charles Lamb, to the life of the lonely places—when once he had been brought among them. He does not spin it out, the visionary fancy, but he had read the *Odyssey*, and he had read the books of chivalry, and he amused himself as he rode by pretending to be a wandering knight, and at Dunvegan he found Phaeacia.

The conventionality of the eighteenth century is an offence to the nineteenth, and it need not be defended nor denied ; it ought to be understood. There is a sort of conventionality that is merely hindrance and nonsense ; absurd as the fat cherubs on tombstones, or the epithets of Darwin's *Loves of the Plants*, or the hairdressing of soldiers, tallow and flour and pigtail. Lord Cochrane suffered that infliction before he went to sea ; it is as good a specimen of painful and foolish convention as one need wish for.

But there is another sort of convention, and in this the literature and other arts of the eighteenth century are strong. It is the convention of a school or a tradition, such as keeps the artists from eccentricity, vanity, and " expense of spirit," the convention which makes an understanding between them as to what is worth doing, and sets them speedily to work, instead of wasting their time considering what they ought to try next. It is this that makes an understanding also between the artist and his customers, and leads to *hilaritas* on both sides, to activity both in production and appreciation.

The eighteenth century is an age, perhaps the last, in which great things, fresh and new things, have been accomplished in discipline and obedience to school traditions.   The next century is filled with the sorrows, the vanities, the glorious achievements of artists who trust in their own might and main, as they say in Iceland, and find out sundry ways of their own.   *Sartor Resartus* struggling through *Fraser's Magazine ;* " done up " from Fraser in fifty or sixty copies ; found unreadable by most respectable judges ;   admired and edited in America, where nevertheless Carlyle's champion, Emerson, complains that glass is meant to be seen through, not to disclose, as Carlyle's glass does, every crystal and lamina in it—there is the nineteenth-century hero as man of letters, belonging to no school, and proud, like Dante, of making a party by himself.   It is this isolation and self-will in the new age that suggests to Peacock his charge against modern poetry.   He finds the poets roving severally over the universe in search of new subjects and sensations, cut off from their fellows and from reasonable society.   Surely this is true of a great deal of nineteenth-century art.   The eighteenth century still retains the sociable quality of the Middle Ages, when the artists worked like members of a guild, for towns that knew what they were doing.

Burns is the poet, after Pope, who is most fully in sympathy with his age, most happy in his audience, most thoroughly economical in his work, and saved from waste of time and energy because he relies upon his literary ancestors and accepts their conventions and their forms.   The result is that his poetry is struck out in full perfection all of one piece, in one volume ; his rendering of the world to which he belonged.   It was Mauchline for religion and other humours ;   for politics it was nothing smaller than the United Kingdom under King George, with the example of Chatham to encourage the king's ministers.   There is nothing like it anywhere for complete security of vision and of utterance ; and this was attained by the man of genius through the school to which he naturally belonged, the conventional and artificial form of Scottish eighteenth-century poetry.

If you look at it in one way you will find the eighteenth century growing stiffer, more conventional, more in want of a change till the change comes. In place of Pope, the imitators of Pope ; in place of Swift and Addison, the formal periods of Johnson and Gibbon. But there are other ways of taking it. " The Peace of the Augustans " does not mean idleness, nor even rest ; it was full of movement and adventure. A great intellectual revolution was accomplished in the eighteenth century with no insurrection, no manifestoes, no conceit. It has often escaped notice. It is a recovery of confidence and courage, an immense revival of energy. It is shown in the work of the novelists, in the work of the historians ; it means that the old cautious ideal of study which is Swift's, as it was More's in earlier times, has given way to something more generous, as large as the education of Gargantua, yet with the style of Hume and Gibbon.

You may say if you will that Gibbon's regular periods are as artificial as *Euphues* ; you may find them as graceful as a minuet :

> He at Philippi kept
> His sword e'en like a dancer—

the important thing is that with this sword, with this style, Gibbon took possession of a thousand years of history. He read as much as the most learned dunce in the *Dunciad*, and his vast work is as elegant as the *Rape of the Lock*, as fine as an ode of Gray.

In this time of war many good people are afraid to
read or think about anything but their most immediate
and pressing cares. Small blame to them. The
learned societies in London have, however, since the
war began taken another resolve about their proper
subjects of discourse. Mr. Gosse has reminded us of
the example of that great scholar and high-minded man
Gaston Paris, lecturing on the *Chanson de Roland*
during the siege of Paris. That is an example of
courage : which is a right opinion about the things
that are to be feared. But this example reminds us
that some subjects are better than others, in time of
siege ; the Song of Roland, I doubt not, since Gaston
Paris spoke about it in 1871, has come to mean more
than it did before for France. I did not choose my
text in order to preach about the honour of England,
but the text is not a bad one for that purpose. The
eighteenth century, which begins with William and
Marlborough, and ends with Nelson and Wellesley,
and which has *Hearts of Oak* in the heart of it, and
Chatham and Wàrren Hastings for its statesmen, is a
time worth thinking about. An heroic age and a time,
I would remind you, of very gallant enmities between
England and France, whi:h may be remembered now
with deep gratitude to the ancestors on both sides of
the water who have left their children so little to be
repented of. The key is set by Prior to Boileau :

old friend, old foe, for such we are,
Alternate as the chance of peace and war.

Later there are such documents as General James
Murray's letter about the surrender of Minorca ; the
correspondence of Vergennes and Washington, when
the French Prime Minister asks for the release of a

young English officer, Captain Asgill ; the testimonial presented by the West Indian merchants after the peace to the French governor who had been over them during the French occupation.   I quote from the *Annual Register*, 1784-85, p. [184] :

" A copy of the above proceedings being presented by the Committee to Monsieur le Marquis de Bouille, his Excellency was pleased to make the following reply :

GENTLEMEN,

I return you my acknowledgements for the very great and distinguished honour you have done me, of which I entertain the warmest sense.

My conduct towards the West Indian Colonies which fell by the fate of war under the dominion of France was such as not only flowed from the examples of magnanimity and justice given by my sovereign, but was the natural result of that high esteem and consideration which I have always held for a nation so respectable and renowned as that of Great Britain.   I cannot, therefore, but wholly attribute the value you are pleased to set on my actions to the generosity of your sentiments, of which I shall preserve a constant remembrance."

I have not composed a peroration ; perhaps this example of the manners of the eighteenth century may do instead.

IV

THOMAS WARTON

THOMAS WARTON represents the history of English poetry, and, more particularly, of English poetry in the Middle Ages—that being the chief part of his study in the volumes he has left behind him. His name is rightly chosen to inaugurate those studies in this Academy, to give an example, from the eighteenth century, of some things which can hardly be bettered at the present day. However much may be erroneous and how much defective in his published work, there is in it, throughout, an example of historical studies springing from a fresh and genuine love of the pursuit.

It may be confessed at once without disguise or palliation that Thomas Warton did not come up to the requirements of a modern University. He was a college tutor all his life, and his method with his pupils was simply and openly to discourage their attendance at lectures. I wonder whether the Academy remembered this when they determined to set up his name and image in their hall as an ancestor to be respected. We might be open to some criticism, in these days of University reform, for choosing an idle Fellow, the editor of the *Oxford Sausage*, a lover of ale and tobacco and low company in taverns, to be commemorated in this way as an authority. Oxford in the eighteenth century is a favourite shocking example, and Thomas Warton in his neglect of his pupils did little, seemingly, to contradict the prevalent opinion about the inefficiency of Oxford teaching at that time. But we were reminded lately by Mr. Dicey, speaking of Blackstone (a friend of Warton's), that the dispraise of Oxford may be overdone ; " the apathy or somnolence of Oxford in the eighteenth century has been the subject of exaggeration " ; among the idlers there were some adventurers, who used their leisure in a right Academic way. Blackstone of All Souls and Warton of Trinity are enough to make the censurers reconsider and modify their estimate of those quiet generations of University life.

It is not very difficult, though it takes some time, to collect the principal dates about the study of the history of poetry. It was part of the literary criticism which followed the Renaissance. Sidney writes the history of English poetry in his *Apology*. It was also part of antiquarian research. Rymer, the editor of the *Foedera*, gives an intelligible short account of old French and Provençal poetry, as an introduction to English poetry, in one of his essays on the Drama. An entry in his table of contents may be worth remembering as a convenient summary of English poetical history :

" Chaucer refin'd our language. Which in perfection by Waller."

Abroad, the connection between antiquarian and literary history is shown more brilliantly by Muratori in some of his essays on the Antiquities of Italy and in his book on the Perfect Italian Poetry. One is inclined at first to keep the antiquarian studies of men like Hickes and Hearne apart from the modern interests of Dryden, Addison, or Pope. But as a matter of fact there was no distinct separation between the antiquities of literature and such modern questions as were discussed in Dryden's prefaces or in the *Spectator*. Rymer had ambitions as a wit and a lively writer; and on the other hand Sir William Temple, the paragon of elegant literature, is ready to notice the discovery of old Scandinavian heroic verse. He quotes the Death-song of Ragnar Lodbrog in his essay *Of Heroic Virtue*; he calls it a sonnet:

" The whole sonnet is recited by Olaus Wormins in his *Literatura Runica* (who has very much deserved from the commonwealth of learning) and is very well worth reading by any that love poetry, and to consider the several stamps of that coin according to several ages and climates.

. . . .

I am deceived, if in this sonnet, and a following ode of Scallogrim . . . there be not a vein truely poetical, and in its kind Pindaric, taking it with the allowance of the different climates, fashions, opinions and languages of such distant countries."

It was from Sir William Temple that Thomas Warton the elder (the father of Thomas and Joseph Warton) got the suggestion and matter of his Runic Ode, published in the posthumous volume of his poems in 1748 :

" A Runic Ode taken from the second volume of Sir William Temple's *Miscellanies* : *Argument* Regner Lodbrog, a King of one of the Northern Nations, being mortally stung by a Viper, before the Venom had reach'd his Vitals, broke out into the following verses."

Here the elder Warton merely translates the two stanzas quoted in Latin by Temple. A more surprising specimen of the good understanding which seems to have obtained between the antiquarians and the modern men of letters is to be found in the *Poetic Miscellany* which was begun by Dryden and continued after his death by the publisher, Jacob Tonson. In the sixth volume, published in 1716, " the sixth part of Miscellany Poems, by the most eminent hands," there is another Runic Ode (though it is not called by that popular name), and this poem, the *Waking of Angantyr*, is taken bodily from Hickes's *Thesaurus* and printed in the original Icelandic :

> *Waknadu Angantyr,*
> *Vekur thig Hervor—*

with Hickes's prose version, and no attempt to modernise it or even to explain.   Such was the courage, or the temerity, of publishers in those days.   The editor of the *Miscellany*, it must be said, was plainly negligent and hurried.   He has kept the original Latin heading as he found it in Hickes, now torn from its context and unintelligible as it stands.   But this very absurdity makes the contrast all the more remarkable between this Northern poem in its old Northern tongue and the other pieces printed by Tonson in this volume.   They are not all of the newest, it should be said ; this *Miscellany* includes Bishop Corbet's " Ballad intituled *The Fairies Farewel*" as well as more modern things like *The Campaign* by Mr. Addison and the *Pastorals* of Mr. Alexander Pope.

The contemporaries of Dryden and Addison, it is clear, did not keep separate the antiquarian and the literary study of poetry.   No more than Sir Philip Sidney were they ashamed to speak of the poetry of barbarous nations or of their own Gothic ancestry. Sir William Temple has been already quoted.   Another significant thing is the little book that was printed at the Oxford Press in 1691 containing the macaronic *Polemo-Middinia*, attributed to Drummond of Hawthornden, and, in black letter, the old Scottish poem of *Christ's Kirk on the Green*.

A Scot will fight for Christ's Kirk on the Green :

—when this was written by Pope he was thinking of Allan Ramsay, whose vigorous revival of old Scottish poetry had already gone far. But Allan Ramsay was not the first to print it, nor was it a mere national prejudice that gave importance to this old comic rhyme. It was published at Oxford by E. G. apparently as a philological diversion and a poetical curiosity. The preface, dated on New Year's Day, explains that it is meant for the Saturnalia and for laughter. The study of burlesque is justified in an historical argument, with reference to the examples set by Homer, Erasmus, and Rabelais ; particular attention is given, of course, to Merlinus Coccaius ; as the original pattern followed in *Polemo-Middinia. Quod felix faustumque sit Reipublicae Iocoseriae.* The notes are full of Teutonic philology, Icelandic and Gothic etymologies set out by the help of the Oxford press with its founts—not yet exhausted—of various type, including even runes, and the alphabet of Ulphilas. The Edda of Snorro Sturlæus, Gawain Douglas's *Æneid*, and Chaucer are frequently quoted. The Marriage of Wit and Learning, of Mercury and Philology, was not broken in those days.

Perhaps, after the Pantagruelist levity of the *Polemo-Middinia* and its preface, it may comfort the Academy to remember that E. G., the author of this philological lark, was Edmund Gibson, afterwards Bishop of London. It is remarkable how many Fathers of the Church have been nursing-fathers of medieval learning—Huet,

Bishop of Avranches, in his discourse on the origin of
Romances, followed by Warburton, controversially, on
the same subject ; Hurd in his essays on Chivalry ;
Percy. Along with these names Bowle should be
remembered—" el reverendo Don Juan Bowle "—the
editor and commentator of *Don Quixote*, to whom
Thomas Warton was indebted for several medieval
notes in his edition of Milton.   If witnesses to character
are required, these names are warrant enough for the
reputation of medieval studies.

The importance of those literary researches in the
eighteenth century is that they were part of a great
reaction, not peculiarly romantic or medieval, against
one of the products of the Renaissance.   The great use
and meaning of them was that they were *history*.
History was what was wanted to provide matter and
substance for the intellect to work on.   In the Revival
of Learning, from the first, there had always been a
danger of formalism—a loss of substance for the sake
of perfection in style, an economy of studies to ensure
perfection within limits, instead of the limitless en-
deavour of Browning's Grammarian.   There was a
nobler motive than the mere admiration for style
which tended to keep some of the leaders of the new
learning from plunging into absorbing researches.   It
was felt that the Humanities, to be really profitable,
must take regard of the conditions of human life.
The enormous schemes of education propounded by
Rabelais and Milton show the spirit of the Renaissance
in its greatest ambition—the spirit of Marlowe's
Faustus.   Another mode was presented in the *Utopia*,
where the aim of study is not infinite knowledge, but
just so much as may be available for the lives of ordinary
men.   The quality of it is carefully chosen, the range

restricted, so that the whole nature of a man may be in good training—not burdened by superfluous knowledge nor distracted from the chief end of life by interests which no life can exhaust. *Utopia* is the nobler counterpart to Browning's Grammarian—not the contrast as Browning gives it :

> This small man goes on adding one to one,
> His hundred's soon hit—

but another sort of man, whose study is so proportioned and arranged that every moment of it is alive, everything in the day's work contributing to the meaning and value of the day.

There is danger in this limited humanism—danger of exhaustion and barrenness. But in the lifetime of Rabelais, Ben Jonson, Burton, and other such extravagant readers the danger was averted. The danger came at the end of the seventeenth century, with the loss of energy which Dryden noted in a famous passage, on the two periods of English drama, before and after the Interregnum :

> Our age was cultivated thus at length,
> But what we gained in skill we lost in strength ;
> Our builders were with want of genius curst,
> The second temple was not like the first.

In this second age, though there was endless and increasing scientific industry of every sort, there was a distrust of science among the chief men of letters. It is seen, curiously, in Samuel Butler, who is in so many things a man of the older fashion ; it is seen most eminently in Swift. *Anima Rabelaesii habitans in sicco ;* Swift might also be described as the spirit of Sir Thomas More without his hopefulness ; the ideal of Swift, as

given in the Second Voyage of Gulliver, is pure Utopia
in its choice and its limitation of studies. Or Swift
might be thought of, again, as Bacon in his negative
and critical aspect, his contempt of fallacies and
futilities—if one could think of Bacon punishing
the follies, without wishing for the advancement, of
learning.

The Renaissance worked itself out in one direction
to a sort of thin culture or polite literature which found
substantial erudition much too laborious and expensive.
Bentley was scoffed at by people with very scanty
furniture of their own. Some of the most famous men
of that time are light in material knowledge, at least
so far as is shown in their writings—Berkeley, for
example, as compared with Hobbes before him or
Hume after him. The great difference between Berkeley
and Hume is that Hume wrote the History of England.
Even Dr. Johnson, who has so much of the old-fashioned
regardless love of reading, makes little use of it in his
works, apart from the *Dictionary ;* his depreciation of
history and historians is well known. But it was from
history that fresh supplies had to be drawn, to save
polite literature from dying of inanition ; and supplies
of this sort were given by Thomas Warton in his
Observations on Spenser, in his Milton, and above all
in his History of Poetry. He was not afraid to plunge,
and he was not too careful about form. The *History
of English Poetry* was censured for its want of method.
But method may be bought too dear, when there is a
want of material ; and method may be applied, when
sufficient material is found. Warton had to work
hard to make his way among the manuscripts of the
Bodleian and Lambeth, the British Museum, and the
Colleges of Oxford and Cambridge. No doubt he took

all the help he could get, and owed much to his advisers and coadjutors ; but with all allowances he had still more than enough to do The main thing wanted was a report on the extant works, and that was what he gave. Method, after all, is far less required in literary than in political. history. The political historian has to extract the essence from masses of documents that in themselves are unmeaning. The historian of literature deals with documents which in themselves are intelligible, which have, or which at any rate were by the authors of them thought to have, an immediate, present, independent value, quite apart from their bearings on other things or the inferences that might be drawn from them. Literary history is more like a guide-book than a geography. It may be amusing in itself at a distance from the realities of which it speaks, but it is not properly effective until it brings the traveller on his way, so that he sees for himself the temples and towers and mountain passes with his bodily eyes. Some historians of literature go wrong, and spoil their work by writing as if their matter were all past, like the events of history ; treating plays and poems like battles or sieges or constitutional reforms, to be described indirectly by a reconstructive gentleman in his study, doing his best to explain what he cannot see. Some part of literary history no doubt is busied conjecturally with epic poems and others which (as Paulin Paris said) have the misfortune not to exist. But the main part of it deals with extant things, which live for the present day when the seeing eye falls on them ; they are unjustly treated when they are kept by the historian at a distance from the eye, as unrealised though permanent possibilities of sensation. That was not Thomas Warton's policy. As well as he could, he put forward the results of his explorations in large samples, and he was right. Those who read his history see and know a good deal of old poetry at first hand ; and those who find what they want will not be troubled at the careless profusion of the show. There are many mistakes, no doubt, which Ritson the accuser was ready to fix upon. But they do not really damage the general character of the book. There are omissions and failures. It is a pity that Warton should have slighted the ironical grace of the dispute between the Owl and the Nightingale, that wonderful anticipation of Chaucer in a rustic thirteenth-century dialect. It is strange that he never found the Cottonian MS. *Nero A. x*, with the *Pearl* and *Sir Gawayne*. But these are accidents.

It seems that Warton deliberately refused to be methodical or philosophical. A scheme of the history of poetry had been drawn by Pope, divided like the history of painting into schools. Gray, who took up the subject after Pope, and who resigned it to Warton, would have put into it more order and construction than his rambling successor.

I cannot here go further without a reference to Mr. Courthope, who has finished what Pope and Gray intended, what Warton did, in part, so well ; and I take leave here, in the first *Warton Lecture*, to offer our Fellow the congratulations of this Society on the accomplishment of his task—a vote of thanks which I imagine might well be ratified by the Parliament of Birds, in their own *Paradise*.

The history of poetry, even when, like Warton's, it is random and informal, is part of history at large. It has its inconveniences and limitations ; it can never be a harmonious work of art, like Gibbon's history, just for the reason already given, that works of art are what it deals with, and that art and literature are living things which assert themselves against the historian and cannot be made into mere matter for a narrative. Nevertheless the history of literature, like political history, is part of the memory of the world ; it is philosophical, like the history of philosophy itself, a record of fashions of thought, of ideas. Thomas Warton, who took up the history of Gothic architecture as well as poetry, had a knowledge of the past life of England most ample, fresh, and variegated. He took an honourable share in that business of historical investigation which was itself the most important new fashion of thought in the eighteenth century. Partly through the store of new matter that it provided for the " reading public," partly through the zest and enthusiasm of its students—the spirit of adventure, which is the same in Warton as in Scott—it did more than any theory to correct the narrow culture, the starved elegance, of the preceding age. It is not to be forgotten that Johnson, who was disrespectful to history in general, and, occasionally, unkind to Warton, became himself an historian of literature in his *Lives of the Poets*.

Warton's historical work began in admiration, particularly of Spenser and of Milton's early poems. This, like Joseph Warton's critical work also, was due to their father. Thomas Warton the elder had discovered the early poems of Milton, in the volume of 1645, when as yet there were few to praise them. (As late as 1782, Joseph Warton in his essay on Pope speaks of Milton's " smaller and neglected poems.") The neglect and the recovery of them is described by Thomas the son in the preface to his edition of " Poems upon several occasions, by John Milton." This is one passage :

" My father used to relate that when he once at Magdalene College, Oxford, mentioned in high terms this volume to Mr. Digby the intimate friend of Pope, Mr. Digby expressed much surprise that he had never heard Pope speak of them, went home and immediately gave them an attentive reading, and asked Pope if he knew anything of this hidden treasure. Pope availed himself of the question : and accordingly we find him soon afterwards sprinkling his *Eloisa to Abelard* with epithets and phrases of a new form and sound, pilfered from *Comus* and the *Penseroso*."

The work of Thomas Warton as a commentator was very largely the tracing of resemblances and possible borrowings—an estimate, in detail, of the reading and book-learning of Spenser and Milton. But it is more than an essay on what is called in so many German professional treatises the *Belesenheit* of authors. Nor is it like the work of those " parallelists " (the word is Warton's own) who " mistake resemblances for thefts." It is a liberal interpretation of the minds of the poets, through their reading. Warton justifies himself, modestly and sensibly, at the end of this chapter " of Spenser's imitations from old romances."

" Many other examples might be alledged, from which it would be more abundantly manifested that our author's imagination was entirely possessed with that species of reading, which was the fashion and the delight of his age. The lovers of Spenser, I hope, will not think that I have been too tedious in a disquisition which has contributed not only to illustrate many particular passages in their favourite poet, but to display the general cast and colour of his poem. Some there are, who will censure what I have collected on this subject as both trifling and uninteresting ; but such readers can have no taste for Spenser."

Without admiration, Warton's work would not have been done; and the same may be said of Joseph Warton's exhilarating criticism. This is even more remarkable, inasmuch as he praises the work of Pope with no mean or ungenerous exceptions or cavillings, while at the same time he refuses to take " acute understanding " as a substitute for " creative and glowing imagination."

The brothers Warton make the same distinction as Hurd in his memorable phrase, between " good sense " and " fine fabling." Thus Thomas Warton in his note on *Comus*, ver. 195, *O thievish Night* : " In the present age, in which almost every common writer avoids palpable absurdities, at least monstrous and unnatural conceits, would Milton have introduced this passage, where thievish Night is supposed for some felonious purpose to shut up the stars in her dark lantern ? Certainly not. But in the present age, correct and rational as it is, had *Comus* been written, we should not perhaps have had some of the greatest beauties of its wild and romantic imagery."

This gives the same antithesis as Joseph Warton puts at the beginning of his essay on Pope, in the dedication to the Reverend Dr. Young, Rector of Welwyn in Hertfordshire. His aim is " to impress on the reader that a clear head and acute understanding are not sufficient alone to make a Poet "—" that it is a creative and glowing imagination, *acer spiritus ac vis*, and that alone that can stamp a writer with this exalted and very uncommon character, which so few possess, and of which so few can properly judge."

Joseph Warton goes much further than Thomas. He speaks of Dante's " sublime and original poem," " which abounds in images and sentiments almost worthy of Homer, but those works he had never seen." Thomas Warton admires Dante too, but is more apologetic—" this wonderful compound of classical and romantic fancy, of pagan and Christian theology, of real and fictitious history, of tragical and comic incidents, of familiar and heroic manners, and of satirical and sublime poetry. But the grossest improprieties of this poem discover an originality of invention, and its absurdities often border on sublimity. We are surprised that a poet should write one hundred cantos on hell, paradise, and purgatory. But this prolixity is partly owing to the want of art and method ; and is common to all early compositions in which everything is related circumstantially without rejection, and not in those general terms which are used by modern writers."

" General terms" is the eighteenth-century prescription for a good style. Joseph Warton will not have it, and what he says might have been said by the young men whose watchword was *hierro*, and who fought the great battle of *Hernani* in 1830. One sentence may be enough : " Among the other fortunate circumstances that attended Homer, it was not one of the least that he wrote before *general* and *abstract* terms were invented." There is much else to the same effect. The brothers are not of one mind about poetic diction, and Thomas is the more old fashioned of the two.

But it does not matter for the success of his work ; and the moral seems to be that it is possible to study medieval literature and get much good from it without being exorbitantly romantic—again a consideration for an Academy. To study the Middle Ages it is not necessary to be medieval, in the sense of any " romantic school." Gray was not, Scott was not, nor were the other workers in this country from the time of Percy and Warton onwards—Tyrwhitt, Ritson, Price (the editor of Warton, too little known), George Ellis,

Leyden. Peacock's Welsh antiquities in the *Misfortunes of Elphin* show how medieval studies may be followed out by a detached ironical mind. The great French scholars who have done most for the history of medieval literature have worked, like Gaston Paris, with a clear light ; while on the other hand the romantic artists do not require the learning of Scott. Victor Hugo did without it, and built his medieval inventions out of the most casual reading ; he did not know as much as Dr. Johnson about the books of chivalry.

What is to be the future of these studies ? Where is advance to be made ?

For one thing, it is becoming plain that more languages are required. We are under the curse of Babel ; those who speak of the glory of poets sometimes forget how narrow and provincial is the fame of most of them, how broken and impeded by differences of language, as compared with the painters and musicians. But that is no reason why the sons of learning should refuse the difficulties ; and for medieval studies all the tongues are needed. Old Irish and Welsh cannot be kept separate from Icelandic and Provençal, if the mind of the Dark and Middle Ages is to be understood. Nor are those studies merely antiquarian. Let us remember Whitley Stokes ; I have no right to speak of his work, but I am proud to think that I knew the man himself, and I know both how he attended to other languages besides the Irish on which he spent his life, and also how he flashed with pleasure at the smallest proof that anything in his work could be made to bear on the living imagination of the present day.

For another thing, much may be done to clear away some literary prejudices about the Middle Ages—for example, those in Lowell's essay on Chaucer. His sentences there on the Provençal poets and their German contemporaries are probably the worst criticism ever written ; he has warned many young ingenuous people away from those regions of poetry with his brisk and complacent slander. He turns from Provence to Germany, to the land and the time of Walther von der Vogelweide, and what he has to say is *Tedeschi lurchi*, " German gluttons." " On the whole it would be hard to find anything more tediously artificial than the Provençal literature, except the reproduction of it by the Minnesingers. The *Tedeschi lurchi* certainly did contrive to make something heavy as dough out of what was light, if not very satisfying, in the canorous dialect of Southern Gaul." It is hard to speak of this as it deserves ; to do so might require another quotation from Dante at the end by way of apology : " È cortesia lui esser villano." It may be enough to use once more the immortal words of *Sartor Resartus* : " All which Propositions I, for the present, content myself with modestly but peremptorily and irrevocably denying."

One may hope to hear a better account of the Provençal lyric poets shortly, when Mr. Alfred Jeanroy comes to London at the invitation of the University, and to find in them what Dante and Petrarch found—or even more than that, for it may prove that they are the original discoverers, followed by half of Christendom ever since in the art of lyric melody.

One is sometimes inclined to envy Warton and the other easy-going men of the older days when one looks at the systematic work of modern scholars—" now when all the claims have been pitched " as the old Greek poet said, thinking regretfully of the time when the ploughs had not been driven as yet through the

V

HORACE WALPOLE

HORACE WALPOLE has received something less than
his due share of gratitude for the gifts he has left
behind him.   It may seem perhaps a trifle exaggerated
and over-emphatic to speak of him as a benefactor :
and yet when one comes to reckon up all that is owing
to him, it is difficult to see what other name is appropriate.   He belongs to a class of writers—he is one of
the most distinguished in a class of writers whose title
to respect is quite different from that of the great
masters, and yet quite as far beyond question, in its
own way.

These are the authors who have left no great monu-
mental work behind them, no epic poem or system of
philosophy or magnificent history—but merely the
record of their life as it appeared to them in its drifting
aspects from day to day and moment to moment.
Their excellence is not to be compared to the excellence
of the great literary artists, but it is quite as singular.
No one is asked to make his choice between Milton's
Paradise Lost and the *Diary of Samuel Pepys*.   But the
very incongruity of the comparison brings home to us
the value of the *Diary*.   The loss and extinction of
it would leave a gap that nothing of Milton's could
supply.

The letters of Horace Walpole form another kind of
history than Gibbon's : and Gibbon could not have
made good the want of them.   They are unlike other
historics and no other history can take their place.
This is admitted even in the solemn and censorious
estimate of Macaulay :

" Walpole is constantly showing us things not of
very great value indeed, yet things which we are
pleased to see, and which we can see nowhere else."

Macaulay's *Essay* has established a sort of conventional opinion in regard to Horace Walpole which it
may be permissible to dispute.   Perhaps he might have
shown him more favour if he had made the essay what
it professes to be, and had kept to his subject.   But
Macaulay chose to pass away from the letters, which
he had set out to discuss, and took up the politics of
the reign of George II.   The greater part of the essay
is a sketch of Sir Robert Walpole's administration, of
his opponents and his fall.   There is no attempt to go
back and raise and modify the harsh judgment with
which the *Essay* begins : and Horace Walpole remains
for readers of Macaulay an example of an unhealthy and
disorganised mind :   " none but an unhealthy and
disorganised mind could have produced such literary
luxuries as the works of Walpole."

It is a little surprising that a rhetorician like Macaulay, fond of crude and striking antitheses and paradoxes, should have made so little of that which lay
ready to his hand, in the fact that Horace was the son
of Sir Robert Walpole.   True history occasionally
indulges in freaks of this sort : and there are few
contrasts in any satire or any comedy more striking
than the contrast of this father and son.   Sir Robert
the robust and cheery squire, the strong prosaic

minister whose political task was to keep himself in office and the king on his throne, to slip out of difficulties and complications, and to pay his way : Horace Walpole a man of taste and sensibility, interested in all trifles if only they had anything of singularity, tolerant of everything except what was commonplace and even of that if he was only allowed to look at it in his own way and touch it off in a caricature. This is the contrast provided by true history—how well Macaulay could have worked it out !

But there is something even strange in the true history, and that is that the father and son were friends : that Sir Robert Walpole as far as we know did nothing to interfere with his son's pursuits and showed no contempt for his frivolities of art and literature : that Horace Walpole, though he spoke his mind about the ways of Norfolk society, had nothing but respect and friendship for his father. Sir Robert Walpole did not appreciate " the finer shades " as his son did, but he was not dull. Horace Walpole was not as robust as his father, but neither was he a fatuous and incapable trifler. The father and son had more in common than appears on the first view. Sir Robert had more interest in his son's pursuits than he commonly gets credit for. One instance at least is given by Horace Walpole in his " Short Notes " of his life, which shows the fallen minister allowing himself to be entertained by these vanities.

" In the summer of 1742 I wrote a *Sermon on Painting* for the amusement of my father in his retirement. It was preached before him by his chaplain." As a matter of fact, Sir Robert was quite as fond of pictures as his son, and they occupied themselves together with the picture gallery at Houghton.

On the other hand, Horace Walpole played well for
his side in the House of Commons.   In one of his
letters he says that " *Sir Robert* shows me no parti-
ality," which means evidently, when taken with the
context, that he left him to fight his own way in
Parliament.   Horace Walpole, though he was not a
great orator nor of much importance to the party,
threw himself into debate with a good deal of vigour
and sometimes with effect.   He took his share in Sir
Robert Walpole's last campaign, and had no reason
to be discontented—as indeed he is not discontented
—with the style of his speeches.   Macaulay says that
his mind was a bundle of whims and affectations, that
his features were covered by mask within mask, that
it is impossible to discover the real man within them.
It is hard to believe that Macaulay when he said this
had any vivid impression of the letters about which
he was writing.   The letters that describe "the
great Walpolian battle " of 1742 certainly do not
leave the impression of insincerity or affectation : if
there was affectation there was beneath it something
stronger.   Horace Walpole like other moralists was
fond of saying that he didn't care ; that there was
nothing new and nothing true and it didn't matter.
But when it came to fighting he could stick by his own
side, and he is not the only critic by whom " young
Mr. Walpole's " speeches are approved.[1]

> Livor edax tibi cuncta negat, Gallosque subactos
> Vix impune feres.
>
> (Whate'er be yours the churls deny you all,
> Look for no mercy since you tam'd the Gaul.)

This quotation from Lucan was made in the course
of the debates on the Hanoverian subsidies after the

[1] ii. 3 n. (ed. Mrs. Paget Toynbee).

Battle of Dettingen, and it was recognised as good.
Horace Walpole doesn't mention it himself. If there
was affectation in quoting Lucan to the House of
Commons, it was an affectation which the House of
Commons did not at that time discourage. This is
only one proof out of a countless multitude, that
Horace Walpole's tastes and studies by no means
tended to make him useless in practical affairs.

Horace Walpole gains very much by the publication
of his collected letters, including many to other corre-
spondents besides Sir Horace Mann. The letters to
Sir Horace Mann, the letters that Macaulay had before
him when he wrote his article for the *Edinburgh Review*,
are perhaps not the best of Walpole's ; taken by themselves they may give a less favourable impression than
is obtained from the whole Correspondence ; though
they hardly bear out Macaulay's judgment. Sir
Horace Mann for one thing was not a very close friend
of Walpole's, though he was an unwearied correspondent ; there are other people who are more sympa-
thetic and bring out better the better side of Walpole's
character.

The earliest letters are among the most valuable of
all, and they belong to the history of English poetry.
Walpole at Eton had formed with three friends what
they called a Quadruple Alliance—one of the four was
Gray. The letters that pass among them, Horace
Walpole and Gray at Cambridge to West at Oxford,
and afterwards from Walpole and Gray on their
Italian travels, are among the most delightful anywhere to be found in any biography. Affectation there
may be, but who is to blame it ? If there had been
no affectation there would have been little wit.

It is not often that one is admitted, as here, to the

confidence of a poet in his youth, with all the world
before him : and to the confidence of his friends.
There is something very attractive in the history of
this early friendship, in the brave hopes, the generous
judgments on life, the air of worldly wisdom, the sentimental reminiscences of the school life that already
seems to lie so far back in the past—two or three years
ago. The friendships were to be clouded and thwarted.
West died young : Ashton took orders and prospered,
and dropped out of intimacy with Gray and Walpole :
Gray and Walpole had a quarrel when they were
travelling, and though they made it up afterwards and
were friends they never quite recaptured the old friendship. But all this change, this after-history does
nothing to spoil the picture of the four students at their
first setting out on their pilgrimage. As to Horace
Walpole there is one thing that comes out strongly in
the early letters, and remains true for the whole of his
life. That is that his interest in books and literature
is absolutely sound and true. It is quite plain that he
took up books not because it was a fine thing to have
a character for learning or taste—though no doubt he
felt the appeal of these motives—but because he could
not choose but hear when the Ancient poets began
their recitations.

He describes to us in the most captivating manner
the character of his early dealings with poetry when
first the charm of Virgil came upon him. It is a quaint
attractive passage out of the early years of that
century : a picture of Eton and the river and its bridge,
and the great castle towering above them all. Walpole
and Gray were not good at the amusements of their
fellows : expeditions against the Thames bargees were
too violent for them. They did not play cricket,

apparently. But there is a probability that though they did not care to " urge the flying ball " they were among those who occasionally dared to " snatch a fearful joy " by going beyond the limits of their little reign : there is no doubt at all that the Windsor landscape became associated to Gray and Walpole with the images of poetry that were beginning to steal into their minds.

" Dear George, were not the playing fields at Eton food for all manner of flights ? No old maid's gown, though it had been tormented into all the fashions from King James to King George, ever underwent so many transformations as those poor plains have in my idea. At first I was contented with tending a visionary flock, and sighing some pastoral name to the echo of the cascade under the bridge. How happy should I have been to have had a kingdom, only for the pleasure of being driven from it, and living disguised in an humble vale ! As I got further into Virgil and Clelia[1] I found myself transported from Arcadia to the garden of Italy ; and saw Windsor Castle in no other view than the *Capitoli immobile saxum.* I wish a committee of the House of Commons may ever seem to be the Senate. . . ."[2]

Those fields and waters have shaped the dreams of many students since Walpole and of later poets than Gray : and the fashion of Walpole's imagination is a little antiquated. But though there may be some complacency in the meditations of this philosopher (aged 19) on the romantic dreams of his youth, there is nothing false. Whatever Walpole liked or disliked, his opinion was an honest one. His judgments have not

---

[1] *Clélie* (Mlle. de Scudéry).
[2] To George Montagu, May 6, 1736 (Paget Toynbee, i. 12-13).

always been confirmed—which is not a matter of much importance—but they were always his own judgments.

He never tampered with his instinctive appreciations of books and authors ; and here at any rate Macaulay might have discovered something of reality under the mask. Walpole's response to a literary touch is infallible—not indeed as a test of the book or the author who appeals to him, but as a test of Walpole's own nature. This may seem to be a truism, but it is nevertheless true. It is not as common as it may seem to get an absolutely genuine answer on things like this. In this matter Walpole had less hypocrisy than most men. From Macaulay we would think that Walpole was an artificial, conventional, mechanical mumbler of perverse or snobbish futilities about all his great contemporaries ; a heartless machine, one of Mr. Carlyle's " digestive apparatus " repeating nothing but formulas. Now it is true that Walpole sometimes speaks disrespectfully of those that were or that have become since Dignitaries in literature. But it is curious that Macaulay should have ignored the unmistakable freshness of all that Walpole says about books and authors. Macaulay speaks as if it were something exceptional to find a man making disproportioned judgments on contemporary authors, and as if it were the symptom of incurable levity, " a diseased and disorganised mind." But what does one really find when one goes to look for the judgments of eminent critics upon their contemporaries ? One finds that Johnson disliked the poetry of Gray, and could not endure the novels of Fielding : one finds that Byron thought the best of his contemporary poets were Crabbe, Campbell, and Rogers, and that Hayley's *Triumphs of Temper* was an immortal work. What

are the literary opinions of Horace Walpole that seem
in need of revision ? He admired, says Macaulay,
that abject thing Crébillon the younger, the profligate
dunce. Well, this admiration he shared with his
friend Gray. It may have been right or wrong : at
any rate it can hardly be called perverse or exceptional.
He would rather, says Macaulay, have written the
most absurd lines in Lee than Thomson's *Seasons*.
This is an instance of the way in which Macaulay,
without literary inaccuracy, produces a wrong impression of the meaning intended.

It will be generally admitted that Horace Walpole
was wrong about Thomson's *Seasons*. They had not
taken his fancy : he confused them with the other
didactic blank verse poems of the time ; he thought
them tame ; he spoke of them in fact in very much
the same contemptuous tone that Macaulay used about
Wordsworth : the *Seasons* were regarded by him very
much as Wordsworth's *Excursion* was regarded by a
number of Wordsworth's contemporaries, " a drowsy
frowsy poem." Walpole with his mercurial quickness, his
antipathy to dulness and solemnity, had sworn a feud
against the pompous authors who droned out their
epic and didactic periods in monotonous and affected
verse. " Now if one has a mind to be read, one must
write metaphysical poems in blank verse, which have
not half the imagination of romances, and are dull
without any agreeable absurdity. Only think of the
gravity of this wise age, that have exploded *Cleopatra*
and *Pharamond*, and approve the *Pleasures of the
Imagination*, the *Art of Preserving Health*, and *Leonidas*!
I beg the age's pardon : it has done approving these
poems and has forgot them." [1]

[1] ii. 248 (Paget Toynbee).

That piece of criticism is sent off to Mr. Conway to amuse him in his garrison at Stirling in the year of Culloden. Who is there that will quarrel with it now? In this passage he says nothing of Thomson: it was unfortunate that Thomson's poetry came to be confounded in Walpole's mind with the poetry that resembled it in outward form. Here is the whole passage from which Macaulay quotes: a letter to Sir Horace Mann, March 29, 1745: " The town flocks to a new play of Thomson's called *Tancred and Sigismunda*: it is very dull; I have read it. I cannot bear modern poetry; these refiners of the purity of the stage, and of the incorrectness of English verse, are most wofully inspired. I had rather have written the most absurd lines in Lee, than *Leonidas* or the *Seasons*; as I had rather be put into the roundhouse for a wrongheaded quarrel, than sup quietly at eight o'clock with my grandmother. There is another of these tame geniuses, a Mr. Akenside, who writes Odes: in one he has lately published he says: ' Light the tapers, urge the fire.' Had not you rather make gods ' jostle in the dark ' than light the candles for fear they should break their heads ? "

Horace Walpole was wrong in coupling the *Seasons* with Glover's *Leonidas*. But Macaulay takes no trouble to understand his point of view. Walpole's criticism may be wrong, but it is unquestionably sane and lively. It is an appeal to the poets. For Heaven's sake spare us your droning platitudes: if we are to have bad poetry, let it at any rate be daring and adventurous; and die nobly.

Is this point of view so very irrational? Surely it is not difficult to sympathise with it. Or is it so very uncommon for readers to find fault with impec-

cable and superior works of edification, to say, Take
away your didactic poem or your philosophical novel,
give me *The Three Musketeers*. This is the temper of
mind that is common with Horace Walpole, and it is
this that makes him so admirable an historian. He
cannot endure being bored : which may be unamiable
and inconsiderate of him : but one result of it is that
he never bores anyone himself.

His cry to be delivered from metaphysical poems in
blank verse is the cry of the generation that was growing
up when Walpole was passing away. His impatience
of dulness in the year 1745, his craving for something
strange and adventurous in literature, is an anticipation
of the impulse that sent Scott on his Liddesdale raids
and Coleridge to the realm of Kubla Khan. Horace
Walpole's experiments in Gothic architecture and the
machinery of medieval romance are easily ridiculed ;
but the meaning of these diversions of his can hardly
be mistaken : the quickness of his nature required
more vivid fancies, more exciting pictures for the mind,
than were commonly provided by contemporary taste.
It is this that explains his severity of judgment on a
number of writers. He cannot help admiring Gibbon's
History, " and yet it has tired me."

To other historians he can be less respectful. " Have
you waded through or into Lord Lyttelton ? How dull
one may be, if one will but take pains for six or seven
and twenty years together ! "

It is wrong no doubt to speak in this light way of
serious and valuable works : but it is still worse to
pretend to be fond of solemn and heavy literature—a
hundred best books or more. There may be many
virtues wanting in Horace Walpole, but at least he
knew his own mind and had confidence in it and didn't

muddle away his time and his wits in trying other people's receipts for improving his mind.

The same freshness and the same ring of sincerity is to be found in all Horace Walpole's opinions even when the language is affected. The journey to Italy along with Gray has left in one of his letters one of the first vivid appreciations in English of romantic and savage landscape, one of the earliest passages of picturesque description. Horace Walpole among his other distinctions—he might not have been proud of it himself—is the first prophet of that extraordinary worship against which Mr. Carlyle lifted up his voice in *Sartor*—the devotion of the scenery hunters. Fresh and clear and solitary were those mountain passes in those days : not crowded as yet with romantic philosophers, or waggonloads of pilgrims in search of the picturesque. Three quarters of a century were to pass before Byron met at Chamouni the travellers, less eloquent than Walpole, who judged that it was all " truly rural." Here is Walpole's account of his discovery : a passage not to be read without some feeling of reverence, appropriate to the sacred well of all the voluminous flood of description that has swept through one century :

" But the road, West, the road ! winding round a prodigious mountain, and surrounded with others, all shagged with hanging woods, obscured with pines, or lost in clouds. Below, a torrent breaking through cliffs, and tumbling through fragments of rocks ! Sheets of cascades forcing their silver speed down channelled precipices, and hasting into the roughened river at the bottom. Now and then an old footbridge, with a broken rail, a leaning cross, a cottage or the ruin of an hermitage. This sounds too bombastic and too romantic to one that has not seen it, too cold for one that has.

If I could send you my letter post between two lovely tempests that echoed each other's wrath, you might have some idea of this noble roaring scene, as you were reading it." [1]

This is the beginning of a great many things. It is strange to find in this passage of a letter written in the time of Pope and Swift so many characteristics of a kind of prose that is hardly yet disused, the *silver speed* of the cataracts that fall into the *roughened river*—one might almost be reading one of the living exponents of the beauties of nature. The manner of Walpole is more attractive than that of some of his successors who are more energetic and more professional in their rhetoric. But for their excesses the leader is not to be blamed. Here as in so many other things the mind of Walpole touches once slightly on a region that was to be explored and exploited after him by a great host of followers. Among his followers are some of the greatest names in literature—Wordsworth, Coleridge, Scott and Byron, and also an innumerable nameless crowd.

It is not without sadness that one traces in these romantic sentences of the year 1739, the beginning of the growth that is accomplished in these latter days in the triumph of the tourist agency, the funicular railway, the organisation of sunrises, and other devices for making things cheap.

It is after the return of Walpole from Italy that the most important and characteristic of his themes is entered on. From that time to his death in 1797 his letters are a picture of the life of England ; and neither Macaulay nor any one else is to be trusted if he attempts to depreciate its value.

[1] Sept. 18, 1739 (Paget Toynbee, i. 38).

For the weight and dignity of its subject this correspondence can be likened to none except the letters of Cicero with their continuous story of the Roman Revolution.   The Revolution of English and European history in Walpole's time was not of less moment even than the mighty changes that put an end to the old Roman Constitution in the time of Cicero.

There is an interest in reading a series of letters like this which is not found even in personal memoirs.   It may be a childish idea, but somehow in reading letters one seems to be nearer to the reality than in reading any other history.   The phantoms of the past rise there less pale and shadowy than in common history, they come nearer to us, the colours deepen, the voices are more distinct.   Letters like those of Cicero are not a record of the time ; they are the life itself, the very accents of the time.   He does not write any more to Atticus or to his brother : he writes to us : he tells us how Cæsar came to stay with him, how they talked at dinner, how they spoke, Cæsar spoke.

There is nothing in all Walpole's letters quite so strange as that quiet party of Cicero's to which all the later generations are admitted as unseen guests.   But there are some things that come very near it in strangeness, as one follows the course of things from month to month, and the glory or the shame of England approaches or withdraws : and the shocks of Fate are repeated as we read on, looking for the next news from America and wondering whether Washington will be caught in a drag-net—though it proves to be more and more unlikely every day.

Macaulay says that about politics in the high sense of the term he knew nothing and cared nothing. Which may very well be true without involving along with it the truth of the common accusation against Walpole that he is a mere retailer of gossip. " It was owing to the peculiar elevation of his character that he cared about a pinnacle of lath and plaster more than about the Middlesex election, and about a miniature of Grammont more than about the American Revolution. Pitt and Murray might talk themselves hoarse about trifles. But questions of government and war were too insignificant to detain a mind which was occupied in recording the scandal of club-rooms and the whispers of the backstairs, and which was even capable of selecting and disposing chairs of ebony and shields of rhinoceros-skin."

It is to be hoped that no one ever was deterred from reading Walpole's letters by this sarcastic description. The scandal of club-rooms may be admitted : the School for Scandal has here in this correspondence one of its most eminent professors. The ebony chairs, the rhinoceros shields, these counts in the impeachment can hardly be denied. But when the chairs and the shields have been confessed, where, it may be asked, is the iniquity ? Is a man not to write to his friends about the things he and they are interested in ? As to the charge that the chairs and the shields and the pinnacles of Strawberry Hill, these and the scandals of the day drive out the weightier matters, it is merely unintelligible. No one was more alive than Walpole to the great achievements of that time. It is almost incredible that Macaulay should have passed over Walpole's descriptions of the inner life of Parliament, and his comments on all the important news that came to him from without, from the great wars with the French in America, India and Germany. Macaulay's statement that " questions of government and war were too insignificant to detain the mind of Walpole " is a misrepresentation which requires, in order to describe it rightly, some of the formulas employed by Macaulay himself about Croker.

From the time when Sir Robert Walpole, after his defeat in 1743, drank the health of Lord Stair and Lord Carteret (who were no friends of his) for the victory of Dettingen, saying he didn't care by whom the thing was done, so long as it was done, Horace Walpole's letters are an index of the fortunes of England at home and abroad. It is true that there was always something unreasoning in his patriotism, and, in spite of all his refinement, something of the spirit that hated the French because they were all slaves and wore wooden shoes. One of his last wishes is to hear that the French are beaten. He did not live long enough to enter into full sympathy with the leader of Macaulay's party, Mr. Fox, and applaud the victories of Bonaparte.

Reading letters like these one has a different sort of experience from that afforded by the stateliest history. Nowhere even in the most vivid and noblest history— not even in Thucydides and in the suspense of the Sicilian expedition, one of the most deeply tragic of all stories—does one get quite the same sort of impression. In reading Horace Walpole you watch the events as they come with the half belief that you are an invisible spectator—a ghost out of the future, permitted to look at the past. Whether is it they or we that are the phantoms ?

So we look on and watch the pageant unrolling— Sir Robert Walpole has gone out, and Mr. Pelham is Prime Minister. You look out of Mr. Walpole's window in Arlington Street to Mr. Pelham's over the way. There is a stir in the street this morning—a number of

the higher clergy have come to show their concern for
the First Lord of the Treasury. You watch the solemn
chariots at the door—then you remember that an
episcopal see is vacant. A year or two later you sit
with Mr. Walpole in Arlington Street, and listen to
the news from Scotland—the news that comes nearer
and nearer—how the Young Pretender is in Edinburgh—he has defeated an English general—he has
passed Carlisle—and all this rumour that we know so
well from other historians, all this story of *Waverley*,
is blended with the rumour of Mr. Walpole's School
for Scandal.

You go with George Selwyn to the trial of the
Scottish Lords, when pitied by gentle hearts Kilmarnock
died, and the half grotesque and wholly courageous and
honest demeanour of Lord Balmerino is followed by
the more violent tragi-comedy of Simon Fraser, Lord
Lovat.

You watch the rise of William Pitt as his contemporaries watched it. You forget that you know the
whole story. No historian can give as these letters
give it, the gradual decline of his greatness and his
genius. Macaulay says that Walpole ignored the distinction of his great contemporaries. It is true : he
ignored it before it was gained—Macaulay may sum up
the character of the Earl of Chatham. Is Walpole to
be blamed because he did not discover in the factious
partisan of 1742, the magnificent and heroic statesman
of the Seven Years War ? But who has made a more
absolute and unconditional acknowledgment of the
magical eloquence of Pitt and his inexhaustible resource
in debate than Walpole has made again and again in
his letters ? And if he touches on the weaknesses of
the great man, his arrogance or whatever is the right

word for it, and his stage effects, where is the harm ?
Are these not to be touched on ? And what would
our knowledge of the great man's character be without
them ?

There may be more generous and more unmeasured
panegyrics of the great achievements of the Seven
Years War. It was not Horace Walpole who wrote
the song of *Hearts of Oak* to " add something more to
that wonderful year," the year of victories, the year of
Minden and Quebec. But it may be doubted whether
any thunders of the artillery of eloquence can do more
for that year than the quiet ironical voice as it notes
these things from day to day—interpolating them in
the scandalous chronicle.

Think of the space that is covered by this series—
the sixty years that saw the rise of Prussia, the American
and French Revolutions—and for England how much
glory and how much the reverse of glorious—General
Braddock and Admiral Byng as well as Chatham and
Burke, Clive and Hastings. When the first of the
letters was written, Pope and Swift were alive and Pope
had still some work to do : before the last was written
Scott and Wordsworth and Coleridge had already
published verses. And thirteen years before his death
Walpole wrote his generous estimate of the poetry of
Crabbe.

To read these letters is for some things like entering
the world imagined by Charles Lamb—the world of
comedy which is only not tragic because your imagination has suspended the laws of the real world. Or it is
like entering a heathen paradise—where not all the
people are happy. The passions and the sins and
miseries that are shown in the magic glass have all but
lost in it their tragic import : there remains only

the phantom of it all—light as the vanity of Vanity Fair.

There are wiser seers than this worldly commentator on the picture of life. But at any rate he was, in his fashion, true to himself. If he seems heartless, it is at least in some measure because he used the ironical manner and does not try to be effusive.

The last words of his last letter have a curious pathetic suggestion—though they are not meant pathetically—of the moods of his great namesake—the Roman Horace—and of the most grave and touching of all the poems of the English Herrick :

" Pray send me no more such laurels. . . . I shall be quite content with a sprig of rosemary thrown after me, when the parson of the parish commits my dust to dust. Till then, pray, Madam, accept the resignation of your

Ancient Servant,

ORFORD."

" Now is the time when all the lights wax dim,
  And thou, *Anthea*, must withdraw from him
  That was thy servant."

VI

THE POLITICS OF BURNS

THIS discourse, whatever result it may come to, is certainly not wrong in its choice of a subject. To think of the politics of Robert Burns is not like some of the idle and irrelevant enquiries about the lives of poets. In every current opinion about him, in every judgment passed on him since the year 1786, he is taken as a representative man, speaking for his nation, or for the rank he belongs to, or for some new reviving spirit of liberty, or for the old traditional Scottish loyalty, or for these two together, as Jacobin-Jacobite.

Of his loyalty to the house of Stuart there can be no doubt, and there is no doubt that he was affected by the spirit of the French Revolution. But neither of these motives made the real politics of Burns. The French Revolution counted for very little in the poetry of Burns, for the good reason that in 1786 the French Revolution was not yet in sight, at any rate from the horizon of Mauchline. It is not wonderful that readers of the life of Burns (in any version of it) should be struck by the story of his later days, and the difficulties of the exciseman who admired the French, and sent them those historical carronades.

The difficulties are well described by Carlyle :

" Meteors of French politics rise before him ; is he not a well-wisher of the French Revolution, a Jacobin, and therefore in that one act guilty of all ? " " These accusations " (Carlyle goes on), " it has since appeared, were false enough : but the world hesitated little to credit them."

And later, we may add, long after the suspicions and jealousies of Dumfries, when Burns's opinions about France have little left in them to irritate the most sensitive Tory, there is another kind of exaggeration connecting Burns and the French Revolution through the Spirit of the Age. You will find this superstition in Matthew Arnold's essay on Gray : " If Gray, like Burns, had been just 30 when the French Revolution broke out, he would have shown perhaps productiveness and animation in plenty."

Now this means evidently that Burns lived in a time of expansion, and had the advantage of this expansion or explosion in his poetical fertility, as contrasted with the small volume of Gray's poems. It is true that Burns was born in 1759, and therefore was 30 in 1789 ; it is true also that the explosion reached his mind. But what had it to do with the Kilmarnock edition of 1786, or the Edinburgh of 1787 ? And how much of Burns's poetry was written after the explosion of 1789 ? That sentence of Matthew Arnold may, I think, be worth noting in an historical society, as an example of one of the Idols of the Theatre, one of the fallacies besetting historical study, especially, I should say, the history of literature. The Spirit of the Age is a dangerous demon, and I cannot but think he has imposed on Matthew Arnold in this reference to Burns. The poems of Burns in which he gave his rendering of

I

Ayrshire life ; the poems which made his fame at once, through all the length of the Island of Britain, were published before the French Revolution ; and further, they show no signs of the coming expansion. The politics of Burns are not, in 1786, affected by the great things coming on ; if there is any high spirit in his politics, and there is much, it is derived from the time of Gray ; the time of depression, as Matthew Arnold counts it. If one is to borrow metaphysical aid to interpret the poetical genius of Burns, why not take the " freits," as we may call them here, which will be interpreted " omens," if this argument is ever repeated in South Britain, why not take the freits from his birth year of 1759 ?

It is not less significant, that date, than 1789 ; it is the " wonderful year," of *Hearts of Oak*, of Minden and Quebec and Quiberon. Burns knew well enough what that year meant, and his hero is William Pitt, Earl of Chatham, and also, for the father's sake chiefly, William Pitt, the son :

> An' Will's a true guid fallow's get,
> A name not envy spairges.

There you have the politics of Burns in 1786, when he was at the height of his power.   It is obvious enough, but seems generally to lack interest for readers of Burns. Yet surely there is something worth considering in the fact, which Scott is one author to note clearly, that Burns for a time was a Pittite :

" You will see he plays high Jacobite . . . though I imagine his Jacobitism, like my own, belonged rather to the fancy than the reason. He was, however, a great Pittite down to a certain period."

Burns shows an extraordinary gift for finding out all

that he wants to know, and he must have wanted to know everything about the Pitts, or he could not have found out Boconnock in Cornwall, the house of the Pitts—regarding which I remember Mr. Phillimore spoke some pleasant things some years ago on a 25th of January—if the newspapers of the 26th are to be trusted. I am sorry I was not there to hear.

There are several points here all at once calling for notice, and seldom getting it from friends of the poet:

The extraordinary talent for history shown by Robert Burns.

His attention to British History in preference to Scottish.

The originality of his views.

He is not fascinated at this time by Charles James Fox. At any rate in his political choice and aims and admirations he refuses to be swayed by the passionate eloquence or the liberal ideas of the statesman with whom we should think he might have had more sympathy. He celebrates him later (1788), without illusion.

Further, and this perhaps when one comes to look into it is the strangest thing of all, his clear, original and careful study of British politics is carried on through the time when his poetical studies are most closely limited to the country he knows—not Scotland, but Ayrshire, and not the whole of Ayrshire.

To understand the politics of Burns it is necessary to think of his position with regard to the scene and the substance of his poetry—the poetry of 1786 and 1787, to which he never added another volume of the same sort in the ten years remaining, and scarcely a poem except *Tam o' Shanter*.

How did Burns come to write the Kilmarnock volume? This problem may be hard to answer, and it is possibly foolish. But there are some misconceptions about his circumstances and education, and his place in literature, which must be cleared away. Carlyle gives his authority to some of these in his review of Lockhart, and his lecture on the Hero as Man of Letters :

" With no furtherance but such knowledge as dwells in a poor man's hut, and the rhymes of a Fergusson or Ramsay for his standard of beauty."

Now we know that his standard of beauty was formed in part upon the rhymes of Ramsay and Fergusson, but we know that it was influenced also by Pope and Steele and Beattie's work, by Shakespeare and Milton, by Thomson, Shenstone, and Gray and Goldsmith. You can tell a man by his quotations ; he quotes *Hamlet*, *Othello*, *King Lear*, *Troilus and Cressida*. He writes to Mrs. Dunlop of his recourse to the dramas of Thomson. He quotes to Clarinda from Gray's *Bard* :

> Dear as the light that visits these sad eyes,
> Dear as the ruddy drops that warm my heart.

Is not the standard of beauty there ?

Carlyle on Burns again, in *Hero-Worship* :

" This Burns appeared under every disadvantage ; uninstructed, poor, born only to hard manual toil ; and writing, when it came to that, in a rustic special dialect, known only to a small province of the country he lived in. Had he written even what he did write in the general language of England, I doubt but he had already become universally recognised as being, or capable to be, one of our greatest men."

I am not quite sure what Carlyle means by a rustic special dialect, known only to a small province of the country he lived in. Of course the language of Kyle

and Carrick has peculiarities of its own.   Burns does
not write exactly the same language as the Scottish
poets of Lothian and the Mearns ; there are words and
phrases in Fergusson, and also let me say for the pleasure of naming them, in *Hamewith* and in *Horace* of the
Ochils, that are not found in Burns.   The language of
Ross of Lochlee, in *Helenore, the Fortunate Shepherdess*
(" Lindy and Nory "), must have been strange to Burns,
though probably more familiar to his father and his
Montrose cousins, but it was no great hindrance to his
understanding and appreciation of " Lindy and Nory " ;
and as for readers in the South, it was in England that
he found at once some of his most enthusiastic admirers,
among some of the most fastidious and most purely
Southern in taste and breeding.   I mean particularly
William Gilpin, the careful and delightful student of
the picturesque, who, if any one, might have been
offended by Scotch drink, Scotch religion and Scotch
manners.   Instead of which Gilpin, the refined and
elegant, chooses precisely from a poem on Scotch drink
a stanza for the death of a hero, and he quotes it at
Killiecrankie for an epitaph on Dundee.   Coleridge in
the *Friend* makes a similar use of the same context,
without the particular reference, though decorously he
omits the line :

> Clap in his cheek a Highland gill.

Wordsworth, speaking of the death of Dundee in one
of his early poems, shows that he had read Gilpin,
and had read Burns as quoted by Gilpin, and did not
disapprove :

> And glad Dundee in faint " huzzas " expired.

It is curious.

There are selections from Burns in the *Annual Register*, as soon as may be after the Edinburgh edition.

Scottish poetry had been regularly within the knowledge of Southern readers for two or three generations before Burns—we may say perhaps ever since *Christ's Kirk on the Green* was published at Oxford by Edmund Gibson. A good example and proof of this is the list of subscribers to *Orpheus Caledonius*, London, 1733; there are many English names among them, more English than Scotch, I should say, guessing roughly—the Rt. Hon. William Pulteney, Esq., Thomas Pitt, Esq., Mrs. Pitt, George Venables Vernon, Esq. (6 sets), Lady Robert Walpole. I believe that Horace Walpole read his mother's copy.

Burns wrote in the language of Kyle, because that was his natural language. But he had not to choose between that and English. Any page of Burns will show that his language is not to be described simply as a special dialect; it has all manner of variations between the pure vernacular and the book-English. It is not, I think, commonly recognised how much an affair of art, an assumed and artificial style, was the Scottish poetry of the eighteenth century; how different in its condition from the poetry of the old " makaris," Dunbar and Douglas and the rest.

Beattie writes a poem to Ross of Lochlee, an occasional diversion, in the familiar stanza :

> O Ross, thou wale o' hearty cocks,
> Sae crouse and canty wi' thy jokes,
> Thy hamely auld warld muse provokes
>   Me for a while
> To ape our guid plain country folks
>   In verse and style.

O bonny are our green sward hows
Where through the birks the burny rows,
And the bee bums, and the ox lows,
    And saft winds rusle,
And shepherd-lads on sunny knows
    Blaw the blythe fusle.

He passes this off as a *tour de force*, a literary joke, and such indeed it was. And so are the Scots verses of Stevenson and of Hugh Haliburton and the author of *Hamewith*, obviously. And so are the Scots verses of Robert Burns and of Allan Ramsay and of Robert Fergusson before him. Burns adopts a literary convention in the same way, though more consistently and thoroughly than Beattie. None of his forms are invented ; all are taken from the tradition which had been founded in the seventeenth century by the *Elegy on Habbie Simson, piper of Kilbarchan*, developed and confirmed by Allan Ramsay. The readers of Burns, his rhyming friends and competitors, all understood this. It is all a game of language, " crambo-clink," with rules and patterns of its own, used for fun by men who wrote their serious business letters in English, and exacted the catechism in English from their children and servants, and sang in English the metrical version of the Psalms by Mr. Francis Rous of Truro, sometime Provost of Eton.

Now when this is understood it will be found, I think, to have some bearing upon the politics of Burns, though possibly I may seem to have wandered away from the proper field of the Historical Society over the borders into philology, if not into mere rhetoric and *belles lettres*.

It is a great thing for an artist to inherit a strong tradition, to belong to a school. It means that he has all the strength of his own and the last generation to draw upon ; he does not waste his time in solitary adventures ; he is not left to himself ; he is saved from caprice and melancholy, from the fate of Chatterton. Think of the difference between the art of Burns, his secure command of all his arguments and all his forms on the one hand, and the poetry of his contemporary Blake on the other—in so many ways miraculous, yet at what an expense of thought and care in finding out the new ways. The poems of Fergusson, as Dr. John Service expressed it, in a true conceit, are the *juvenilia* of Burns ; and Fergusson himself worked in a traditional way.

The security of Burns as a poet with the inherited forms and examples of Ramsay and Fergusson goes along with security and confidence in the choice of themes. His poetry, for all its rustic character and language, has the distinctive mark of aristocratic literature. It is self-possessed, at ease and sure of itself ; classical. It is not restless, or self-conscious or anxious or experimental or *arriviste*. It has the true dignity, like that of the man who knows he is master in his own house, and is accustomed to converse with his equals, and has no reason to go craving for what he has not got.

When Keats came up by Glen App, and so by Ballantrae and Girvan and Maybole to Alloway, thinking rightly about Burns, more than most men, he saw Arran over the sea, and wondered why the vision of the island had never passed into Burns's poetry. Arran had been before him all his days, and there is no word of it anywhere, in any of his prose or rhyme. For this disregard there was probably good reason. Burns has left out of his poetry many other things which must have been equally within his knowledge, and might have been wrought into the fabric of his verse. He was thought by some to be indifferent to the beauties of nature. He was certainly irresponsive when people gave utterance to their hearts of sensibility :

" He disliked to be tutored in matters of taste, and could not endure that one should run shouting before him whenever any fine object appeared." (Cunningham, Chambers II. 156 n.). Andrew Lang, in a sonnet written under the influence of Wordsworth, has uttered the same complaint of those who shout

> To me, to me the poet, O look there !

But it is not only in matters of this sort that Burns is economical and reticent. The Kilmarnock volume, which expresses so much of the life of Ayrshire, leaves out a great deal. Burns keeps to the region he knows ; neighbouring provinces are left unnoticed, though he might easily have touched upon them, and brought back profitable things. Why does he go down to the sea, and no further ? Why does he make nothing of the contraband trade with which he came to be acquainted at Kirkoswald ? If he was too proud to speak of the Arran hills which did not belong to him, might he not have gone sailing with fishermen of Girvan or Ayr, Dunure or Turnberry ? No, they were not his own people ; his own people are the farmers or their cotters, and it was not his business to go looking for subjects. The fishermen are left out. So on the other side the further moorlands and their shepherds are left out. He takes the Doon where it comes near him ; he does not wander up to talk with the lonely shepherds on the Galloway border ; Loch Doon he never thinks about, nor the wild uplands where his river comes down from the granite of Loch Enoch, and houses are far between.

While he thus restricted himself in his choice of Ayrshire themes, he was attending to contemporary history. He must have read the newspapers and probably also the *Scots Magazine* with extraordinary care. And he does not read under the influence of that Scottish prejudice which he was proud to confess in the well known and often quoted words : " the spirit of Wallace poured a Scottish prejudice into my veins, which will boil along there till the floodgates of life shut in eternal rest."

He is not particularly good at Scottish history. His Scottish politics are determined by Scotch drink. But the politics of the United Kingdom of Great Britain in his own lifetime were noted by him with a diligence which the biographers and commentators of Burns have passed over very lightly.

This historical study comes out in two poems particularly : the birthday poem to the King and the historical fragment on the American war and the parliamentary vicissitudes following—" When Guilford good our pilot stood." His carefulness is proved through one of the conventions of that sort of lyrical satire. The rule is that persons are not to be named by their right names, if another name can be provided. It is that rule (together with the need for a rhyme to *winnock* and *bannock* and *Nanse Tinnock*) that puts *Boconnock* for *Pitt* or *Chatham*. Hence *Guilford* and not *Lord North*, *Montague* for *Lord Sandwich*, *Grenville* for the statesman commonly called *Lord Temple*. *The Duke of York* is *Right Reverend Osnabrug* (of course there are other obvious motives here). *Lord George Germaine* appears under his other name of *Sackville*. A note in the Centenary Edition, from an autograph manuscript

seen by the editors, shows that Burns originally wrote
Germaine :

> And bauld G——ne wham Minden's plain
> To fame will ever blaw, man.

Altered :

> And Sackville doure, wha stood the stoure
> The German chief to thraw, man.

I believe that Burns thought of changing it because
Germaine was the right name, and therefore the wrong
name for his purpose.

It does not look as if he were working with an index
or a peerage at his side. He knows the names and
titles of these persons of quality because he is interested
in British history. Boconnock comes to his mind because he has found out some time before what he wants
to know about the family of Pitt ; just as he does not
need a file of newspapers, or a set of the *Scots Magazine*,
or the *Annual Register*, when he finds his old soldier
among the Jolly Beggars :

> My prenticeship was past where my leader breathed his
>   last,
> When the bloody die was cast on the heights of Abram ;
> I served out my trade when the gallant game was played,
> And the Moro low was laid at the sound of the drum.
>
> I lastly was with Curtis among the floating batteries,
> And there I left for witness an arm and a limb,
> Yet let my country need me, with Elliot to lead me,
> I'll clatter on my stumps at the sound of a drum.

The fragment " When Guilford good " looks at first
like a rigmarole of mere annals turned into burlesque
rhyme. But it works up to a climax, and it is not a
fragment ; it is the war-song of William Pitt, the young
hero. It turns into that, whatever Burns may have first
intended, or even if he intended nothing in particular

when he began. And he certainly had the whole history in his mind when he began, and also his judgment on the characters. You may notice that his alteration of *Germaine* proves this. It is not merely a conventional vague illusion to Lord George Sackville's notorious cowardice at Minden. It is so, in the first version ; but the second, the authorised version, shows that Burns knew what happened at Minden, and he has put this into a phrase so mischievous that the point of it may easily escape notice and Sackville be mistaken for a hero :

> wha stood the stoure
> The German chief to thraw, man.

It looks at first like heroic resistance ; till you remember that the German chief, Ferdinand of Brunswick, was Lord George Sackville's commander, that the *stoure* means the repeated order to charge, with a prophetic allusion to the trial that followed. " The German chief to thraw " is not to confound the enemy, but to disappoint his own general.

Burns's politics at this time are clear enough. Chatham is his great hero because he knows about Minden and Quebec, and the taking of Havana, " when the Moro low was laid." And William Pitt the younger has his regard partly for his father's sake, and partly for his own courage and his resistance to the coalition of Fox and North, which Burns could not stand because it was meanness and knavery. He does not object to Fox because of his tinkler jaw or dicing box and sporting lady. Fox's gambling was merely a good thing for a satirical poet, as in the address to the Prince of Wales in the *Dream* :

> That e'er ye brak Diana's pales,
> Or rattl'd dice wi' Charlie.

But he seriously did not like " yon mixtie maxtie queer
hotch potch, the Coalition," and he seriously regarded
Pitt as a high-spirited young man breaking through the
intrigues of party politics and likely to go further.
And this is what he puts into his rhyme of the American
war and Rockingham and Shelburne and the Coalition,
and Fox's India Bill, and Temple's message from the
King, " a secret word or twa, man," and Pitt's courageous adventure—a long way from Mauchline, but
touched off with the same intensity as Black Russell
and Moodie and Peebles from the Waterfoot :

> But word an' blow, North, Fox, and Co.
>   Gowff'd Willie like a ba', man,
> Till Suthron raise an' coost their claise
>   Behind him in a raw, man :
> An' Caledon threw by the drone,
>   An' did her whittle draw, man ;
> An' swoor fu' rude, thro' dirt an' bluid,
>   To mak it guid in law, man.

The Dream of the 4th of June, 1786, is the other
example of Burns's interest in the history of his country,
which is not politically Scotland, but Great Britain.
Also of the quickness and readiness with which he followed the news from London.   *The Dream* is suggested
by Thomas Warton's periodical birthday ode published
in the newspapers.   It is worth mentioning that while
the ode of 1786 prompted Burns's poem, the ode of the
previous year was the occasion of the notorious burlesque Probationary Odes, the sequel of the *Rolliad*.
So that Burns here again had his eye on the same sort
of things as attracted the wits of London.   He has
nothing much to learn from them in the art of satirical
poetry.   Here again, though here only by the way,
Pitt comes in as the statesman to be respected ; and
Burns appears as the champion of the Navy against

retrenchment in a passage which may possibly have been quoted, though I have never noticed it, in speeches of knights and squires who represent our burghs and shires :

> I'm no mistrusting Willie Pitt,
>   When taxes he enlarges,
> (An' Will's a true guid fallow's get,
>   A name not envy spairges),
> That he intends to pay your debt,
>   An' lessen a' your charges ;
> But, God sake ! let nae saving fit
>   Abridge your bonie barges
>   An' boats this day.

" Burns was a great Pittite down to a certain period," and that period was the end of his free, unimpeded work as a poet.   He is a poet for the rest of his life, but never again with that irresistible command of his art, that certainty in all his various themes and moods which went with the volume of poems chiefly in the Scottish dialect.   After that he is distracted.   His work in the songs, as we watch it in his correspondence with Johnson and Thomson, is of a different sort, often painful and laborious.   He wastes his time thinking about impossible plans for Scottish drama and Scottish opera.   And his political opinions change.   His important Whig friends make him unsure of himself ;   he has to ask Henry Erskine whether it will do to print " When Guilford good our pilot stood."   He takes to wearing the buff and blue, and owes allegiance to Mr. Fox.   At the same time he makes more than in early days of his Jacobite sentiment ;   he writes his worst verse in a poem on the name of Stuart :

Though something like moisture conglobes in my eye.

To make up for that :

> It was a' for our rightfu' king.

But before he had forgotten his earlier studies and interests he wrote a deliberate argument which may be quoted here.

I cannot see anything wrong in Burns's letter to the *Star*, Nov. 8, 1788, protesting against some of the Whig rhetoric over the centenary of the glorious Revolution ; it seems to me right in history and right in sentiment, with a shrewd stroke at the orators who blamed the tyranny of the Stuart kings and ignored the tyranny of parliaments.

To the Editor of " The Star."

Nov. 8th, 1788.

Sir,—Notwithstanding the opprobrious epithets with which some of our philosophers and gloomy sectarians have branded our nature—the principle of universal selfishness, the proneness to all evil, they have given us ; still, the detestation in which inhumanity to the distressed, and insolence to the fallen, are held by all mankind, shows that they are not natives of the human heart. Even the un-happy partner of our kind who is undone—the bitter consequence of his follies or his crimes—who but sympa-thizes with the miseries of this ruined profligate brother ? We forget the injuries, and feel for the man.

I went, last Wednesday, to my parish church, most cordially to join in grateful acknowledgment to the AUTHOR OF ALL GOOD, for the consequent blessings of the glorious Revolution.   To that auspicious event we owe no less than our liberties, civil and religious ; to it we are likewise indebted for the present Royal Family, the ruling features of whose administration have ever been mildness to the subject, and tenderness of his rights.

Bred and educated in revolution principles, the principles of reason and common sense, it could not be any silly political prejudice which made my heart revolt at the harsh abusive manner in which the reverend gentleman mentioned the house of Stuart, and which, I am afraid, was too much the language of the day.   We may rejoice sufficiently in our deliverance from past evils, without cruelly raking up the ashes of those whose misfortune it was, perhaps as much as their crime, to be the authors of those evils, and we may bless God for all his goodness to us as a nation, without at the same time cursing a few ruined, powerless exiles, who only harboured ideas, and made attempts, that most of us would have done, had we been in their situation.

The " bloody and tyrannical House of Stuart," may be said with propriety and justice, when compared with the present royal family, and the sentiments of our days ; but is there no allowance to be made for the manners of the times ? Were the royal contemporaries of the Stuarts more attentive to their subjects' rights ? Might not the epithets of " bloody and tyrannical " be, with at least equal justice, applied to the House of Tudor, of York, or any other of their predecessors ?

The simple state of the case, Sir, seems to be this :—At that period, the science of government, the knowledge of the true relation between king and subject, was like other sciences and other knowledge, just in its infancy, emerging from dark ages of ignorance and barbarity.

The Stuarts only contended for prerogatives which they knew their predecessors enjoyed, and which they saw their contemporaries enjoying ; but these prerogatives were inimical to the happiness of a nation and the rights of subjects.

In this contest between prince and people, the con- sequence of that light of science which had lately dawned over Europe, the monarch of France, for example, was victorious over the struggling liberties of his people ; with us, luckily, the monarch failed, and his unwarrantable pretentions fell a sacrifice to our rights and happiness. Whether it was owing to the wisdom of leading individuals, or to the justling of parties, I cannot pretend to determine ; but, likewise happily for us, the kingly power was shifted into another branch of the family, who, as they owed the throne solely to the call of a free people, could claim nothing inconsistent with the covenanted terms which placed them there.

The Stuarts have been condemned and laughed at for the folly and impracticability of their attempts in 1715 and 1745. That they failed, I bless God : but cannot join in the ridicule against them. Who does not know that the abilities or defects of leaders and commanders are often hidden until put to the touchstone of exigency ; and that there is a caprice of fortune, an omnipotence in particular accidents and conjectures of circumstances, which exalt us as heroes, or brand us as madmen, just as they are for or against us ?

Man, Mr. Publisher, is a strange, weak, inconsistent being : who would believe, Sir, that in this our Augustan age of liberality and refinement, while we seem so justly sensible and jealous of our rights and liberties, and animated with such indignation against the very memory of those who would have subverted them—that a certain people under our national protection should complain, not against our monarch and a few favorite advisers, but against our WHOLE LEGISLATIVE BODY, for similar oppression, and almost in the very same terms, as our forefathers did of the House of Stuart ! I will not, I cannot, enter into the merits of the cause ; but I dare say the American Congress, of 1776, will be allowed to have been as able and enlightened as the English Convention was in 1688 ; and that their posterity will celebrate the centenary of their deliverance from us, as duly and sincerely as we do ours from the oppressive measures of the wrong-headed House of Stuart.

To conclude, Sir, let every man who has a tear for the many miseries incident to humanity, feel for a family, illustrious as any in Europe, and unfortunate beyond historic precedent ; and let every Briton (and particularly every Scotsman), who ever looked with reverential pity on the dotage of a parent, cast a veil over the fatal mistakes of the kings of his forefathers.

R. B.

Burns's opinions about the French Revolution have nothing dishonourable in them, and nothing very difficult to understand. They are like Wordsworth's, but of course without Wordsworth's intimate knowledge of France, and with sympathies less intense. He hates the invaders of France, and there is deadly contempt in his rude rhyme :

You're welcome to Despots, Dumourier !

But, like Wordsworth, he turns to think of his own country when his country is in danger. There is no discord or contradiction between *A man's a man for a' that*, Jan. 1795 (" two or three good prose thoughts inverted into rhyme "), and the song for the Dumfries Volunteers (*Dumfries Journal*, May 5th, 1795) :

> Be Britain still to Britain true
>   Amang oursels united,
> For never but by British hands
>   Maun British wrangs be righted !
>
> .   .   .   .   .
>
> The wretch that would a tyrant own,
>   And the wretch, his true-born brother,
> Who'd set the mob above the throne,
>   May they be damn'd together !
> Who will not sing *God save the King !*
>   Shall hang as high's the steeple ;
> But while we sing *God save the King !*
>   We'll not forget the people !

Whatever may be the value of his later thoughts in prose or rhyme, they have not the significance or the force of the miraculous volume of 1786, with the other poems written but not printed at that time. Burns as a poet is to be judged by the work of those years ; the more this is studied the clearer is the relation between his command of the world of Mauchline and Ayr, and his political understanding of what is meant by Great Britain.

VII

JOSEPH RITSON

You have conferred on me a great honour, and imposed a very pleasant duty. I do not mean the obligation to make a speech, but the charge that will remain with me when this compulsory sermon is ended ; the thought that I have been chosen one of the captains of a band of adventurers, whose province is the ocean of stories, the fortunate isles of romance, kingdoms of wonders beyond the farthest point of the voyage of Argo. The business of your president is like that of Francis Drake taking his men to the treasure-house of the world. I hope to be forgiven by the countrymen of Lope de Vega for this allusion to their enemy ; there is nothing malign in it, I hope. For happily where our treasure is, there is no grudging, no chance of quarrels about sharing : each man's gain is the profit of all, and the riches multiply under the eyes of the adventurers, instead of being tucked away in hiding places on the " Dead Man's Chest." There is a spirit of youth and confidence and hope in our Society : it is only a pity that presidential formalities should hinder any of us from the real work —when I think of the books waiting to be read—the poets of Provence, the Spanish plays in their thousands,

the chroniclers of Portugal, the memoirs of France.
Nos manet oceanus circumvagus. Let us pay a visit to
Mr. Aubrey Bell on his Atlantic shore, where, far from
committees, he spends the time happily with the
redondilhas of Gil Vicente. And there is all the Northern region waiting ; how many Englishmen have
ventured into the old Laws of Norway ? how many
have found for themselves the value of Icelandic verse ?
I will go no further in this rehearsal now. But I will
ask leave to make a claim and to draw a line.

I draw the line at the report addressed to the President of the Board of Education on the teaching of
English. It is useful as a statement of most things
which our Association does not want. It prescribes
for Universities a study of language which must not go
too far, and particularly not too far back ; it is suspicious of Anglo-Saxon and Middle English. It treats
the student as if his salvation were all included in what
he is expected to study in the " School."

If the later literature, so much easier of approach, be
crowded out, the humane influence which English should
exercise is only too likely never to come into play at all.
It would be a mistake to sacrifice Burke and Johnson,
Wordsworth and Shelley, for the sake of things of an appeal
so much more remote as early language and early literature
must inevitably be.

No hope, you see, for Burke and Johnson, Wordsworth
and Shelley, if students, studying English, are asked
to study English ! The poor victim of Sweet's *Reader*
is cut off from *Rasselas* and the *Present Discontents.*
That is the assumption ; his head is unanointed with
oil ; he has no time for more than his masters allow
him. His pitiable case resembles that of an older day
as rhymed in an Oxford poem :

Say, shall our authors from Morris to Malory
Languish, untaught, on their several shelves ?
Say shall, for want of a reader (with salary),
Students be forced to read Keats for themselves ?

The law of our Association was not made for pupil teachers : " I hate a pupil teacher," the noble words of Milton in *Areopagitica*, might be taken for one of our impresses. If we want to learn Dutch or Danish, we set about it ; we are not impeded in our grammar by any craving for soft unphilological influences. We know where to find these if we want them ; as Henry Sweet himself did, a lifelong lover of romance. If we are suspicious of any sort of learning, which we would not willingly be, it is the learning that asks for quick returns, that places bounds and puts up forbidding notices, " by order," where the glades open into the wood.

There is perhaps one other variety of narrow learning which may be mentioned here as a possible danger in modern research. It is that which is limited to the Degree and the Dissertation ; it is at its worst in Germany and America. Our former acquaintance, Dr. Aloys Brandl, once published a statement that after Goethe, the great work of Germany was the schools of research in America. The same defects may be found in both ; particularly in the research commanded by the Professor, and got up by the pupil just well enough to pass, with results laboriously acquired and useful, and unutterably spiritless and disheartening to anyone who looks into them and sees how they have been compiled. I refer, for example, to a German dissertation on the life and writings of Frere which I read some time ago—a painstaking meritorious essay which had got up everything obtainable about Frere, and could not be trusted to wander an inch beyond (or even within) the understood limits of the subject. Frere was British Minister at Madrid in 1802-1804, dangerous years. Spain declared war at the end of 1804, when Godoy was the chief personage at Court : Godoy, Prince of the Peace, by his Spanish title. The German author clearly had never heard of Godoy before, and had not troubled to read any Spanish history ; he was interested in John Hookham Frere, and in nobody and nothing else, for the time, and he consequently takes the title " Prince of Peace " as part of Frere's fun—an ironical epithet for the adversary. He had of course been given to understand that Frere was a jester. This same student in modern humanities, I remember, gave proof how useful the ancient humanities may be at a pinch. Frere is Whistlecraft, the author of *The Monks and the Giants*, and our poor German commentator was pulled up in this admirable poem by the spectacle of a giant footstep with six toes :

> Then to the traces of gigantic feet,
> Huge, wide apart, with half a dozen toes.   (iv. 53.)

He did not take the allusion to the giants of Gath, 2 Sam. xxi. 20. A sound religious education is desirable for foreigners and others whose researches and humanities compel them to understand a British joke.

I have chosen Joseph Ritson as a theme for this afternoon ; you will readily understand my motive. Ritson belonged to the great age of the adventurers, the *conquistadores*, Percy, Warton, Tyrwhitt, Scott, Ellis, Leyden, not to speak of their great contemporaries on the Continent—the brothers Grimm, Ferdinand Wolf, Raynouard. Unfortunately, I have to complain that

Joseph Ritson has suffered from the same kind of half-baked research as his contemporary Frere. His American biographer,[1] with many excellent qualities, suffers from a want of the least tincture of Ritson's spirit of curiosity. Nothing leads him out of his way : he mentions Leyden without a word of the *Complaynt of Scotland*, and his note on Ritson's *Caledonians* exhibits this information about the Picts :

The first mention of the Picts is about 300, when they are referred to by Cæsar, Tacitus and others as enemies to the Britons.

Joseph Ritson, on the whole, has had less than justice. It is one of his misfortunes that Lockhart did not understand him. Many people read Lockhart's slighting and self-contradictory remarks, for one who reads Scott on Ritson :

This narrow-minded, sour, and dogmatical little word-catcher had hated the very name of a Scotsman, and was utterly incapable of sympathising with any of the higher views of his new correspondent. Yet the bland courtesy of Scott disarmed even this half-crazy pedant ; and he communicated the stores of his really valuable learning [N.B. the word-catcher had really valuable learning] in a manner that seems to have greatly surprised all who had hitherto held any intercourse with him on antiquarian topics. (Lockhart's *Life of Scott*, ii. p. 62.)

Lockhart himself had not taken the trouble to find out, or to remember, what Sir Walter really thought of his quaint friend. Ritson however need not be put to shame ; with Scott and Surtees to understand him, with Scott and George Ellis helping him and accepting his help, there cannot be much wrong with him. George Ellis translated for Ritson's *Ancient Songs* the

[1] *Joseph Ritson, a critical biography*, by Henry Alfred Burd (University of Illinois Studies, vol. ii. No. 3, August, 1916).

old French lament for Simon de Montfort, MS. Harl. 2253 :

> In song my grief shall find relief,
>   Sad is my verse and rude,
> I sing in tears our gentle peers
>   Who fell for England's good.
> Our peace they sought, for us they fought,
>   For us they dared to die ;
> And where they sleep, a mangled heap,
>   Their wounds for vengeance cry.
> On Evesham's plain is Montfort slain,
>   Well skill'd the war to guide,
> Where streams his gore shall all deplore
>   Fair England's flower and pride.

Scott, for the same selection, translated 344 lines of the *Recollections of Chatelain*. Scott and Ellis did not find Ritson a " word-catcher," but a discoverer of the sort of precious things that they themselves enjoyed.

Joseph Ritson was a successful man ; he made his fortune, and was able to help his family, particularly a nephew who was not ungrateful and who did well for his uncle's memory. He was born in 1752 at Stockton-on-Tees. Articled to a solicitor there, by the time he was twenty he seems to have learned to make the best of both worlds. Without neglecting the law, he found time for reading, and particularly for antiquarian studies. He walked to Edinburgh, and visited the Advocates' Library when he was twenty-one ; he spent so much on books, including Pitscottie's *Chronicle*, that he could not pay his lodging. A stranger helped him, persuaded by Ritson's description of Flodden. He was not in those days morose ; the year before 1772 he had addressed " Verseës " to the ladies of Stockton (he spells already as in the " Romanceës " thirty years later) ; his poem was printed in the *Newcastle Miscellany*. About the same time he made the acquaint-

ance of the Newcastle poet, John Cunningham. He
had already, by the time he was twenty-one, all the
tastes that went to make his work as a scholar and
historian ; he was already an antiquary, and at the
same time he was a lover of literature, a servant of the
Muses.

Then (end of 1775) he went to London and worked
as clerk to a firm of conveyancers. How he lived it is
difficult to make out ; he was trusted and approved
by his employers, Masterman and Lloyd ; he cannot
have been remiss in his conveyancing work ; yet at the
same time he was reading hard at the British Museum.
In 1784 he was appointed High Bailiff of the Liberty
of the Savoy. Jan. 25, 1786, he was granted the Patent
of the office for life. He was called to the Bar from
Gray's Inn, May 20, 1789. He must have had something of a conveyancing practice. At the same time
he was writing legal antiquities.[1] And for many years
he had been working as an editor of old poetry, a
disputant who would stand no nonsense.

In 1782 he had published one of the most characteristic of all his works ; the letter to Thomas Warton,
Observations on the first three volumes of the *History
of English Poetry*. The cruelty of the language, the
accuracy of the criticism, the ingenious malignity of the
form—4°, so that it might be conveniently bound up
at the end of Warton's third volume—all are Ritson.
Then he turned to Shakespeare, with *Remarks Critical
and Illustrative* on Steevens, and began and continued
his delightful series of collections : *English Songs*, 1783 ;
the *Bishoprick Garland or Durham Minstrel*, Stockton,

---

[1] *A Digest of the Proceedings of the Court Leet of the Manor and
Liberty of Savoy*, 1789. *The Jurisdiction of the Court Leet*, 1791.
The Office of Constable, 1791.

1784 ; *Gammer Gurton's Garland or the Nursery Parnassus*, Stockton, 1784.

The next collection had a strange fate : the *Caledonian Muse* was ready printed in 1785, when a fire destroyed the introductory matter and stopped the publication. Long afterwards, in 1821, the surviving sheets, that is to say, the poems, were published by Robert Triphook, 23 Old Bond Street.

Ritson's Essay on the author of *Christ's Kirk on the Green*, his notes and glossary, are lost.

Now this *Caledonian Muse*, printed in the year before Burns, has in it, you might say, the whole of Burns's poetical ancestry : *Peblis to the Play* and *Christ's Kirk on the Green*, the originals from which are derived *Hallowe'en* and the *Holy Fair* ; Montgomerie's poem of the *Cherrie and the Slae* ; and the *Elegy on Habbie Simson*, Piper of Kilbarchan. These are the three chief forms or types which in the next year were to come out at Kilmarnock. Joseph Ritson was the forerunner ; his *Caledonian Muse* of 1785 was partly a symbolical vision of the antique world from which the poetical life of the Kilmarnock volume was drawn.

And so he goes on ; publishing *Ancient Songs*, printed 1787, published 1792, dated 1790, and pieces of *Ancient Popular Poetry*, and all the time engaged with the Jurisdiction of the Court Leet, and the office of Constable. The *English Anthology* in three volumes appeared in 1793-94. It contains specimens of Chatterton. Ritson was not deceived by the *Rowley Poems* ; neither was he prejudiced against them, as poetry.

Scottish Songs appeared in 1794.

So far, except for his observations on Warton and his use of MSS. for his *Ancient Songs*, Ritson had not dealt very particularly with old English literature.

He had, it is true, discussed and debated medieval questions ; but so far his literary publications had been all of the nature of anthologies. He might have been mistaken for a compiler of elegant extracts ; he is, plainly, a lover of many varieties of verse. His *English Anthology* is the mind of a student of poetry, who gathers all the good things he can, not as a commentator, or as one supporting a thesis. In 1795 he broke new ground with his edition of Laurence Minot ; and it is on his Minot and his Metrical Romances that his reputation chiefly depends as a critic of the older English language. I pass over his *Robin Hood*, 1795, and other works, to speak more particularly of his share in the revival of Middle English studies.

This was no new thing : English philology, not in all respects harsh or crabbed, had continually been touching upon poetry and upon the popular taste. Percy's *Reliques of Ancient Poetry* are not the first of their kind : they carry on what Tonson had done in his *Poetical Miscellany*, what Gibson had accomplished in his edition of *Christ's Kirk on the Green*. By some amazing good luck it happened that the older English literature was not kept separate from polite literature of the modern fashion, nor did Greek and Latin make every mind incapable of Anglo-Saxon. The proof, almost miraculous, of this liberality, this right comprehension, is given by Frere's translation of the *Brunanburh* poem into what we now have learned from Jacob Grimm to call Middle English. Frere did this when he was a boy at Eton, it should be remembered.

George Ellis was working at the English metrical romances when Ritson came out of his seclusion to visit Scott at Lasswade. It is now for the first time that we really see Ritson ; coming to Scott to get and

give what he can with regard to the *Border Minstrelsy*,
and also *Sir Tristrem*, it should be noted : Scott, Ellis,
and Ritson all at the same time are reading Middle
English MSS., and in their several ways making their
contents accessible. How Ritson appreciated Scott is
shown in his language about the presentation copy of
the *Border Minstrelsy*, " the most valuable literary
treasure in his possession." Scott's respect for Ritson
is significantly shown in his lending Ritson Hogg's
original copy of *Auld Maitland*. Writing to Ellis,
Scott says : " I wish him to see it *in puris naturalibus*."
In the same letter he says :

As for Mr. Ritson, he and I still continue on decent terms ;
and in truth he makes *patte de velours*; but I dread I shall
see a whisker first and then a claw, stretched out against
my unfortunate lucubrations.

Scott was not quite easy in his mind over the *Border
Minstrelsy* ; he knew that his own methods were too
free for Ritson's accuracy, too much resembling the
ways of Bishop Percy.

Scott's memoir of Leyden (*Edinburgh Annual
Register*, 1811) referring to Leyden's edition (1801) of
the *Complaynt of Scotland* tells a characteristic story of
both the humorists :

This singular work was the means of introducing Leyden
to the notice and correspondence of Mr. Ritson, the celebrated antiquary, who in a journey to Scotland during the
next summer found nothing which delighted him so much
as the conversation of the editor of the *Complaynt of Scotland*,
in whose favour he smoothed down and softened the natural
asperity of his own disposition. The friendship however
between these two authors was broken off by Leyden's
running his Border hobbyhorse a full tilt against the Pytha-
gorean palfrey of the English antiquary. Ritson, it must
be well remembered, had written a work against the use of

animal food ; Leyden, on the other hand, maintained it was part of a masculine character to eat whatever came to hand, vegetable or animal, cooked or uncooked ; and he concluded a tirade to this purpose by eating a raw beef steak before the terrified antiquary, who never afterwards could be prevailed upon to regard him except as a kind of learned ogre. This breach, however, did not happen till they met in London, previous to Leyden's leaving Britain.

Leyden sailed for the East Indies in April, 1803.

Another characteristic story is given in Scott's *Essay on Border Antiquities*, speaking of the Roman Wall, and particularly of Glenwhelt, near Gilsland Spaw :

Its height may be guessed from the following character-istic anecdote of the late Mr. Joseph Ritson, whose zeal for accuracy was so marked a feature in his investigations. That eminent antiquary, upon an excursion to Scotland, favoured the author with a visit. The wall was mentioned, and Mr. Ritson, who had been misinformed by some ignorant person at Hexham, was disposed strongly to dispute that any relics of it yet remained. The author mentioned the place in the text, and said there was as much of it standing as would break the neck of Mr Ritson's informer were he to fall from it. Of this careless and metaphorical expression Mr. Ritson failed not to make a memorandum, and after-wards wrote to the author that he had visited the place with the express purpose of jumping down from the wall, in order to confute what he supposed a hyperbole. But he added, that, though not yet satisfied that it was quite high enough to break a man's neck, it was of elevation sufficient to render the experiment very dangerous.

Ritson's most elaborate piece of research, *Annals of the Caledonians, Picts and Scots, and of Strathclyde, Galloway and Murray*, was published by his nephew in 1828. Scott reviewed it in the *Quarterly Review* for July, 1829. It is the old debate between Sir Arthur Wardour and Mr. Jonathan Oldbuck, whether the Picts were Celtic or Gothic. Scott was never fully convinced that the Gothic theory was impossible, but he had to surrender most of the Antiquary's positions. Ritson's argument is a collection from all available authorities of all the relevant passages : it is the method of Wilhelm Grimm in his *Deutsche Heldensage*. Scott salutes him :

George Chalmers raised a banner against Pinkerton on the other side, and long previous to the publication of his great work of *Caledonia*—a work unequalled, if we consider it as a mass of materials assembled by the labour of a single man—Joseph Ritson, an antiquary of the first order, had embraced the same side with much vehemence. Of this last writer we may say with justice, that allowing for a certain portion of irritability (a constitutional *disease*) he possessed in a degree surpassing his contemporaries the patience, the ardour, and the industry necessary for anti-quarian researches. He was firm and somewhat obstinate in his opinions, as was natural in one who had adopted them after much thought. But he piqued himself on the most profound honesty in research and quotation, and if you brought him sufficient evidence to convince him of his error, he was the first to avow his conviction to the world. His violence, though often to be regretted, was always sincere and unaffected ; while that of Pinkerton was sus-pected by some of his friends to be in a great measure assumed, for the sake of attracting attention.

We are now at the end of the story. Ritson's active mind and irritable soul wore out long before old age : he died Sept. 23, 1803, a few days short of fifty-one years. His best epitaph is by Scott, who reviewed Ritson's *Romances*, 1802, and Ellis's *Specimens of Romance*, 1805, together, in the *Edinburgh Review*, 1806. Ritson's favourite subject for dissertation was Minstrelsy, partly through direct interest, and partly through opposition to Percy. Scott takes occasion to expostulate with Ritson over his violent language in controversy :

Surely neither the gallant Sir Lancelot nor the courteous Sir Gawain would have given a reverend Bishop the lie direct, on account of a disputed reading in the old song of *Maggie Lauder*.

On the main question of Minstrelsy Scott has a discovery to announce. It is strange to think that Ritson died before Scott had finished his study of Thomas the Rhymer; before he found in the Lincoln MS. of Thomas of Erceldoune the proof " that tongue is chief of minstrelsy." Ritson all his life had maintained the opposite; that minstrels were not poets but only jugglers and harpers. Scott quotes:

> Harping, he said, ken I non,
> For tong is chefe of mynstrelsie,

and continues:

From this decisive declaration which a poet and minstrel made on the nature of his own profession, it appears plainly that in more ancient times the minstrel's principal and most honourable occupation referred to poetry rather than music, and the Rhymer might have been justly described as one " who united the arts of poetry and music and sang verses to the harp of his own composing," if he had not disdained the musical skill to which it was Mr. Ritson's persuasion that the talents of the minstrel were exclusively limited. We should have been anxious to have heard what reply his keen and eager spirit could have suggested; but poor Ritson is probably now deciphering the characters upon the collar of Cerberus, or conversing in unbaptized language with the Saxon and British chiefs of former times,

> " With Oswald,
> Vortigern, Harold, Hengist, Horsa, Knute
> Allured, Edgar and Cunobeline."

Upon the whole it occurs to us from a careful perusal of this essay that Mr. Ritson's talents were better adapted to research than to deduction, to attack than to defence, to criticism than to composition ; and that he has left us a monument of profound industry and extensive study, undirected by any attempt at system, and tarnished by the splenetic peculiarities of an irritable temperament. Still, let it be remembered to his honour that, without the encouragement of private patronage or of public applause ; without hopes of gain and under the certainty of severe critical censure, he has brought forward such a work on national antiquities as in other countries has been thought worthy of the labour of universities and the countenance of princes.

When this was written *Annals of the Caledonians* had not been published : the *Life of King Arthur*, 1825, has also to be added to the list of Ritson's works : Scott in 1806 did not know all that Ritson had done.   His praise of Ritson will remain unchallenged, and will bear testing : we need not try to improve on it.

VIII

SIR WALTER SCOTT

WHEN I was asked to choose a subject for a lecture at the Sorbonne, there came into my mind somehow or other the incident of Scott's visit to Paris when he went to see *Ivanhoe* at the Odéon, and was amused to think how the story had travelled and made its fortune :

It was an opera, and, of course, the story sadly mangled and the dialogue in great part nonsense. Yet it was strange to hear anything like the words which (then in an agony of pain with spasms in my stomach) I dictated to William Laidlaw at Abbotsford, now recited in a foreign tongue, and for the amusement of a strange people. I little thought to have survived the completing of this novel.

It seemed to me that here I had a text for my sermon. The cruel circumstances of the composition of *Ivanhoe* might be neglected. The interesting point was in the contrast between the original home of Scott's imagination and the widespread triumph of his works abroad—on the one hand, Edinburgh and Ashestiel, the traditions of the Scottish border and the Highlands, the humours of Edinburgh lawyers and Glasgow citizens, country lairds, farmers and ploughmen, the Presbyterian eloquence of the Covenanters and their descendants, the dialect hardly intelligible out of its own region, and not always clear even to natives of Scotland ; on the other hand, the competition for Scott's novels in all the markets of Europe, as to which I take leave to quote the evidence of Stendhal :

Lord Byron, auteur de quelques héroïdes sublimes, mais toujours les mêmes, et de beaucoup de tragédies mortellement ennuyeuses, n'est point du tout le chef des romantiques.

S'il se trouvait un homme que les traducteurs à la toise se disputassent également à Madrid, à Stuttgard, à Paris et à Vienne, l'on pourrait avancer que cet homme a deviné les tendances morales de son époque.

If Stendhal proceeds to remark in a footnote that " l'homme lui-même est peu digne d'enthousiasme," it is pleasant to remember that Lord Byron wrote to M. Henri Beyle to correct his low opinion of the character of Scott. This is by the way, though not, I hope, an irrelevant remark. For Scott is best revealed in his friendships ; and the mutual regard of Scott and Byron is as pleasant to think of as the friendship between Scott and Wordsworth.

As to the truth of Stendhal's opinion about the vogue of Scott's novels and his place as chief of the romantics, there is no end to the list of witnesses who might be summoned. Perhaps it may be enough to remember how the young Balzac was carried away by the novels as they came fresh from the translator, almost immediately after their first appearance at home.

One distinguishes easily enough, at home in Scotland, between the novels, or the passages in the novels, that are idiomatic, native, home-grown, intended for his own people, and the novels not so limited, the romances of English or foreign history—*Ivanhoe, Kenilworth, Quentin Durward*. But as a matter of fact these latter, though possibly easier to understand and better suited to the general public, were not invariably preferred. The novels were the " Scotch novels." Although Thackeray, when he praises Scott, takes most of his examples from the less characteristic, what we may call the English group, on the other hand, Hazlitt dwells most willingly on the Scotch novels, though he did not like Scotsmen, and shared some of the prejudice of Stendhal—" my friend Mr. Beyle," as he calls him in one place—with regard to Scott himself. And Balzac has no invidious preferences : he recommends an English romance, *Kenilworth*, to his sister, and he also remembers David Deans, a person most intensely and peculiarly Scots.

One may distinguish the Scotch novels, which only their author could have written, from novels like *Peveril of the Peak* or *Anne of Geierstein*, which may be thought to resemble rather too closely the imitations of Scott, the ordinary historical novel as it was written by Scott's successors. But though the formula of the conventional historical novel may have been drawn from the less idiomatic group, it was not this that chiefly made Scott's reputation. His fame and influence were achieved through the whole mass of his immense and varied work ; and the Scots dialects and humours, which make so large a part of his resources when he is putting out all his power, though they have their difficulties for readers outside of Scotland, were no real hindrances in the way of the Scotch novels : Dandie Dinmont and Bailie Nicol Jarvie, Cuddie Headrigg and Andrew Fairservice were not ignored or forgotten, even where *Ivanhoe* or *The Talisman* might have the preference as being more conformable to the general mind of novel readers.

The paradox remains : that the most successful novelist of the whole world should have had his home and found his strength in a country with a language of its own, barely intelligible, frequently repulsive to its nearest neighbours, a language none the more likely to win favour when the manners or ideas of the country were taken into consideration as well.

The critics who refuse to see much good in Scott, for the most part ignore the foundations of his work. Thus Stendhal, who acknowledges Scott's position as representative of his age, the one really great, universally popular, author of his day, does not recognise in Scott's imagination much more than trappings and tournaments, the furniture of the regular historical novel. He compares Scott's novels with *La Princesse de Clèves*, and asks which is more to be praised, the author who understands and reveals the human heart, or the descriptive historian who can fill pages with unessential details but is afraid of the passions.

In which it seems to be assumed that Scott, when he gave his attention to the background and the appropriate dresses, was neglecting the dramatic truth of his characters and their expression. Scott, it may be observed, had, in his own reflections on the art of novel-writing, taken notice of different kinds of policy in dealing with the historical setting. In his lives of the novelists, reviewing *The Old English Baron*, he describes the earlier type of historical novel in which little or nothing is done for antiquarian decoration or for local colour ; while in his criticism of Mrs. Radcliffe he uses the very term—" melodrama "—and the very distinction—melodrama as opposed to tragedy—which is the touchstone of the novelist. Whatever his success might be, there can be no doubt as to his intentions. He meant his novels, with their richer background and their larger measure of detail, to sacrifice nothing of dramatic truth. *La Princesse de Clèves*, a professedly historical novel with little " local colour," may be in essentials finer and more sincere than Scott. This is a question which I ask leave to pass over. But it is not Scott's intention to put off the reader with details and decoration as a substitute for truth of character and sentiment. Here most obviously, with all their differences, Balzac and Scott are agreed : expensive both of them in description, but neither of them inclined to let mere description (in Pope's phrase) take the place of sense—*i.e.* of the life which it is the business of the novelist to interpret. There is danger, no doubt, of overdoing it, but description in Balzac, however full and long, is never inanimate. He has explained his theory in a notice of Scott, or rather in a comparison of Scott and Fenimore Cooper (*Revue Parisienne*, 1840), where the emptiness of Cooper's novels is compared with the variety of Scott's, the solitude of the American lakes and forests with the crowd of life commanded by the author of *Waverley*. Allowing Cooper one great success in the character of Leather-stocking and some merit in a few other personages, Balzac finds beyond these nothing like Scott's multitude of characters ; their place is taken by the beauties of nature. But description cannot make up for want of life in a story.

Balzac shows clearly that he understood the danger of description, and how impossible, how unreasonable, it is to make scenery do instead of story and characters. He does not seem to think that Scott has failed in this respect, while in his remarks on Scott's humour he proves how far he is from the critics who found in Scott nothing but scenery and accoutrements and the rubbish

ciated, unless one remembers that the author of this
and other charges against chivalry is also the historian
of the feud between the Shepherdsons and the Granger-
fords, equal in tragedy to the themes of the *chansons
de geste* : of *Raoul de Cambrai* or *Garin le Loherain*.
Mark Twain in the person of Huckleberry Finn is committed to the ideas of chivalry neither more nor less than
Walter Scott in *Ivanhoe* or *The Talisman*. I am told
further—though this is perhaps unimportant—that
Gothic ornament in America is not peculiarly the taste
of the South, that even at Chicago there are imitations
of Gothic towers and halls.

Hazlitt, an unbeliever in most of Scott's political
principles, is also the most fervent and expressive
admirer of the novels, quite beyond the danger of
modern progress, his judgment not corrupted at all by
the incense of the cotton-factory or the charm of the
locomotive. Hazlitt's praise of Scott is an immortal
proof of Hazlitt's sincerity in criticism. Scott's friends
were not Hazlitt's, and Scott and Hazlitt differed both
in personal and public affairs as much as any men of
their time. But Hazlitt has too much sense not to be
taken with the Scotch novels, and too much honesty
not to say so, and too much spirit not to put all his
strength into praising, when once he begins. Hazlitt's
critical theory of Scott's novels is curiously like his
opinion about Scott's old friend, the poet Crabbe :
whose name I cannot leave without a salute to the
laborious and eloquent work of M. Huchon, his scholarly
French interpreter.

Hazlitt on Crabbe and Scott is a very interesting
witness on account of the principles and presupposi-
tions employed by him. In the last hundred years or
so the problems of realism and naturalism have been

canvassed almost too thoroughly between disputants who seem not always to know when they are wandering from the point of wearying their audience with verbiage and platitudes. But out of all the controversy there has emerged at least one plain probability—that there is no such thing as simple transference of external reality into artistic form. This is what Hazlitt seems to ignore very strangely in his judgment of Crabbe and Scott, and this is, I think, an interesting point in the history of criticism, especially when it is remembered that Hazlitt was a critic of painting, and himself a painter. He speaks almost as if realities passed direct into the verse of Crabbe; as if Scott's imagination in the novels were merely recollection and transcription of experience. Speaking of the difference between the genius of Shakespeare and Sir Walter Scott, he says:

It is the difference between *originality* and the want of it, between writing and transcribing. Almost all the finest scenes and touches, the great master-strokes in Shakespeare, are such as must have belonged to the class of invention, where the secret lay between him and his own heart, and the power exerted is in adding to the given materials and working something out of them: in the author of *Waverley*, not all, but the principal and characteristic beauties are such as may and do belong to the class of compilation—that is, consist in bringing the materials together and leaving them to produce their own effect. . . .

No one admires or delights in the Scotch Novels more than I do, but at the same time, when I hear it asserted that his mind is of the same class with Shakespeare, or that he imitates nature in the same way, I confess I cannot assent to it. No two things appear to me more different. Sir Walter is an imitator of nature and nothing more; but I think Shakespeare is infinitely more than this. . . . Sir Walter's mind is full of information, but the "*o'er informing power*" is not there. Shakespeare's spirit, like fire, shines through him; Sir Walter's, like a stream, reflects surrounding objects.

I may not at this time quote much more of Hazlitt's criticism, but the point of it would be misunderstood if it were construed as depreciation of Scott. What may be considered merely memory in contrast to Shakespeare's imagination is regarded by Hazlitt as a limitless source of visionary life when compared with the ideas of self-centred authors like Byron. This is what Hazlitt says in another essay of the same series :

Scott " does not ' spin his brains ' but something much better." He " has got hold of another clue—that of Nature and history—and long may he spin it, ' even to the crack of doom ! ' " Scott's success lies in not thinking of himself. " And then again the catch that blind Willie and his wife and the boy sing in the hollow of the heath—there is more mirth and heart's ease in it than in all Lord Byron's *Don Juan* or Mr. Moore's *Lyrics*. And why ? Because the author is thinking of beggars and a beggar's brat, and not of himself, while he writes it. He looks at nature, sees it, hears it, feels it, and believes that it exists before it is printed, hotpressed, and labelled on the back *By the Author of ' Waverley.'* He does not fancy, nor would he for one moment have it supposed, that his name and fame compose all that is worth a moment's consideration in the universe. This is the great secret of his writings—a perfect indifference to self."

Hazlitt appears to allow too little to the mind of the author of *Waverley*—as though the author had nothing to do but let the contents of his mind arrange themselves on his pages. What this exactly may mean is doubtful. We are not disposed to accept the theory of the passive mind as a sufficient philosophical explanation of the Scotch novels. But Hazlitt is certainly right to make much of the store of reading and reminiscence they imply, and it is not erroneous or fallacious to think of all Scott's writings in verse or prose as peculiarly the fruits of his life and experience. His various modes of writing are suggested to him by the way, and he finds his art with no long practice when the proper time comes to use it. After all, is this not what was meant by Horace when he said that the subject rightly chosen will provide what is wanted in art and style?

> Cui lecta potenter erit res
> Nec facundia deseret hunc nec lucidus ordo.

It was chosen by Corneille as a motto for *Cinna*; it would do as a summary of all the writings of Scott.

The Waverley Novels may be reckoned among the works of fiction that have had their origin in chance, and have turned out something different from what the author intended. Reading the life of Scott, we seem to be following a pilgrimage where the traveller meets with different temptations and escapes various dangers, and takes up a number of duties, and is led to do a number of fine things which he had not thought of till the time came for attempting them. The poet and the novelist are revealed in the historian and the collector of antiquities. Scott before *The Lay of the Last Minstrel* looked like a young adventurer in the study of history and legend, who had it in him to do solid work on a large scale (like his edition of Dryden) if he chose to take it up. He is not a poet from the beginning like Wordsworth and Keats, devoted to that one service; he turns novelist late in life when the success of his poetry seems to be over. His early experiments in verse are queerly suggested and full of hazard. It needs a foreign language—German—to encourage him to rhyme. The fascination of Bürger's *Lenore* is a reflection from English ballad poetry; the reflected image brought out what had been less remarkable in the original. The German devices of

terror and wonder are a temptation to Scott; they
hang about his path with their monotonous and
mechanical jugglery, their horrors made all the more
intolerable through the degraded verse of Lewis—a
bad example which Scott instinctively refused to follow,
though he most unaccountably praised Lewis's sense of
rhythm. The close of the eighteenth century cannot
be fully understood, nor the progress of poetry in the
nineteenth, without some study of the plague of ghosts
and skeletons which has left its mark on *The Ancient
Mariner*, from which Goethe and Scott did not escape,
which imposed on Shelley in his youth, to which Byron
yielded his tribute of *The Vampire*. A tempting subject for expatiation, especially when one remembers—
and who that has once read it can forget?—the most
glorious passage in the *Memoirs* of Alexandre Dumas
describing his first conversation with the unknown
gentleman who afterwards turned out to be Charles
Nodier, in the theatre of the Porte Saint-Martin where
the play was the *Vampire*: from which theatre Charles
Nodier was expelled for hissing the *Vampire*, himself
being part-author of the marvellous drama. I hope
it is not impertinent in a stranger to express his
unbounded gratitude for that delightful and most
humorous dialogue, in which the history of the Elzevir
Press (starting from *Le Pastissier françois*) and the
tragedy of the rotifer are so adroitly interwoven with
the theatrical scene of Fingal's Cave and its unusual
visitors, the whole adventure ending in the happiest
laughter over the expulsion of the dramatist. I may
not have any right to say so, but I throw myself on
the mercy of my hearers: I remember nothing in
any chronicle so mercurial or jovial in its high spirits
as this story of the first encounter and the beginning

of friendship between Charles Nodier and Alexandre Dumas.

The Vampire of Staffa may seem rather far from the range of Scott's imagination ; but his contributions to Lewis's *Tales of Wonder* show the risk that he ran, while the White Lady of Avenel in *The Monastery* proves that even in his best years he was exposed to the hazards of conventional magic.

Lockhart has given the history of *The Lay of the Last Minstrel*, how the story developed and took shape. It is not so much an example of Scott's mode of writing poetry as an explanation of his whole literary life. *The Lay of the Last Minstrel* was his first original piece of any length and his first great popular success. And, as Lockhart has sufficiently shown, it was impossible for Scott to get to it except through the years of exploration and editing, the collection of the Border ballads, the study of the old metrical romance of *Sir Tristrem*. The story of the Goblin Page was at first reckoned enough simply for one of the additions to the Border Minstrelsy on the scale of a ballad. Scott had tried another sort of imitation in the stanzas composed in old English and in the metre of the original to supply the missing conclusion of *Sir Tristrem*. It was not within his scope to write an original romance in the old language, but Coleridge's *Christabel* was recited to him, and gave him a modern rhythm fit for a long story. So the intended ballad became the *Lay*, taking in, with the legend of Gilpin Horner for a foundation, all the spirit of Scott's knowledge of his own country.

Here I must pause to express my admiration for Lockhart's criticism of Scott, and particularly for his description of the way in which the *Lay* came to be

And *The Lady of the Lake* is all that the Highlands
meant for Scott at that time.   But *Rokeby* has little
substance, though it includes more than one of Scott's
finest songs.   *The Lord of the Isles*, though its battle is
not too far below *Marmion*, and though its hero is
Robert the Bruce, yet wants the original force of the
earlier romances.   When Scott changed his hand from
verse to prose for story-telling and wrote *Waverley*, he
not only gained in freedom and got room for a kind of
dialogue that was impossible in rhyme, but he came
back to the same sort of experience and the same
strength of tradition as had given life to the *Lay*.   The
time of *Waverley* was no more than sixty years since,
when Scott began to write it and mislaid and forgot
the opening chapters in 1805 ;   he got his ideas of the
Forty-five from an old Highland gentleman who had
been out with the Highland clans, following the lead of
Prince Charles Edward, the Young Chevalier.   The
clans in that adventure belonged to a world more
ancient than that of *Ivanhoe* or *The Talisman* ;   they
also belonged so nearly to Scott's own time that he
heard their story from one of themselves.   He had
spoken and listened to another gentleman who had
known Rob Roy.   *The Bride of Lammermoor* came to
him as the Icelandic family histories came to the historians of Gunnar or Kjartan Olafsson.   He had known
the story all his life, and he wrote it from tradition.
The time of *The Heart of Midlothian* is earlier than
Waverley, but it is more of a modern novel than an
historical romance, and even *Old Mortality*, which is
earlier still, is modern also ;   Cuddie Headrigg is no
more antique than Dandie Dinmont or the Ettrick
Shepherd himself, and even his mother and her Cove-
nanting friends are not far from the fashion of some

enthusiasts of Scott's own time—*e.g.* Hogg's religious uncle who could not be brought to repeat his old ballads for thinking of " covenants broken, burned and buried." *Guy Mannering* and *The Antiquary* are both modern stories : it is not till *Ivanhoe* that Scott definitely starts on the regular historical novel in the manner that was found so easy to imitate.

If *Rob Roy* is not the very best of them all—and on problems of that sort perhaps the right word may be the Irish phrase *Naboclish!* (" don't trouble about that ! ") which Scott picked up when he was visiting Miss Edgeworth in Ireland—*Rob Roy* shows well enough what Scott could do, in romance of adventure and in humorous dialogue. The plots of his novels are sometimes thought to be loose and ill-defined, and he tells us himself that he seldom knew where his story was carrying him. His young heroes are sometimes reckoned rather feeble and featureless. Francis Osbaldistone, like Edward Waverley and Henry Morton, drifts into trouble and has his destiny shaped for him by other people and accidents. But is this anything of a reproach to the author of the story ? Then it must tell against some novelists who seem to work more conscientiously and carefully than Scott on the frame of their story—against George Meredith in Evan Harrington and Richard Feverel and Harry Richmond, all of whom are driven by circumstances and see their way no more clearly than Scott's young men. Is it not really the strength, not the weakness, of Scott's imagination that engages us in the perplexities of Waverley and Henry Morton even to the verge of tragedy—keeping out of tragedy because it is not his business, and would spoil his looser, larger, more varied web of a story ? Francis Osbaldistone is less severely tried. His story sets him travelling, and may we not admire the skill of the author who uses the old device of a wandering hero with such good effect ? The story is not a mere string of adventures—it is adventures with a bearing on the main issue, with complications that all tell in the end ; chief among them, of course, the successive appearances of Mr. Campbell and the counsels of Diana Vernon. The scenes that bring out Scott's genius most completely—so they have always seemed to me—are those of Francis Osbaldistone's stay in Glasgow. Seldom has any novelist managed so easily so many different modes of interest. There is the place—indifferent lights—the streets, the river, the bridge, the Cathedral, the prison, seen through the suspense of the hero's mind, rendered in the talk of Bailie Nicol Jarvie and Andrew Fairservice ; made alive, as the saying is, through successive anxieties and dangers ; thrilling with romance, yet at the same time never beyond the range of ordinary common sense. Is it not a triumph, at the very lowest reckoning, of dexterous narrative to bring together in a vivid dramatic scene the humorous character of the Glasgow citizen and the equal and opposite humour of his cousin, the cateran, the Highland loon, Mr. Campbell disclosed as Rob Roy—with the Dougal creature helping him ?

Scott's comedy is like that of Cervantes in *Don Quixote*—humorous dialogue independent of any definite comic plot and mixed up with all sorts of other business. Might not Falstaff himself be taken into comparison too ? Scott's humorous characters are nowhere and never characters in a comedy—and Falstaff, the greatest comic character in Shakespeare, is not great in comedy.

Some of the rich idiomatic Scottish dialogue in the novels might be possibly disparaged (like Ben Jonson) as " mere humours and observation." Novelists of lower rank than Scott—Galt in *The Ayrshire Legatees* and *Annals of the Parish* and *The Entail*—have nearly rivalled Scott in reporting conversation. But the Bailie at any rate has his part to play in the story of *Rob Roy* —and so has Andrew Fairservice. Scott never did anything more ingenious than his contrast of those two characters—so much alike in language, and to some extent in cast of mind, with the same conceit and self-confidence, the same garrulous Westland security in their own judgment, both attentive to their own interests, yet clearly and absolutely distinct in spirit, the Bailie a match in courage for Rob Roy himself.

Give me leave, before I end, to read one example of Scott's language : from the scene in *The Antiquary* where Monkbarns bargains with the fish-wife. It is true to life : memory and imagination here indistinguishable :

" What are ye for the day, your honour ? " she said, or rather screamed, to Oldbuck ; " caller haddocks and whitings—a bannock-fluke and a cock-padle."

" How much for the bannock-fluke and cock-padle ? " demanded the Antiquary.

" Four white shillings and saxpence," answered the Naiad.

" Four devils and six of their imps ! " retorted the Antiquary ; " do you think I am mad, Maggie ? "

" And div ye think," rejoined the virago, setting her arms a-kimbo, " that my man and my sons are to gae to the sea in weather like yestreen and the day—sic a sea as it's yet outby—and get naething for their fish, and be misca'd into the bargain, Monkbarns ? It's no fish ye're buying— it's men's lives."

" Well, Maggie, I'll bid you fair—I'll bid you a shilling for the fluke and the cock-padle, or sixpence separately—

and if all your fish are as well paid, I think your man, as you call him, and your sons, will make a good voyage."

"Deil gin their boat were knockit against the Bell-Rock rather! it wad be better, and the bonnier voyage o' the twa. A shilling for thae twa bonnie fish! Od, that's ane indeed!"

"Well, well, you old beldam, carry your fish up to Monkbarns, and see what my sister will give you for them."

"Na, na, Monkbarns, deil a fit—I'll rather deal wi' yoursell; for though you're near enough, yet Miss Grizel has an unco close grip—I'll gie ye them" (in a softened tone) "for three and saxpence."

"Eighteen-pence, or nothing!"

"Eighteenpence!!!" (in a loud tone of astonishment, which declined into a sort of rueful whine, when the dealer turned as if to walk away)—"Ye'll no be for the fish then?" —(then louder, as she saw him moving off)—"I'll gie ye them—and—and—and a half-a-dozen o' partans to make the sauce, for three shillings and a dram."

"Half-a-crown then, Maggie, and a dram."

"Aweel, your honour maun hae't your ain gate, nae doubt; but a dram's worth siller now—the distilleries is no working."

"And I hope they'll never work again in my time," said Oldbuck.

"Ay, ay—it's easy for your honour, and the like o' you gentle-folks to say sae, that hae stouth and routh, and fire and fending, and meat and claith, and sit dry and canny by the fireside—but an ye wanted fire, and meat, and dry claes, and were deeing o' cauld, and had a sair heart, whilk is warst ava', wi' just tippence in your pouch, wadna ye be glad to buy a dram wi't, to be eilding and claes, and a supper and heart's ease into the bargain, till the morn's morning?"

Do we at home in Scotland make too much of Scott's life and associations when we think of his poetry and his novels? Possibly few Scotsmen are impartial here. As Dr. Johnson said, they are not a fair people, and when they think of the Waverley Novels they perhaps do not always see quite clearly. Edinburgh and the

Eildon Hills, Aberfoyle and Stirling, come between their minds and the printed page :

> A mist of memory broods and floats,
>   The Border waters flow,
> The air is full of ballad notes
>   Borne out of long ago.

It might be prudent and more critical to take each book on its own merits in a dry light. But it is not easy to think of a great writer thus discreetly. Is Balzac often judged accurately and coldly, piece by piece, here a line and there a line ? Are not the best judges those who think of his whole achievement altogether—the whole amazing world of his creation—*La Comédie Humaine ?* By the same sort of rule Scott may be judged, and the whole of his work, his vast industry, and all that made the fabric of his life, be allowed to tell on the mind of the reader.

I wish this discourse had been more worthy of its theme, and of this audience, and of this year of heroic memories and lofty hopes. But if, later in the summer, I should find my way back to Ettrick and Yarrow and the Eildon Hills, it will be a pleasure to remember there the honour you have done me in allowing me to speak in Paris, however unworthily, of the greatness of Sir Walter Scott.

IX

SIR WALTER SCOTT'S SCOTLAND

THE fame of " The Waverley Novels " in all countries
and languages throughout the world has naturally not
preserved everywhere the full value of Scott's local
knowledge and personal experience. He succeeded far
and wide as an author of historical romances. *Ivanhoe*
and *Kenilworth* were examples on which scores of
romances were founded in every land. The Scottish
humour, like the dialect of Andrew Fairservice and
Cuddie Headrigg, could not be translated or exported.
But it is wrong to suppose that " the Scotch novels,"
as they were commonly called, lost their effect in England through their Scotch peculiarities. It is true that
there were some objectors ; but for more than a century
England had been ready to listen to songs and poems
in Scottish dialect. Burns had won English readers
in spite of his language, and the language of " The
Waverley Novels " is not as difficult as the Ayrshire
idiom of Burns. And the difficulty, great or small,
ought to be faced and conquered, for it is only in
Scotland, or with Scottish characters (as in *The Fortunes of Nigel*), that Scott's excellence as a novelist
really comes out to the full. *Ivanhoe, Kenilworth, The
Talisman* may be nearly equalled in French or Flemish,
German or Italian historical novels ; but there is

nothing abroad like the peculiar strength of *The Antiquary*, *Rob Roy*, and *The Heart of Midlothian*.

In Scott's wide success as an author of historical
romance—success to which his tales in rhyme contributed not a little—it is sometimes forgotten how closely
he keeps to his own time in the novels that made his
fame. *Waverley* we read now as an historical novel of
the Forty-five : but when the novel was begun the
Forty-five was no more than " sixty years since " ; no
further off than, for us, the substance of Mr. Drink-
water's *Abraham Lincoln* ; the world of Mr. Hardy's
Dynasts is twice as far off from our day.   Scott heard
the adventures of the Young Chevalier from a Highland
gentleman who had taken his share in the Forty-five,
and before that had fought a duel with Rob Roy ;
the Porteous Riot was still in living memory when
Scott was young ; Helen Walker, the original of Jeanie
Deans, died when Scott was seventeen.   The time of
The Bride of Lammermoor is a good deal earlier, but
the story on which the novel is based was known to
Scott by tradition, not made up out of books : as he
tells his readers in the Introduction to the tale :

A lady, very nearly connected with the family, told the
author that she had conversed on the subject with one of
the brothers of the bride, a mere lad at the time, who had
ridden before his sister to church. He said her hand,
which lay on his as she had her arm round his waist, was
as cold and damp as marble. But, full of his new dress,
and the part he acted in the procession, the circumstance,
which he long afterwards remembered with bitter sorrow
and compunction, made no impression on him at the time.

The bridal feast was followed by dancing ; the bride and
bridegroom retired as usual, when of a sudden the most
wild and piercing cries were heard from the nuptial chamber.
It was then the custom, to prevent any coarse pleasantry
which old times perhaps admitted, that the key of the

nuptial chamber should be intrusted to the brideman.   He
was called upon, but refused at first to give it up, till the
shrieks became so hideous that he was compelled to hasten
with others to learn the cause.   On opening the door, they
found the bridegroom lying across the threshold, dreadfully
wounded and streaming with blood.   The bride was then
sought for : she was found in the corner of the large chimney,
having no covering save her shift and that dabbled in gore.
There she sat grinning at them, mopping and mowing, as I
heard the expression used ; in a word, absolutely insane.
The only words she spoke were, " Tak up your bonny
bridegroom."   She survived this horrible scene little more
than a fortnight, having been married on the 24th of August,
and dying on the 12th of September, 1669.

The unfortunate Baldoon recovered from his wounds but
sternly prohibited all inquiries respecting the manner in
which he had received them.   If a lady, he said, asked him
any question upon the subject, he would neither answer
her nor speak to her again while he lived ; if a gentleman,
he would consider it as a mortal affront, and demand
satisfaction as having received such.   He did not very long
survive the dreadful catastrophe, having met with a fatal
injury by a fall from his horse, as he rode between Leith
and Holyrood House, of which he died the next day, 28th
March, 1682.   Thus a few years removed all the principal
actors in this frightful tragedy.

Old Mortality depends more on the author's reading,
and is more like what is commonly counted an historical
novel.   But here comes in Scott's independence of
dates when he is dealing with the people of his own
country.   Cuddie Headrigg belongs to the reign of
Charles II. just about as much as Mrs. Quickly belongs
to the year of Agincourt.   Cuddie's mother, Mause
Headrigg, in her religious eloquence may be thought
to have more of the fashion of her time ; but in fact
there was no want of real life, when Scott wrote, corre-
sponding to the ideas and language of Mause Headrigg
or David Deans.   The humour of Richie Moniplies in

The Fortunes of Nigel or of Oliver Proudfute in *The Fair Maid of Perth*, at a date supposed to be much earlier, is not antiquated ; Scott may try occasionally to give the effect of a past age by putting old-fashioned language in the mouth of his characters, but the humorous Scotch characters speak with no antiquarian touches.   Sir Dugald Dalgetty of course has his " Lion of the North," Gustavus Adolphus, and his reminiscences of the art of war suffice to give him his date, but the man himself is not an antiquity.

Scott as a lawyer and the son of a lawyer is at home in Edinburgh ; the Highlands and the Borders, till he went to live on the Tweed, he knew only on holiday excursions, and his Tweedside houses, Ashestiel and Abbotsford, were mainly for holidays.   Edinburgh was for business, and for intervals of business.   Scott escaped to the country as often and as quickly as he could ; he used regularly to come to the Parliament House on Saturday morning dressed in his country clothes, to be ready to start with no delay when the Court was up.   But with all his love of country life Edinburgh held his imagination, and there is nothing better than his Edinburgh scenes, in *The Heart of Midlothian*, all through ; in *Guy Mannering*, the visit of Colonel Mannering to Counsellor Pleydell ; the opening of *The Antiquary* (Lovel meeting Mr. Oldbuck at the unpunctual start of the Queensferry coach).

The Edinburgh passages in *Redgauntlet* are rather different from these, being more in the nature of reminiscences worked up for the purposes of the novel, and turned deliberately from Scott's own experience into the early lives of Alan Fairford and Darsie Latimer. The " Kittle Nine Steps " on the Castle Rock (which make the origin of Scottish mountaineering), the art

to " pin a lozen " (throw a stone through a window
pane), to " head a bicker " (lead a general fight with
stones, High School boys against the street boys of the
town), this business is simply Scott's youth transferred
to imaginary names. Truth here is livelier than fiction ;
there is nothing in the novel as good as the heroism of
Green Breeks, told by Scott in the General Introduction to " The Waverley Novels." The life of the High
School was not confined to any definite bounds. It
took in Arthur's Seat and the Salisbury Crags, where
Scott used to wander with his friend John Irving to
spin yarns of endless romance ; Walter " the Historio-
grapher," John " the Geographer," so they were called
in the High School, as the present writer was told by a
friend of an older generation who knew John Irving.
Those scenes of the schoolboy story-telling were later
to have their place in *The Heart of Midlothian*—St.
Leonard's Crags, St. Anthony's Chapel, Muschat's
Cairn, and the Hunter's Bog. All this scenery had
been analysed and described by the great student of
the picturesque, William Gilpin, when Scott was a boy ;
Gilpin particularly sets down the view of Edinburgh
from the east as " not picturesque but romantic."
The famous prospect in *Marmion* is from the south
and the epithet has a different sense in " mine own
romantic town."

Every reader of Scott is bound to know more or less
distinctly the difference between the old and the new
town of Edinburgh. The old town is clustered about
the Castle and all down the tail of the Castle Rock,
along the line of the High Street which is Lawn Market
at the top and Canongate at the foot of the hill leading down to the Palace of Holyrood. On the north
side of the Castle Rock and the old town is a valley

which now holds Princes Street Gardens and the North British Railway where used to be the water of the Nor' Loch. The other side of the valley opposite the Castle is a long ridge, which on the other side slopes down to the Firth of Forth. The ridge had the new town built on it, beginning not long before the time of Scott's birth (August 15, 1771). The regular well-built streets and squares of the new town make strong contrast even now to the old town ; a contrast which was much greater before any improvements were made in the old town. The following passage is taken from Robert Chambers's *Illustrations of Waverley*, first published in 1822 :

At the period when Mr. Crosbie flourished, all the advocates and judges of the day dwelt in those obscure " wynds " or alleys leading down from the High Street, which, since the erection of the new town, have been chiefly inhabited by the lower classes of society, the greater part, for the sake of convenience, living in the lanes nearest to the Parliament House—such as the Advocate's Close, Writer's Court, the West Bow, the " Back Stairs," the President's Stairs in the Parliament Close, and the tenements around the Meat market. In these dense insalubrious obscurities they possessed what were then the best houses in Edinburgh which were considered such till the erection of Brown's Square and the contiguous suburbs, about the beginning of the last king's reign, when the lawyers were found the first to remove to better and more extensive accommodations, being then, as now, the leading and most opulent class of the Edinburgh population. This change is fully pointed out in *Redgauntlet* where a Writer to the Signet is represented as removing from the Luckenbooths to Brown's Square about the time specified—which personage, disguised under the name of Saunders Fairford, we have no doubt was designed for Sir Walter Scott's own father, a practitioner of the same rank, who then removed from the Old Town to a house at the head of the College Wynd, in which his distinguished son, the Alan Fairford of the romance, was born and educated.

This is in the chapter illustrating *Guy Mannering*, and it is in *Guy Mannering*, in the scenes already referred to, that Scott has made the most lively use of his knowledge of Edinburgh.

The scenes of *Guy Mannering* show different aspects of Scott's life and imagination. The house of Dandie Dinmont on the Borders and the visit of Colonel Mannering to Edinburgh are taken from real life, from the most vivid memories; the Galloway coast and the smuggling business have much more fancy work in them; there Scott is not at home; he relies on his general knowledge of Scottish life and character without the particular local truth which belongs to his recollections of Edinburgh and Liddesdale.

Dandie Dinmont is a portrait with more than one original : Scott knew the Border farmers well, their independence, their good sense mixed with recklessness, their love of sport, especially of fox hunting in their own fashion. The Peppers and Mustards who carry on Dandie's name are descended from terriers who had hard work to do, going in to tackle the fox in his hole among the crags and stones. The following passage shows one side of the man as Scott conceived him :

Dinmont, who had pushed after Mannering into the room, began with a scrape of his foot and a scratch of his head in unison. " I am Dandie Dinmont, sir, of the Charlies-hope —the Liddesdale lad—ye'll mind me ? It was for me ye won yon grand plea."

" What plea, you loggerhead ? " said the lawyer ; " d'ye think I can remember all the fools that come to plague me ? "

" Lord, sir, it was the grand plea about the grazing o' the Langtae-head," said the farmer.

" Well, curse thee, never mind ; give me the memorial, and come to me on Monday at ten," replied the learned counsel.

" But, sir, I haena got ony distinct memorial."

" No memorial, man ? " said Pleydell.

" Na, sir, nae memorial," answered Dandie ; " for your honour said before, Mr. Pleydell, ye'll mind, that ye liked best to hear us hill-folk tell our ain tale by word o' mouth."

" Beshrew my tongue that said so ! " answered the counsellor ; " it will cost my ears a dinning.—Well, say in two words what you've got to say—you see the gentleman waits."

" Ou, sir, if the gentleman likes he may play his ain spring first ; it's a' ane to Dandie."

" Now, you looby," said the lawyer, " cannot you conceive that your business can be nothing to Colonel Mannering but that he may not choose to have these great ears of thine regaled with his matters ? "

" Aweel, sir, just as you and he like, so ye see to my business," said Dandie, not a whit disconcerted by the roughness of this reception. " We're at the auld wark o' the marches again, Jock o' Dawston Cleugh and me. Ye see we march on the tap o' Touthop-rigg after we pass the Pomoragrains ; for the Pomoragrains, and Slackenspool, and Bloodylaws, they come in there, and they belang to the Peel ; but after ye pass Pomoragrains at a muckle great saucer-headed cutlugged stane, that they ca' Charlies Chuckie, there Dawston Cleugh and Charlies-hope they march. Now, I say, the march rins on the tap o' the hill where the wind and water shears ; but Jock o' Dawston Cleugh again, he contravenes that, and says that it hauds down by the auld drove-road that gaes awa' by the Knot o' the Gate ower to Keeldar-ward—and that makes an unco difference."

" And what difference does it make, friend ? " said Pleydell. " How many sheep will it feed ? "

" Ou, no mony," said Dandie, scratching his head ; " it's lying high and exposed—it may feed a hog or aiblins twa in a good year."

" And for this grazing, which may be worth about five shillings a year, you are willing to throw away a hundred pound or two ? "

" Na, sir, it's no the value of the grass," replied Dinmont, " it's for justice."

" My good friend," said Pleydell, " justice, like charity,

should begin at home. Do you justice to your wife and family, and think no more about the matter."

Dinmont still lingered, twisting his hat in his hand—"It's no for that, sir—but I would like ill to be bragged wi' him—he threeps he'll bring a score o' witnesses and mair—and I'm sure there's as mony will swear for me as for him, folk that lived a' their days upon the Charlies-hope, and wadna like to see the land lose its right."

"Zounds, man, if it be a point of honour," said the lawyer, "why don't your landlords take it up?"

"I dinna ken, sir" (scratching his head again); "there's been nae election-dusts lately, and the lairds are unco neighbourly, and Jock and me canna get them to yoke thegither about it a' that we can say—but if ye thought we might keep up the rent"——

"No! no! that will never do," said Pleydell—"confound you, why don't you take good cudgels and settle it?"

"Odd, sir," answered the farmer, "we tried that three times already—that's twice on the land and ance at Lockerby fair. But I dinna ken—we're baith gey good at single-stick, and it couldna weel be judged."

"Then take broadswords, and be d—d to you, as your fathers did before you," said the counsel learned in the law.

"Aweel, sir, if ye think it wadna be again the law, it's a' ane to Dandie."

"Hold! hold!" exclaimed Pleydell, "we shall have another Lord Soulis' mistake—Pr'ythee, man, comprehend me; I wish you to consider how very trifling and foolish a lawsuit you wish to engage in."

"Ay, sir?" said Dandie, in a disappointed tone. "So ye winna take on wi' me, I'm doubting?"

"Me! not I—Go home, go home, take a pint and agree."

Possibly Scott's liking for Dandie Dinmont made him rather indifferent to some other types of character in Scotland. He did not know much of the industrial life of the country though he does full justice to the prosperity of Glasgow in *Rob Roy*. Galt's *Annals of the Parish*—an Ayrshire parish—represents much of Scotland which Scott hardly notices. On the other

hand it is strange that Burns, well acquainted with
the Kilmarnock weavers (who have no interest for
Scott as a story teller) takes little or no account of
people like Dandie Dinmont, or of the shepherds in
lonely cottages high up among the hills. Poets and
novelists have left large parts of Scotland out of their
records. The east and north-east are not without
honour, but neither the author of *Helenore* nor the
author of *Hamewith*, neither Robert Falconer nor
Johnnie Gibb have the fortune to be known all over
the world like the people of Burns's *Hallow-e'en* or the
household of Dandie Dinmont. Scott's representation
of his fellow-countrymen is not complete ; and it may
have been that his understanding of the Liddesdale
character led him to undervalue the weavers and mis-
understand the political agitations of the year 1820—
the Radical cry for freedom. Talk of freedom being
wanted in Scotland may have seemed to him an absurdity, when he thought of the simple people he knew,
like Dandie Dinmont, living independent lives, as
sensitive as any laird to whatever might touch their
honour.

The business life of Glasgow makes a considerable
part of *Rob Roy*, and for a hundred years Glasgow has
paid respect to the memory of Bailie Nicol Jarvie.
Scott's son-in-law, Lockhart, has celebrated another
eminent Glasgow man, Captain Paton, " so affable and
courteous," hospitable, " with limes from his planta-
tion in Trinidad that grow." The industrial life of the
west of Scotland and the motives of the Radical war
were probably misunderstood both by Scott and Lockhart ; to this day no poet or romancer has made anything of the political sentiments of that time in the
west. A sufficient account for most readers is to be

found in Henry Cockburn's *Memorials of his Time* and *Life of Lord Jeffrey*, which may be supplemented from Peter Mackenzie's *Reminiscences of Glasgow*, published " sixty years since."

Though Scott was not himself a west-land man some of his most successful characters belong to the west. Clydesdale is the region of " Old Mortality," and Andrew Fairservice belongs, no less than the Bailie, to the west. The contrast of these two characters is the best proof of Scott's imaginative accuracy and skill.   Andrew and the Bailie are in a sense types of the west of Scotland ; they have common qualities very well fitted for laugh- able scenes in a novel or play, qualities that are thought to be recognisable to-day in their native country, a cheerfulness and complacency which is not like Edin- burgh conceit or Aberdeen self-confidence. At the same time the difference between Andrew and the Bailie, in spite of their likeness of speech and gesture, is absolute on every point where honour is concerned. The Bailie is as courageous as any knight in *Ivanhoe* ; his garrulous vanity does nothing to spoil his integrity, his good sense and good feeling. Andrew Fair- service, decent enough in his own way, a master of expressive idiom, is not to be trusted when the qualities of true metal are required.   The moral differences be- tween the characters are not to be lightly passed over as the affair of the moralist merely, and no concern of the novel reader who wishes to be amused.   The amusement of Andrew's conversation is indistinguish- able from his small ignoble self-respecting habit of mind.

Having accepted his courtesy, I [that is, Francis Osbal- distone] asked him if he had long been a domestic at Osbaldistone Hall ?

" I have been fighting with wild beasts at Ephesus,"
said he, looking towards the building, " for the best part of
these four-and-twenty years, as sure as my name's Andrew
Fairservice."

" But, my excellent friend, Andrew Fairservice, if your
religion and your temperance are so much offended by
Roman rituals and southern hospitality, it seems to me
that you must have been putting yourself to an unnecessary
penance all this while, and that you might have found a
service where they eat less, and are more orthodox in their
worship. I dare say it cannot be want of skill which
prevented your being placed more to your satisfaction."

" It disna become me to speak on the point of my
qualifications," said Andrew, looking round him with great
complacency ; " but nae doubt I should understand my
trade of horticulture, seeing I was bred in the parish of
Dreepdaily, where they raise lang-kale under glass and force
the early nettles for their spring kale.—And, to speak
truth, I hae been flitting every term these four-and-twenty
years ; but when the time comes, there's aye something
to saw that I would like to see sawn,—or something to maw
that I would like to see mawn,—or something to ripe that
I would like to see ripen,—and sae I e'en daiker on wi' the
family frae year's end to year's end. And I would say for
certain, that I am gaun to quit at Candlemas, only I was just
as positive on it twenty years syne, and I find mysell still
turning up the mouls here, for a' that. Forbye that, to
tell your honour the evendown truth, there's nae better
place ever offered to Andrew. But if your honour wad
wush me to ony place where I wad hear pure doctrine, and
hae a free cow's grass, and a cot, and a yard, and mair
than ten punds of annual fee, and where there's nae leddy
about the town to count the apples, I'se hold mysell muckle
indebted t'ye."

" Bravo, Andrew ; I perceive you'll lose no preferment
for want of asking patronage."

" I canna see what for I should," replied Andrew ; " it's no
a generation to wait till ane's worth's discovered, I trow."

From no place in Scotland, not even Edinburgh in
rhyme or prose, has Scott derived more notable effects
of scenery or more romantic touches of association than

Glasgow.   The Sunday spent by Francis Osbaldistone in Glasgow is better accounted for than any day in Scott's stories.   The spirit of the place works into the narrative ; without any long set descriptions the reader gets an idea of the various scenes ; the river, the bridge, the green, the cathedral and its crypt, the college and its garden where Francis encounters his cousin Rashleigh, the prison where the plot of the novel comes to one of its chief moments in the discovery of Rob Roy Macgregor by his cousin the Bailie, in the presence of Francis Osbaldistone who had known the outlaw familiarly as Mr. Campbell.   These and all the rest of it make an imaginary story in which the character of the place is truly kept with incalculable effect in the adventures and speeches reported.

The Antiquary preceded *Rob Roy* and has not been omitted here out of any want of consideration : something in these rambling notes led from *Guy Mannering* to Glasgow.   *The Antiquary* after the first chapter is not very closely connected with any definite place, any small east coast town and its neighbourhood will do. But the Edinburgh scene at the start is one of the truest things in Scott, and the landlord of the Queensferry Inn should not be forgotten, a stout and victorious advocate of claret against the port which was encouraged by " the Saxon tyrant."   The plot of the novel required something rather like melodrama, but the more theatrical characters are never allowed to take command.   Edie Ochiltree, the Blue Gown, is mixed up in some sensational passages for the discomfiture of the German impostor, but he talks like reality to Mr. Oldbuck.   The famous scene of Saunders Mucklebackit and his boat is characteristic of Scott in every way.

" I am glad," he [the Antiquary] said, in a tone of sympathy—" I am glad, Saunders, that you feel yourself able to make this exertion."

" And what would ye have me to do," answered the fisher gruffly, " unless I wanted to see four children starve because one is drowned ? It's well wi' you gentles, that can sit in the house wi' handkerchers at your een when ye lose a friend ; but the like o' us maun to our wark again, if our hearts were beatin' as hard as my hammer."

Without taking more notice of Oldbuck he proceeded with his labour ; and the Antiquary, to whom the display of human nature under the influence of agitating passions was never indifferent, stood beside him, in silent attention, as if watching the progress of the work. He observed more than once the man's hard features, as if by the fact of association, prepare to accompany the sound of saw and hammer with his usual symphony of a rude tune hummed or whistled, and as often a slight twitch of convulsive expression showed that, ere the sound was uttered, a cause for suppressing it rushed upon his mind. At length, when he had patched a considerable rent, and was beginning to mend another, his feelings appeared altogether to derange the power of attention necessary for his work. The piece of wood he was about to nail on was at first too short ; then he chose another equally ill adapted for the purpose. At length, throwing it down in anger, after wiping his dim eye with quivering hand, he exclaimed, " There is a curse either on me or on this auld black bitch of a boat, that I have hauled up high and dry, and patched and clouted sae mony years, that she might drown my poor Steenie at the end of them, and be d——d to her ! " and he flung his hammer against the boat, as if she had been the intentional cause of his misfortunes. Then recollecting himself, he added, " Yet what needs ane be angry at her, that has neither soul nor sense ?—though I am no muckle better mysell. She's but a rickle o' auld rotten deals nailed thegither, and warped wi' the wind and sea—and I am a dour cark, battered by foul weather at sea and land till I am maist as senseless as hersell. She maun be mended though again' the morning tide—that's a thing o' necessity."

Thus speaking, he went to gather together his instruments and attempt to resume his labour, but Oldbuck took him kindly by the arm. " Come, come," he said, " Saunders, there is no work for you this day—I'll send down Shavings, the carpenter, to mend the boat, and he may put the day's work into my account—and you had better not come out to-morrow, but stay to comfort your family under this dispensation, and the gardener will bring you some vege- tables and meat from Monkbarns."

" I thank ye, Monkbarns," answered the poor fisher ; " I am a plain-spoken man, and hae little to say for mysell ; I might hae learned fairer fashions frae my mither lang syne, but I never saw muckle gude they did her ; however, I thank ye. Ye were aye kind and neighbourly, whatever folk says o' your being near and close ; and I hae often said in thae times when they were ganging to raise up the puir folk against the gentles—I hae often said, ne'er a man should steer a hair touching to Monkbarns while Steenie and I could wag a finger—so said Steenie too. And, Monk- barns, when ye laid his head in the grave, (and mony thanks for the respect,) ye saw the mouls laid on an honest lad that likit you weel, though he made little phrase about it."

The learned quarrel about the Picts between Mr. Oldbuck and Sir Arthur Wardour may be thought rather overdone by modern readers who do not know the fury of antiquarians, and the rage of Ritson against Pinkerton over the same subject. Mr. Oldbuck offends his Highland nephew, Hector Macintyre, by his scep- ticism in an equally dangerous question, the merits of Ossian ; it is worth mentioning that Hector (and there- fore Scott) had found out some of the true Ossianic Gaelic poetry ; Captain Macintyre does not rely on the forgeries of Macpherson. The alarm of invasion and the rally of volunteers make the most notable passage of contemporary history worked into the Waverley Novels. For a right judgment of Scott's attitude to politics it ought not to be forgotten that Mr. Oldbuck, who in so many respects is Scott himself, is not of Scott's political party ; he is a Whig, and Scott

language of Helen Macgregor to Bailie Nicol Jarvie is high flown rhetoric, and does not belong to the same world as the lively characteristic natural language of her husband in the earlier scenes.   Rob Roy, himself, talks a little like Roderick Dhu when he tells Mr. Osbaldis-tone that his foot is on his native heath.   Scott knew very little of the Gaelic language, though, as has been already remarked, he managed somehow to get very near to the truth about Ossianic poetry.   But in spite of all his disadvantages it is wonderful what variety of character is shown in his Highland personages, from Fergus McIvor to "the Dougal Creature."   Ever since the publication of Macpherson's Ossian, the Highlands of Scotland had been a region of sentimental romance for Europe and America.   There is an amusing record of a young American enthusiast for Ossian in the travels of the French geologist Faujas de Saint Fond in 1784.   (This book, translated by Sir Archibald Geikie, may be recommended to every lover of the Highlands ; it makes a third with Johnson's *Journey to the Western Isles* and Boswell's *Tour in the Hebrides*.) Scott's *Lady of the Lake* did not begin the popular in-terest in Highland scenery.   The Trossachs were famous already, as is proved by the tour of Wordsworth and his sister in 1803.   But *The Lady of the Lake* caught up and carried further the interest which had begun in Ossian, and in "picturesque" travellers like Gilpin. Scott remade the imaginary world of the Highlands, and gave the Highlands such importance in English opinion that when King George IV. visited Edinburgh in 1822 he appeared in Highland dress, as likewise did an Alderman of London on the same occasion.   The Highlands had come to mean the whole of Scotland, mainly through Scott's romantic work in verse and prose. Yet in spite of this unreality Scott knew the Highlands as they really were ; not intimately as he knew Edinburgh and Ettrick Forest, but accurately as far as he chose to go. *The Fair Maid of Perth*, which some judges think the best of his historical novels, is true to the life of the Highland clansmen.

X

QUENTIN DURWARD ; ST. RONAN'S WELL

THE foreign victories of the Waverley Novels began, as Lockhart notes, with *Quentin Durward*. Scott's venture in French history had an immediate success in France ; and it is from *Quentin Durward* that the popularity of Scott took its rise and travelled abroad, through translations and imitations, all over Europe, with a vogue to which Stendhal at once bore witness. "The man himself counts for little," said M. Beyle, already cited, "but this is the man for whom all the professional translators are competing, in every tongue and every market." From Chapter I., "The Contrast" —*le chapitre des deux cousins*, as Balzac quotes it— from the contention of Louis XI. and Charles the Bold, sprang the Historical Novel as a new idea, a source of invention and profit for innumerable literary men. They had their pattern provided for them, and all the mills were busy for years repeating and varying, as the several operators saw their way and proved their skill.

It is easy to understand how the French scene and story won applause in France ; but the foreign readers of Scott had no prejudice against his English plots when once they discovered what entertainment he was providing. Victor Hugo turned *Kenilworth* into the drama of *Amy Robsart*, and Scott, when he visited Paris, heard the opera of *Ivanhoe*. " The Scotch Novels," properly so called, were not less acceptable : Jeanie Deans and her father were as well appreciated in France as in England, and *Les Eaux de Saint-Ronan* is taken by Balzac as one of the masterpieces of Scott. In this last there was something different from the success of the historical novel ; but it seems clear that the historical novel *Quentin Durward* found for its author thousands of readers before one of them turned back to *Old Mortality* (*Les Puritains d'Écosse*) or *The Heart of Midlothian* (*La Prison d'Édimbourg*). There is nothing strange in this ; *Quentin Durward* is one of the lightest and quickest of the Waverley Novels : Quentin himself is a hero whom any one can admire and follow with the comforting belief that he, the reader, would have acted even so and could not have done much better. There is more to think about in the contradictory and conflicting motives of Edward Waverley and Henry Morton, in the drifting fortunes of Francis Osbaldistone or Nigel Oliphant, but the clear youthful wits of Quentin and his ready courage are better entertainment for the ingenuous readers who put themselves in his place. Scott knew what he was about—he tells us so himself —when he chose the Scottish archer for his hero and made him a different sort of man from the fluctuating, uncertain minds that come so near to a tragic crisis in *Waverley* and *Old Mortality*. And the adventures happen in the old unfailing best fashion of a perilous journey. Quentin in a more modern world is the successor of Sir Gareth of Orkney and Sir Libeaus in the old romances, champions travelling along with damsels in distress ; and he sets an example for D'Artagnan in his ride from Paris to the sea, the glory of the greatest of all prose epics in the succession of Scott. The

historical business of the novel is for Scott himself no
mean adventure ; he takes all the risks, and pays not
too much attention to the prudent advisers who say
that it is a mistake in historical novels to put great
historical characters in the front of the stage. This is
very reasonable, good advice, in a general way ; but it
does not count when there is given in sober history
" The Contrast " of Chapter I., the two rival powers of
Lewis and Charles, together with the incident (however
Scott may have played with historical particulars) of
the King of France putting himself in the power of the
Duke of Burgundy.

It is not very profitable to ask whether Scott has
succeeded or failed in his characters of the two great
adversaries. It is not quite fair to remember Shakespeare's drama of *Richard II.* and *Henry IV.*—another
of the epigrammatic contrasts which are plentiful
enough in plain ordinary history. Scott is not writing
tragedy on a groundwork of Philippe des Commines.
Is he superficial ? King Lewis's hatband, and his
leaden saints and prayers, may seem no more than any
tiro would remember to put in, given the task of doing
a sketch of Louis XI. Still, there would be no point
in leaving the King unfurnished with those properties.
And if we compare (for example) Scott's Lewis with his
Duke of Buckingham in *Peveril*, the King comes out
with much more to his credit than the Duke, who is
too obviously made to fit the pattern of Dryden's Zimri,
and hardly exists when the tags of Dryden's satirical
commentary are deducted. Lewis is recognisable without his hatband, and alive, apart from the mannerisms
of his conventional piety. Scott has made just the
right use of the traditional picture of Lewis. The quaint
touches help and do not hinder the expression of his

character ; and his character, when it is tried in the great ordeal, when the least mistake might let down the whole threatening weight of Charles's anger and revenge, is such as to win over even the most innocent hearts to take sides with this devilish person who plays so well. No one wants him to be beaten. After all, he makes the fortune of Quentin Durward. It is pleasant to remember here his dealings with Gringoire in Théodore de Banville's play. Whether the happiest of French poets owed much, or little, or nothing to *Quentin Durward*, it remains true that the King, listening in disguise to the ballad-monger's rhyme of " King Lewis his orchard close," is the same dangerous humorist as in Scott's novel.

Ludovic Lesley, " le Balafré," deserves all the praise he has won from Thackeray and others. Thackeray himself understood and could render with similar skill the processes of the honest slow mind, moving with fair comfort in a world where much may be gained without excessive subtlety. The clever ones and their cunning games are small concern to le Balafré. As for the Scottish archers in general, there is little wrong with them, except that none of them ever appeals to St. Ninian, St. Ringan, whose name, Saint Treignan, meant all Scotland to the companions of Pantagruel, so frequent was he in the mouth of the Scot abroad.

In the romance of the two lovers Scott himself found a new version of the squire of low degree " who loved the King's daughter of Hungary " ; for although Quentin and his uncle are allowed their claim to very gentle blood, yet Quentin is landless, an adventurer, with all the enormous danger of the lady's relations and obligations against him—the danger of high place and authority thwarting the course of true love which

was continually present to the minds of medieval poets
dealing in allegory and sentiment, and which needed
no help from antiquarian learning to give it a place in
Scott's memory and imagination. We may find in
Quentin Durward the author's own early reveries : the
fortunate lover is what he himself might have been ; it
is a dream story, like Gregory's in *The Earthly Paradise.*
At the end it is clear that the happy dream is vanishing ;
the later history of Quentin and his bride is beyond the
author's reach ; he lets them go, and merely asks the
reader to believe what he will about their happiness
ever after. The play is over, and the audience go away
well satisfied. They have something besides a good
story to carry with them in the song of County Guy,
which has this advantage, beyond itself, that it sets
one remembering and reckoning up all the other magical
verses of Scott, in the novels and out of them—a
pleasant occupation and never untimely.

St. Ronan's Well is possibly one of Scott's masterpieces, as Balzac thought : whatever its merits, they
are different from those of *Quentin Durward.* Others
of Scott's novels—*The Antiquary* in particular—are not
far from his own day. *St. Ronan's Well*, in its time of
action, comes within the last ten years before the date
of its publication in 1823. For John Mowbray and
Captain MacTurk are in time for the end of the Penin-
sular War—which might have saved a good deal of
trouble if it had drawn off some of the other idle people
earlier. It does not seem to have occurred to them
that opportunities for visiting the Continent might be
found with a little influence, which, while they would
have reduced the profits of the new hotel, would have
protected their young blood from the devastating
elegance of Lady Penelope and the many portfolios of

Mr. Winterblossom. But the author understood what he was doing ; the society of " Spaw " is delineated from real life, and the natural history of that strange menagerie is explained in the introduction. Bath and Clifton could not find room for all the tedious unoccupied humanity of Britain ; and not every shady adventurer found it necessary to live in the Isle of Man. Scott in one sentence of *Peveril* had been able to touch off the queer raffish set which in his day was able to exist in that kingdom—a field for the satirical observer which seems never to have had its due. Are there any extant memoirs of the smart set in Man during the great war a hundred years ago ? It was not Scott's proper concern, and he knew the Isle of Man only by report. In *St. Ronan's Well* his motive was not in the first place to describe the oddities of the " Spaw," but something deeper, more in the vein of Crabbe. His old friend, at the beginning of their acquaintance, had marked down Scott as a likely person to provide him with details of crime, for his own purposes, relying for this end on what he knew of Scott's professional work as a lawyer. Crabbe's letter is amusingly innocent and vague with regard to Scott's official capacity, but his request was well directed. A story of real life, too horrible for Lockhart to repeat, was in Scott's mind when he resolved to try what could be made of the present day and a town like Melrose, Peebles, or Innerleithen as a subject for a novel. So *St. Ronan's Well* came to follow *Quentin Durward*.

Balzac's high estimate of *Les Eaux de Saint-Ronan*, if there is anything more definite in it than his ready and hearty admiration of Scott, *l'Homère du genre*, may be taken as partly due to Scott's anticipation of his own methods and favourite subjects. The St. Ronan's

Hotel was just the right place for Balzac, allowing for
difficulties of a foreign land and language. The Maison
Vauquer shows what he could have made of it, and
Scott makes no less, though the work is rather uncongenial. The Cleikum is another story ; Mrs. Margaret
Dods is one of his own people, and her life and language
must have been a relief to him after the humours of
the new hotel. But he was interested in these also ;
humours they are, in Ben Jonson's sense, and there is
something like Ben Jonson's method, which is also a
good deal like Balzac's, in the unsparing exhibition of
malformed human nature.

Scott in the story of Clara Mowbray got into difficulties which are not accurately described by Lockhart,
and not fully explained by the discovery of the cancelled sheet, which was published in the *Athenæum* by
J. M. Collyer in 1893 (February 4). In the story as
Scott originally thought it out, Clara Mowbray had
suffered more grievous wrong than in *St. Ronan's Well*
as published. According to Lockhart, the villainy
which was too much for Scott's moral advisers was
that the deception of Clara Mowbray by Bulmer did
not stop at the mock marriage. But it was not so in
the printed sheet, the cancelled proof, which was found
among Constable's papers. What Hannah Irwin confessed to Mr. Cargill, the minister, is summarised in
Mr. Cargill's very natural question : " Wretch ! " exclaimed the clergyman ; " and had you not then done
enough ? Why did you expose the paramour of one
brother to become the wife of another ? "

It was the lawless love of Clara and Tyrrel, not an
outrage like that of Lovelace, which had to be left out
of the novel in compliance with the prudery or the
commercial judgment of Ballantyne. Scott's contemp-

tuous words as he yielded are more intelligible now than
they are in Lockhart ; there would have been no
prudery, he thought, if it had been only the love affair
of a country lass.   Scott may have been right ; at the
same time it is possible to see other objections than
those of prudery to the tale as told by Hannah Irwin.
Disclosures coming at the end of a story are always
awkward and apt to fail in their effect on the reader.
The confession of Elspeth in *The Antiquary* is an example of this difficulty ; and Hannah Irwin's confession
is still more open to cavilling criticism.   It is bad narrative, because it comes too late and includes too much :
the reader has too much given to him all at once, and
finds it hard to accept the steady, calculated malignity
of Bulmer and his agent Solmes ; the envious perfidy
of Hannah Irwin herself requires too much explanation.
It is possible to defend Ballantyne and hold that the
novel is better as it now is : not because the love-story
of Clara and Tyrrel is unfit for the young person, but
because Hannah Irwin's confession is not the right way
to tell it.   The passion of Clara Mowbray is no more
tragic, no deeper or more interesting, for the woman
Irwin's confession or Mr. Cargill's comment.   If Clara
herself has nothing to say, the author should not have
left the truth to come out as a mere fact of evidence.
In *St. Ronan's Well* Scott makes the same mistake as
(now and then) his contemporaries Galt and Miss
Ferrier—whom we naturally think of when we find
Scott approaching the world of *The Entail* and
Marriage.   All three novelists have fits of melodrama,
which does not agree well with their humorous comedy
of Scottish life and manners.   The villains of *St.
Ronan's Well* are too obvious, too mechanically per-
sistent.   And they are dull devils, too : the theft of the

XI

BYRON

BYRON'S poetry is made difficult for the critics in the same way as Pope's. It is almost impossible to get to it through the tumult of conflicting opinions. Was Byron a great poet ? The question and the doubt are obstacles in the way of the reader, just as a similar question prevents many from enjoying Pope. Colonel Newcome, we all remember, had to make what he could of the opinion that Lord Byron was not a great poet, though he was a very clever man ; and something like this judgment of the case crosses the minds of most modern readers of Byron. They take up the book in order to prove or disprove this or some other formula ; it is hard to read the poems frankly for their own sake. We read as advocates or attorneys, and we read in a restless, noisy room : the voices of competing and contradictory arguments make confusion and distraction. How can anyone read quietly and simply when he has it drummed into his ears that Byron is the voice of Revolution, or the spirit of 1848, or the one modern English poet who is recognised over all the Continent ?

Few authors have gained more apparent advantage and few have suffered more real injustice from the Spirit of the Age and theories of representative men. Byron and Isaiah go together in a splendid stanza of

Victor Hugo's ; Byron is the spokesman and champion of a new era. The orators who have to state their objections to kings, priests, and the Congress of Vienna are apt to think well of Byron. But the poet as representative man, especially as representative of political ideas, draws the votes of a reading public not wholly or mainly concerned with poetry. The representative man is an abstraction : not unreal, but abstract. Mr. John Morley many years ago, in an essay on Byron which does not neglect his poetry, was inclined to make most of him as a preacher and disputant. Incidentally, he uses the representative formula in a way that brings out the danger of the process. " Dante, the poet of Catholicism," he says : but how much do we learn of Dante through this mode of thinking ? Leaving out of account Dante's distribution of Popes in his comedy as possibly irrelevant, we cannot help asking what Catholicism has to do with the poetry of Dante as he himself explains it—with the *dolce stil nuovo* or with any particular beautiful lines that come to the memory. " Shakespeare, the poet of Feudalism " (*ibidem*) : what do we get from his representative valuation, either for Feudalism or for Shakespeare ? Except indeed, what is not to be despised, a prompting of the mind to range from *Love's Labour's Lost* to the *Tempest*, from the *Comedy of Errors* to *Antony and Cleopatra*, looking for Feudalism and finding other things by the way.

But representative is not a vain word : it is one of Byron's own terms, and it is not out of place in speaking of him. It is Goethe's way of thinking about Byron, and what Goethe thought of Byron is worth considering, in spite of Swinburne's refusal to attend. Swinburne thought that Goethe's excessive praise of Mérimée

proved him a despicable judge of art. "No array of
terms can say how much I am at peace about Goethe's
opinions on modern poetry." But Goethe does not
speak of Byron merely in passing, carelessly. He
thought more about Byron than about any contemporary poet. He made him the *representative* of modern
poetry in his allegorical *Helena* ; he reviewed him, and
he explained to Eckermann what he (Goethe) thought
and meant when he declared deliberately that Byron
was the greatest poet of his age. He did not mean that
Byron was the voice of Revolution : he was thinking
of poetry, as well as of its foundation in real life.
Byron, he told Eckermann, is neither antique nor
romantic ; he is the present day.

More partial critics than Goethe might cavil here over
" antique " and " romantic," might say that Byron is
antique, or classical, in some respects as those terms
are commonly used : in his admiration for Pope, and
his observance of the Dramatic Unities. Goethe (to
Eckermann, again) is amused over Byron's dramatic
unities—to see the great Rebel entangled in that stale
convention ! It makes no real difference ; only a
trifling piece of vanity. To most contemporary readers
of Byron he was all romance : romance in the spirit,
romance in scenery and dresses ; romance in the
intensive mode of passion ; romance all abroad dis-
played in its outward glow. *The Giaour* and *The Bride
of Abydos*, *The Corsair* and *Lara*, seemed to give both
aspects of romance, to be all that anyone could wish :
sweet, strong, fiery, plentiful, showy, tumultuous. But
Goethe, who was tired of the nickname romantic, knew
that the so-called Romantic School in Germany had a
spirit different from Byron's for good or evil. Byron
was not attached to any school. Byron was the poetical

genius of the present day : forty years younger than Goethe, and as strongly bent as Goethe on finding all possible instruments and modes of poetry, to express himself and to get what he could for poetry out of life. Goethe was not prejudiced, and he was not extravagant : he saw that some things were wrong in Byron's art ; that Byron was cramped in his dramatic unities, and that his dark misanthropy was overdone. But these defects were nothing compared with Byron's energy and variety. Goethe never cavils at Byron's choice of a theme, never complains that his subject is not the Duke of Wellington or Lord Castlereagh, but the two Foscari and Sardanapalus. Byron for him is the great explorer, trying everything. Is Goethe wrong ? However that may be, his judgment is not to be dismissed as merely a foreigner's pardonable error. At the lowest it is worth something as an offset to the political valuation of Byron as given by Mazzini and Mr. John Morley. Goethe spent his time in praising :

To praise you search the wide world over ;

he could find riches in every region of the world (excepting, unhappily, the gods, heroes, and poets of Denmark, Norway, Sweden, and Iceland), and he always knew why he praised, and always kept his sense of form and style. Success in form and style overbore all other considerations ; and when he finds in Byron the perfection of comic poetry, it does not occur to him to mention that comic poetry is less noble than some other works of the Muses. What is important is that Byron's poetry is alive ; so full of life indeed that it threatens other more dignified sorts of poetry : *let fire go out of the bramble and devour the cedars of Lebanon.* This is Goethe's quotation when

Eckermann draws him on to Tasso—Tasso's influence
on Byron, a comparison of Tasso and Byron, and so
forth. Goethe, if anyone, might be expected to defend
and praise Torquato Tasso ; but he cannot maintain
his cause against Byron. Byron is the flaming bramble
who reduces the saintly cedar to ashes : *der brennende
Dornstraüch, der du heilige Ceder des Libanon in Asche
legt.* One line of *Don Juan* is enough to kill the whole
of *Jerusalem Delivered.*

Speaking shortly after the death of Byron with regret
and admiration for his abundant versatile genius—" a
great man, good at many things "—Goethe says that
there was probably nothing left for Byron to invent.
He had come to the height and limit of his powers in
his astounding *Vision of Judgment. In dem unbegrei-
flichen Gedicht seines Jungsten Gerichts hat er das
Aeusserste gethan was er zu thun fähig war.* The poem
had been read to him, we know, by Crabb Robinson,
on the same day as *Samson Agonistes,* and Goethe was
content. His critical opinions are disparaged by Swinburne ; here, with regard to the *Vision of Judgment,*
Swinburne and Goethe think alike. Here Byron
left behind him the easier successes of romance, the
cloudy ambitions of tragedy, and came out secure,
triumphant, himself at last, with his proper voice and
expression :

> Sharp sleet of arrowy shower against the foe.

So have I seen a hailstorm in winter going east over
the sea, cracking and flashing, with a rainbow following
from the low sun, and a new power of breathing in the
air. But, as Goethe says, it is indescribable. The
meeting of Michael and Satan is everything that
Byron had aimed at in his poetical life, and much

more. It is a great discovery, and words are useless to explain it.

> He and the sombre silent spirit met—
>   They knew each other both for good and ill ;
> Such was their power that neither could forget
>   His former friend and future foe, but still
> There was a high immortal proud regret
>   In either's eye, as if 'twere less their will
> Than destiny to make the eternal years
> Their date of war, and their *champ clos* the spheres.

I offer some remarks on the poetical forms in Byron —a subject not so imposing as the Revolution, or Byron the forerunner of 1848, but more immediately concerning the study of poetry.

There may be doubt how far we are justified in taking any poet as the representative of his age, even in poetry ; but in every poet something of his age is represented : there are streams of tendency, fashions and changes of fashion independent of any one particular human mind, and in poetry they claim attention from the critic and historian. Sometimes you will find a poet attacked by a fashionable vanity, showing the symptoms for a time, then throwing it off and going his own independent way. The most interesting case is Milton's temporary short and violent fit of conceits in his poem on the *Passion* : Milton (for example) proposing to write his poem with his tears, making white letters on a black ground, and so on—all the time more or less conscious that his " flatter'd fancy " is absurd. When Byron and Shelley began to make verses, they fell into a common bad fashion of the time which is shown in a remarkably hideous set of measures moving not happily in anapæsts. " The triplex is a good tripping measure " (Shakespeare said so), but the dancing

feet of the triple cadence need the skill of a good piper
to help them along ; and by the end of the eighteenth
century the art was not well understood.   Byron
achieved it later in *Sennacherib*, but first he had to take
a course of couplets, to get clear of the feeble verse of
Hours of Idleness.

> On Marston with Rupert, 'gainst traitors contending,
> Four brothers enrich'd with their blood the bleak field,
> For the rights of a monarch their country defending
> Till death their attachment to royalty seal'd.

It was well for Byron that he should leave this tune
and take to the old-established verse of Satire.   *English
Bards and Scotch Reviewers* is a poem not now much
regarded, but it is one of the last of a great family, and
no discredit to the old tradition.   Byron was to return
to the heroic couplet later, and show in *The Corsair*
and *Lara* that the measure of Dryden might be used
in the nineteenth century without the satiric point of
epigram, for stories of action and adventure.   In *The
Corsair* Byron was deliberately giving up the various
measures, partly borrowed from Scott, which had
helped so much in the success of *The Giaour* and the
following romances.   I quote from his preface :   the
dedication of *The Corsair*, January 2, 1814, to Thomas
Moore.   Byron is so often blamed for carelessness and
want of art that it is a duty to remember his technical
notes on versification :

   " In the present composition I have attempted, not
the most difficult, but perhaps the best adapted measure
to our language, the good old and now neglected heroic
couplet.   The stanza of Spenser is perhaps too slow and
dignified for narrative, though I confess it is the measure
most after my own heart.   Scott alone of the present
generation has triumphed over the fatal facility of the

octosyllabic verse, and this is not the least victory of his fertile and mighty genius ; in blank verse Milton, Thomson, and our dramatists are the beacons that shine along the deep, but warn us from the rough and barren rock on which they are kindled. The heroic couplet is not the most popular measure certainly ; but as I did not deviate into the other from a wish to flatter what is called public opinion, I shall quit it without further apology, and take my chance once more with that versification in which I have hitherto published nothing but compositions whose former circulation is part of my present, and will be of my future, regret."

The stanza of Spenser was to come again in the third and fourth cantos of *Childe Harold*. Most readers agree that Byron did well when he took up the Italian octave instead ; that is his proper tune ; his poetic life is infinitely more various in the octave than in the longer stanza of *Childe Harold* or the couplets of *Lara*. But the Spenserean stanza from the first was used by Byron in the same way as the octave. His model was not the *Faerie Queene*, but Beattie's *Minstrel* and Thomson's *Castle of Indolence*. He tells us so in his preface (February 1812), and he joins with theirs the name of Ariosto :

" The stanza of Spenser, according to one of our most successful poets, admits of every variety. Dr. Beattie makes the following observation : ' Not long ago I began a poem in the style and stanza of Spenser, in which I propose to give full scope to my inclination, and be either droll or pathetic, descriptive or sentimental, tender or satirical, as the humour strikes me ; for, if I mistake not, the measure which I have adopted admits equally of all these kinds of composition.' Strengthened in my opinion by such authority, and by

some in the highest order of Italian poets, I shall make
no apology for attempts at similar variations in the
following composition ; satisfied that if they are unsuccessful, the failure must be in the execution rather
than in the design, sanctioned by the practice of
Ariosto, Thomson, and Beattie."

The Italian *ottava rima* (we gather from this) serves
the same purpose as the longer stave of Beattie and
Thomson. The English poets and Ariosto are alike as
using stanzas for capricious and humorous poetry ; for
poetry that claims the freedom of Roman satire, with
larger range of poetical music than either the Roman
or the English conventional form, the verse of Juvenal
or of Johnson.

This early preface shows that Byron was consistent
in his aim and ambition. From the start of *Childe
Harold* to the last rhyme of *Don Juan* he had for his
chief object a kind of poetry that would let him say
anything he pleased :

Nella chiesa
Coi santi, ed in taverna coi ghiottoni—

if I may apply a text of Dante thus : in church with
the saints, at the wine-shop with skinkers—which by
the way proves that Dante, before the octave was
fashionable in Italy, knew all about the freedom of
satiric verse—there is a good deal of Dionysiac old
Comedy mingled in the Divine. Byron's *Vision of
Judgment* is not Dante's, but it is possibly nearer
Dante's spirit than the poem which Byron wrote under
Dante's name.

Ottava rima, which Chaucer refused to copy in English, was frequent from the time of Daniel and Drayton,
most successful in Fairfax's Tasso, but seldom so as to
gain any peculiar advantage over other known types.

Between the Spenserean tradition and the reforms of Waller and Denham, the octave had no special favour. Once or twice it comes out with anticipations of later melodies :

> Art thou not Lucifer ? he to whom the droves
>   Of Stars, that gild the morn in charge were given ?
> The nimblest of the Lightning-wingèd loves ?
>   The fairest and the first-born smile of Heav'n ?
> Look in what pomp the Mistress Planet moves,
>   Rev'rently circled by the lesser seven ;
> Such, and so rich, the flames that from thine Eyes
> Opprest the common-people of the Skies.

One might ask whether this is Byron learning from Shelley, or Shelley borrowing thunder from Byron. It is Crashaw translating Marino, and there is more of it, well worth attention.

Gay had been reading Ariosto, more particularly the forty-sixth canto of *Orlando Furioso*, where the poet imagines his ship coming home to harbour, and all his friends meeting him, to the sound of bells and trumpets and general cheering. From this original Gay proceeded to invent *Mr. Pope's Welcome from Greece*. How was it that this refreshing good example was taken up by no one ? It is the only thing before Whistlecraft that is like Byron's octaves.

> See generous Burlington with goodly Bruce
>   (But Bruce comes wafted in a soft sedan)
> Dan Prior next, belov'd by every Muse ;
>   And friendly Congreve, unreproachful man !
> (Oxford by Cunningham hath sent excuse ;)
>   See hearty Watkins come with cap and can,
> And Lewis who has never friend forsaken ;
> And Laughton whispering asks—" Is Troy Town taken ? "

I say nothing now of Byron's reading in the Italian poets, or his pride in his translation from the *Morgante*

Maggiore ; it is enough for the present that he found his right measure, partly through accident, but also through long-established liking for that kind of verse, and through his treatment of the Spenserean stanza.

Byron is sometimes treated as if he were no more than a rhetorical poet : *The Isles of Greece* his highest achievement in lyric, and that without attaining the true character which distinguishes song from oratory. But many readers will not believe that lyric is a wrong name for the musical phrases that come to their minds from Byron's shorter poems :

> There be none of Beauty's daughters
> With a magic like thee.

> I enter thy garden of roses. . . .

> She walks in beauty, like the night
> Of cloudless climes and starry skies.

Those beginnings mean true poetry to many who remember little more. Therefore in justice to Byron let us take one poem which has suffered some injustice ; partly through being too well known to be thought of ; partly through a defect inherent in English verse, for which Byron is not to blame :

> The Assyrian came down like the wolf on the fold. . . .

That is the beginning of a faultless poem. Before any-one rises to take up this challenge, I would ask him to be sure that he understands the scope of the poem. It is an artifice, something like the *Lays of Ancient Rome* —a ballad such as a Hebrew might have written at the time if ballads had been allowable (and I am not sure that they were not). It is a short, simple lyrical poem of a tragical time, a great deliverance. Its aim is to

give the whole meaning truly, without conceit, without
breaking the simple frame :

> And there lay the steed with his nostril all wide,
> But through it there roll'd not the breath of his pride ;
> And the foam of his gasping lay white on the turf,
> And cold as the spray of the rock-beating surf.
>
> And there lay the rider distorted and pale,
> With the dew on his brow, and the rust on his mail ;
> And the tents were all silent, the banners alone,
> The lances uplifted, the trumpet unblown.
>
> And the widows of Ashur are loud in their wail,
> And the idols are broke in the temple of Baal ;
> And the might of the Gentile, unsmote by the sword,
> Hath melted like snow in the glance of the Lord !

Is it not well done ?   There is, as I have said, a
hindrance, but it is not a real thing, and it is not Byron's
fault.   He has mastered the triple cadence ; but this
measure does not make itself absolutely clear to all
readers ; it is not certainly fixed in English.   From the
mere words, it might be hard to find difference of
measure between the *Laird of Cockpen* and *Lochaber no
more !*   The slower form of the triplex is better taken
not as anapæsts, but as a short syllable followed by
two longs ; this is Bentley's suggestion in his preface
to Terence, where he finds equivalents in English verse
for the Latin varieties used by this poet.   The English
triplex he scans as bacchiac.   Mr. Walter Leaf, in his
Hafiz, translates the same measure from the Persian :

$$\cup - - \,|\, \cup - - \,|\, \cup - - \,|\, \cup - \,|$$

> So prate not of wisdom : the hour comes for all.
> Aristo departs like the Kurd midst the kine.

In his note Mr. Leaf says [1] : " The metre of this ode

[1] W. Leaf : *Versions from Hafiz*, an essay in Persian metre, 1898,
Ode xlv., note, p. 74.

is the traditional epic measure ; that used, for instance,
by Firdousi in the *Shahnamah*. . . . I must make a
special appeal to the benevolent reader to do his best
to prevent the metre falling into a lumbering anapæstic
jingle—a tendency which I find almost incurable, to
the point that I have been tempted to omit the translation altogether.''

Rhythm and metre are dangerous branches of
learning. Some poets and lovers of poetry refuse to
think of them, and consequently live more comfortable
lives, and give less anxiety to their friends. But this
business of the triple cadence really needs some attention : enough, at any rate, to prevent one from reading
Sennacherib in the same way as *Young Lochinvar*.

One of Byron's lyrical poems, seldom quoted, is a
proof of what may be gained in the history of poetry and
the enjoyment of verse by a study of mere metrical form :

> Could Love for ever
> Run like a river,
> And Time's endeavour
>   Be tried in vain—
> No other pleasure
> Like this could measure ;
> And like a treasure
>   We'd hug the chain.
> But since our sighing
> Ends not in dying,
> And formed for flying,
>   Love plumes his wing ;
> Then for this reason
> Let's love a season,
> But let that season be only Spring.

The art of Byron is little admired in the finer, slighter
sorts of rhyme. Swinburne never quotes this nor says
a word about it either in his praise or blame of Byron.
He includes it in the selection from Byron for which he

wrote the better tempered of his two essays, in 1865.
Anima Anceps was written about that time :

> Till death have broken
> Sweet life's love token,
> Till all be spoken
>   That shall be said,
> What dost thou praying
> O soul, and playing
> With song and saying
>   Things flown and fled ?
> For this we know not—
> That fresh springs flow not,
> And fresh griefs grow not,
>   When men are dead ;
> When strange years cover
> Lover and lover,
> And joys are over
>   And tears are shed.

It is a very old form of verse—one of those shadows of
music that seem to wander all over the world till the
lucky moment when they get a poet to hear them.
The airy melody of Byron's verse here is translated
from the Drinking Song of his friend Curran :

> If sadly thinking, with spirits sinking,
> Could more than Drinking my cares compose,
> A cure from sorrow for sighs I'd borrow,
> And hope to-morrow would end my woes.
> But as in wailing there's nought availing,
> And Death unfailing will strike the blow,
> Then for that reason and for a season
> Let us be merry before we go !

The history of this metrical idea goes much farther
back ; for readers of Byron it is not necessary, though
it may be pleasant, to trace the whole pedigree. This
lyric of Byron's is a discovery ; with admirable skill
he has detected the finer shades in a riotous song.
When it is observed that Byron's stanza is the same as

The Groves of Blarney and Swinburne's *Anima Anceps*, the successful craft of Byron may be recognised.

I will add two remarks, and one, I am sure, is right : that the dealings of Scott and Byron bring out each of them at his best.   Scott's review of *Childe Harold*, III., in the *Quarterly* (1816) was felt by Byron to be a very generous and well-timed act.   When the fourth canto appeared Scott reviewed that also in an article which showed not only his friendship for Byron but his discriminating good sense.   The passage about Venice and Italy, not often read, is a good specimen :

Byron " might have spared his regret for the loss of that freedom which Venice never possessed. . . .   It is surely vain to mourn for a nation which if restored to independence could not defend or support itself, and it would be worse than vain, were it possible, to restore the Signoria with all its oligarchical terror of denunciation, and secret imprisonment, and judicial murder. What is to be wished for Italy is the amalgamation of its various petty States into one independent and well-governed kingdom, capable of asserting and maintaining her place among the nations of Europe."

Scott, writing just after Byron's death in 1824, anticipates the opinion of Mazzini that Democracy has yet to learn what it owes to Byron, and provides, in no unprejudiced way, some materials for that account. He quotes Byron :   " Do not let us suffer ourselves to be massacred by the ignoble swarms of ruffians who are endeavouring to throttle their way to power." And again, from *Don Juan* :

> It is not that I adulate the people :
>   Without *me* there are demagogues enough,
> And infidels, to pull down every steeple,
>   And set up in their stead some proper stuff.

Whether they may sow scepticism to reap hell,
    As is the Christian dogma rather rough,
I do not know :—I wish men to be free
    As much from mobs as kings—from you as me.

About another topic I am not so certain. It has occurred to me that the resemblance between Dr. Edward Young and Lord Byron, which has often been noticed in particulars, is closer than their common taste for skulls as ornaments and for gloom as a regular habit.

There is in Young and Byron the same tendency to comply with the popular taste, and the same sort of independence. Young writes fashionable poems : his *Last Day* is in the fashion ; his Satires are contemporary with Pope's, and like Pope's in form. His tragedies are not much different from usual tragedies, except for Zanga in *The Revenge*, one of the first Byronic personages. Byron was Zanga, as he tells us, one Speech Day at Harrow :

I once more view the room, with spectators surrounded,
Where, as Zanga, I trod on Alonzo o'erthrown.

This, of course, is from *Hours of Idleness* in the trivial verse of that period. Zanga might be a character of Byron, or of Victor Hugo—an abstraction of the essence of Iago ; pure revenge personified.

In the *Night Thoughts* Young does not follow the popular taste as he had done in the Satires ; or he follows it in a more subtle manner. The *Night Thoughts* is an original poem in a blank verse which is not that of any other poet, not like the Miltonic imitators. Young, like Byron, after many experiments found a style of his own ; found also, like Byron, that the proper matter of his poetry was whatever came into his head to say.

These comparisons and resemblances are of doubtful profit. But whatever may be the correspondence and affinity between these poets, Young in his latest work, the *Conjectures on Original Composition*, in a letter addressed by the Rector of Welwyn to the author of *Sir Charles Grandison*, gave definite expression to a claim for freedom for poetry ; after all his compliances, all his experiments, he comes to this conclusion : that there has been too much compliance, too much imitation ; that the wide world lies open to the poets if they will only trust their own genius. Is it not something like Byron's escape from models and precedents ? At any rate, it was in 1759 (the wonderful year) a remarkable prophecy of a new age coming on, and a realm of poetry about which the prophet could say nothing, except that it would have a life of its own. Is it not rather like Goethe's description of Byron, neither antique nor romantic, but simply the poet of the present day ?

XII

KEATS

I AM greatly honoured by an invitation to give a lecture on the poetry of Keats and find myself involved, rather pleasantly, in difficulties such as students know when subjects are imposed on them for essays. I had not previously wanted to say anything particular about Keats ; it is not easy to say anything new and true. The British Academy lately paid reverence to the memory of Keats, on February 23rd, with Mr. de Sélincourt for their orator ; Sir Sidney Colvin was there present, the biographer of Keats giving his countenance to the latest and most careful editor of Keats's poetry. Think of all the essays on Keats written by poets and critics, Matthew Arnold, Swinburne, Robert Bridges, Bradley, Mackail, John Bailey, Sir Sidney Colvin and Mr. de Sélincourt. Now turn the pages of the recent Memorial Volume where some of those reapers appear again as gleaners : Mr. Bradley writing on Keats and " Philosophy," Mr. Mackail on the English landscapes in *Endymion*, Sir Sidney Colvin on the *Ode to a Nightingale*, with others like Mr. Herford, who writes on the Mountains—and I ask you and myself what there is left to do or say.

Very willingly would I evade the proper subject, the impossible task, and instead of that go wandering with

Keats and Brown on Skiddaw or along the coast of
Galloway and Carrick, until they came to a wan water,
I think they call it Clyde, and my fellow-townsman,
not sober, expressed his not unreasonable opinion of
Keats waving his arms in front of him on the Glasgow
street and saying, " Well, I have seen all foreigners,
bu-u-ut I never saw the like o' you "—and so on by
Loch Lomond and Glencoe to Inveraray, to Oban,
Kerrara, Mull, Iona, Staffa : thus the mind goes wandering when it ought to be at work. It is not indeed all
irrelevant waste of time to remember Keats's walking
tour, a piece of very hard travelling, as hard though
not as far as the journey of Jones and Wordsworth
twenty-eight years earlier from Calais southward across
the Alps. Wordsworth and Keats were regarded as
soft fellows by literary men of their time who never
did anything like those pilgrimages. To think of
Keats walking through the rough country of the Isle
of Mull, not easier going than Iceland, is enough
to make an answer if that were necessary to the
villainous noise of *Blackwood* over the Cockney School
of Poetry.

Criticism, being analytical discourse, is naturally
subject to the common danger of language, the misleading qualities of words, such as Bacon, Hobbes and
Locke and other philosophers have indicated. Those
difficulties are very evident in the criticism of Keats,
and particularly where Keats's saying about Beauty and
Truth has been taken as a challenge to moralists and
an occasion for debate about the ethics of art. I cannot
help venturing on this ground, for Keats has often been
mistaken both by opponents and defenders, and thought
to be " on the other side of Good and Evil " when really
like all true poets he is on the other side of conventional

W.K.E.   P

definitions and distinctions. " Poetry divorced from moral ideas is poetry divorced from life." This is Swinburne dealing with Matthew Arnold and Wordsworth : what does this amount to, and why should it be treated as something worth talking about ? Only, I should say, because the words " moral " and " morality," which are concerned with life and nothing else, have come to be so misused and so hackneyed that they seem to imply want of life, a negative attitude. This implication Swinburne rightly refuses ; moral ideas are summaries of the meaning of human life. But here comes the point of my quotation. I have not given you the whole sentence. Swinburne says this : " Poetry divorced from moral ideas is poetry divorced from life "—and adds a parenthesis : " Even John Keats would not deny this."

This seems to me a singular example of that danger of words and terms of which I have spoken, that Swinburne with his poetic sense and judgment, his lifelong concern not only with dramatic poetry but with the casuistry of innumerable novels, should say " even John Keats " and thus slip into the erroneous judgment which he himself has done so much to refute of Keats as a being entirely given over to the sort of poetical cookery and confectionery which Plato made the ground of his charge against poets.

Keats's letters show that he thought about life in a large, noble and original way. He had nothing like Shelley's philosophical education in Plato and Hume ; as Mr. Bradley remarks, he seems to condemn *Political Justice* without reading it. He had little training in the use of abstract language, in the familiar gambits and openings of philosophical discussion. But he discovers things for himself, his own principles of life ; and language is not wanting to express what he means. Thus for example he says what he thinks about logical debaters (to George Keats, September 24th, 1819) :

... Dilke is a man who cannot feel he has a personal identity unless he has made up his mind about everything. The only means of strengthening one's intellect is to make up one's mind about nothing—to let the mind be a thoroughfare for all thoughts, not a select party.... All the stubborn arguers you meet are of the same brood. They never begin upon a subject they have not preresolved on. They want to hammer their nail into you, and if you have the point, still they think you wrong. Dilke will never come at a truth as long as he lives, because he is always trying at it. He is a Godwin Methodist.

Two of his letters are by this time famous and even in some danger of too frequent reference and repetition : to Reynolds, May 3rd, 1818, on Wordsworth and *Tintern Abbey*, the Chamber of Maiden-Thought, the Burden of the Mystery ; there is much more in it, the *May Day Ode* ; and the Vale of Soul-making, in the long journal letter to his brother in America which contains *La Belle Dame sans Merci*.

I would say two things about those arguments in Keats's letters, and they both bear upon Keats's poetry. First, in the letter to Reynolds the sentences about Wordsworth and Milton show an amazing steadiness of judgment and mature freedom from prejudice : Keats was prejudiced in many ways, and he particularly did not like Puritanism, but in summing up Milton he lets nothing of this intrude ; he is a sane historian and sees Milton in relation to Milton's own time. Secondly, in all his speculations you feel that he is giving out his own life, that he has lived through what he expresses as thoughts, that his intellectual life is vision and hardly distinguishable from the vision of poetry :

> Beauty is truth, truth beauty ;—that is all
> Ye know on earth, and all ye need to know.

He could not help saying that—and of course it has been taken up and discussed and debated and mis-understood—it was not his fault. Only when you read his letters may you see what he really means. Truth for him is not what you get at by thinking about things. He does not think *about* the real world—he thinks *in* it —his thought is real life. Take for example the letter to Reynolds and the passage on *Tintern Abbey*—the stages of Wordsworth's life which he finds are his own stages, and consider his phrase :

We see not the balance of good and evil—we are in a mist—*we* are now in that state. We feel the " burden of the Mystery." To this point was Wordsworth come, as far as I can conceive, when he wrote *Tintern Abbey*, and it seems to me that his Genius is explorative of those dark Passages. Now if we live, and go on thinking, we too shall explore them.

We are now in that state : it is the language of a man who is living and thinking directly, telling how far he has come, not discoursing, as a superior person, about life. He sees Truth in the same way as he sees Beauty, through life and experience, and he finds them the same.

Shelley has a different way of thinking : trained in philosophy, a reader of Plato and Hume, a prose author of many arguments, capable of dealing philo-sophically, scientifically, in regular form, with moral and political questions.

The dialogue of Keats and Shelley, as one might call it, is one of the strangest things ; strangest of all,

their failure to meet oftener when both were travelling
the same way. They were acquainted through Leigh
Hunt ; the three poets met, and on one occasion in
February, 1818, wrote sonnets in competition on the
River Nile. But Keats and Shelley did not understand
one another ; Keats was shy, and afraid of Shelley's
influence on his own poetry : " I refused to visit Shelley,
that I might have my own unfettered scope," he wrote
to Bailey (October, 1817) when he had finished *Endymion* and was anxious and irritated through Leigh
Hunt's want of confidence in him and his adventure.

Shelley becomes more and more generous as time
goes on ; he did not indeed see all the beauty at once
of the volume of 1820 ; he praised at first only *Hyperion*.
But he had the book with him on the boat and was
reading it when the squall took them and he was
drowned. He wrote to Mrs. Leigh Hunt (November
11th, 1820) : " Where is Keats now ? I am anxiously
expecting him in Italy, when I shall take care to bestow
every possible attention on him. I consider his a most
valuable life, and I am deeply interested in his safety.
I intend to be the physician both of his body and his
soul ; to keep the one warm, and to teach the other
Greek and Spanish. I am aware, indeed, in part, that
I am nourishing a rival who will far surpass me ; and
this is an additional motive, and will be an added
pleasure."

This was some months after he had written to Keats
(July 27th, 1820) inviting him to stay at Pisa, and
after Keats's letter in answer (August 20th), hearty
enough and grateful, but showing no very sufficient
understanding of the *Cenci* and no great eagerness to
receive the promised gift of *Prometheus*. One of life's
ironies. It is in that letter that Keats writes the

often-quoted sentence : " You, I am sure, will forgive
me for sincerely remarking that you might curb your
magnanimity, and be more of an artist, and load every
rift of your subject with ore." And it is in acknowledgment of the *Cenci* that Keats writes this, the most
solid, the strongest of all Shelley's poems. The two
poets were working in different ways, and probably
Keats had not taken time to read the tragedy with
proper attention. He might have written in the same
sense to Milton complaining that *Paradise Regained*
was less splendid than *Paradise Lost*, or that *Samson
Agonistes* had no interludes like *Paradise Regained*, no
knights of Logres or of Lyonesse, no utmost Indian
isle Taprobane.

The two poets had been working in very different
ways and each was too near his own work to understand
the other. It is only after some interval that we see
how near they were in the high region of their fancies,
that we can explain what hindered and kept them
apart. Keats's poetical life was a continual progress,
breaking through and away from one achievement to
another till *Hyperion* is reached, and abandoned.
Shelley's progress is not less wonderful, but it is not
steady all through. When he leaves the *Revolt of Islam*
behind him and goes on to *Prometheus Unbound* it is
true that he gains in the same way as Keats did when
he came to *Hyperion* ; here you may say is progress,
the argument of the two poems is the same, the first
is confusion, the second clear and triumphant success.
But the *Cenci* seems to have no preparation, no antece-
dents—a miracle, a different thing entirely from all
that had gone before. And it has no successor, and
Epipsychidion is a fall from the height of tragedy.

The difference between Keats and Shelley in temper

of intellect is shown very curiously and significantly in
their views of Milton, and those different opinions of
theirs explain a good deal of the difference between
Hyperion and *Prometheus Unbound*, which were written
nearly about the same time.

Paradise Lost included all that Shelley most detested
and most admired. On the one hand for hatred the
jealous God who for him was sufficient proof of the
Necessity of Atheism; the tyrannical arbitrary creator
of a godless world : on the other hand for admiration
the character of Satan and all the poetry of the poem.
So Shelley proceeds and rewrites the argument of
Milton, as he conceives it, into Prometheus, the mind
of Man, and Asia, the spiritual life of the world, opposing and confounding the tyrant Jupiter. The value of
the poem is of course quite independent of the opinion
about *Paradise Lost* in the preface. Satan, the hero of
that magnificent fiction, as he calls it, is not faultless.
" Prometheus is, in my judgment, a more poetical
character than Satan, because, in addition to courage,
and majesty, and firm and patient opposition to omni-
potent force, he is susceptible of being described as
exempt from the taints of ambition, envy, revenge,
and a desire for personal aggrandisement, which, in
the Hero of *Paradise Lost*, interferes with the interest."

Keats does not read into Milton a meaning which
Milton would have rejected with horror. He takes
Milton as the man of Milton's own time. He comes to
the point in the letter to Reynolds from which I have
already quoted, immediately after his comment on
Wordsworth and *Tintern Abbey*. And it is a very
notable thing that this same deliberate historical
judgment, which really amounts to an interpretation
of the whole of history, should rise in the mind of Keats

when he is most deeply conscious of the burden of his own personal life. His reflection on his own experience is not selfish or egotistical. He is as much concerned with Wordsworth and with Milton as with himself.

To this point was Wordsworth come . . . when he wrote *Tintern Abbey*, and it seems to me that his Genius is explorative of those dark Passages. Now if we live and go on thinking we too shall explore them—He is a genius and superior to us, in so far as he can, more than we, make discoveries and shed a light in them—Here I must think Wordsworth is deeper than Milton, though I think it has depended more upon the general and gregarious advance of intellect, than individual greatness of mind—From the *Paradise Lost* and the other works of Milton, I hope it is not too presuming, even between ourselves, to say, that his Philosophy, human and divine, may be tolerably understood by one not much advanced in years. In his time, Englishmen were just emancipated from a great superstition, and Men had got hold of certain points and resting-places in reasoning which were too newly born to be doubted, and too much opposed by the Mass of Europe not to be thought ethereal and authentically divine. . . . He did not think into the human heart as Wordsworth has done—Yet Milton as a Philosopher had sure as great powers as Wordsworth—What is then to be inferred? O many things—It proves there is really a grand march of intellect; It proves that a mighty providence subdues the mightiest Minds to the service of the time being, whether it be in human Knowledge or Religion.

Is it not clear from this that Keats had a large, sane, comprehensive mind? Do we not see here too how his reading of Milton gives him the motive of *Hyperion*, just as Shelley's reading of Milton helps him to *Prometheus Unbound*? Keats in talking about exploration of the dark passages has already explored and come through, has made his way from the meaning of *Endymion* to the meaning of *Hyperion*. The purport

of his sentences on *Tintern Abbey* is that he and his
friend are not yet old enough, that Wordsworth must
go ahead and guide them. Yet before the end of the
letter he shows that his thought is mature ; that he
himself has won a new " resting-place and seeming sure
point of reasoning," and this is nothing less than the
argument of *Hyperion*, which was to be, though Keats
does not explicitly say so, for the nineteenth century
such an heroic poem as *Paradise Lost* had been for the
seventeenth. Shelley on the suggestion of Milton
wrote *Prometheus Unbound* with the like ambition.
Prometheus and *Hyperion* are each intended by the
author for a prophetic book, to include the whole
meaning of the universe. Keats's reading of the riddle
is given in prose in this letter ; the argument is the
same as in the speech of Oceanus in *Hyperion* :

> We fall by course of Nature's law, not force
> Of thunder, or of Jove. Great Saturn, thou
> Hast sifted well the atom-universe ;
> But for this reason, that thou art the King,
> And only blind from sheer supremacy,
> One avenue was shaded from thine eyes,
> Through which I wander'd to eternal truth.
> And first, as thou wast not the first of powers,
> So art thou not the last ; it cannot be :
> Thou art not the beginning nor the end.
> From chaos and parental darkness came
> Light, the first fruits of that intestine broil,
> That sullen ferment, which for wondrous ends
> Was ripening in itself. The ripe hour came,
> And with it light, and light, engendering
> Upon its own producer, forthwith touch'd
> The whole enormous matter into life.
> Upon that very hour, our parentage,
> The Heavens and the Earth, were manifest :
> Then thou first born, and we the giant race,
> Found ourselves ruling new and beauteous realms.

Now comes the pain of truth, to whom 'tis pain ;
O folly ! for to bear all naked truths,
And to envisage circumstance, all calm,
That is the top of sovereignty.   Mark well !
As Heaven and Earth are fairer, fairer far
Than Chaos and blank Darkness, though once chiefs ;
And as we show beyond that Heaven and Earth
In form and shape compact and beautiful,
In will, in action free, companionship,
And thousand other signs of purer life ;
So on our heels a fresh perfection treads,
A power more strong in beauty, born of us
And fated to excel us, as we pass
In glory that old Darkness : nor are we
Thereby more conquer'd, than by us the rule
Of shapeless Chaos.   Say, doth the dull soil
Quarrel with the proud forests it hath fed,
And feedeth still, more comely than itself ?
Can it deny the chiefdom of green groves ?
Or shall the tree be envious of the dove
Because it cooeth, and hath snowy wings
To wander wherewithal and find its joys ?
We are such forest-trees, and our fair boughs
Have bred forth, not pale solitary doves,
But eagles golden-feather'd, who do tower
Above us in their beauty, and must reign
In right thereof ; for 'tis the eternal law
That first in beauty should be first in might :
Yea, by that law, another race may drive
Our conquerors to mourn as we do now.
Have ye beheld the young God of the Seas,
My dispossessor ?   Have ye seen his face ?
Have ye beheld his chariot, foam'd along
By noble winged creatures he hath made ?
I saw him on the calmed waters scud,
With such a glow of beauty in his eyes,
That it enforc'd me to bid sad farewell
To all my empire : farewell sad I took,
And hither came, to see how dolorous fate
Had wrought upon ye ; and how I might best
Give consolation in this woe extreme.
Receive the truth, and let it be your balm.

Much has been made of the allegory in *Endymion* ; here in *Hyperion* the allegory is almost too clearly explained. Yet neither for the one poem nor the other is allegory more than a makeshift word. In allegory properly speaking there is a separate existence for the reality intended and for the symbol, emblem, picture. In poetical work like *Endymion* or *Hyperion* there is no such division. Endymion *is* the true lover ; the older and the younger gods in *Hyperion* do not merely represent but *are* the different orders through whose succession the life of the world is carried on.

Endymion, though Keats was not satisfied with it and wished to forget it and go on to something new, is a finished poem and has its own place and rank unmistakably. Mr. Mackail's account of his own experience with regard to *Endymion* will be found true I think by many readers. When you read it first you think you have come upon all the poetry in the world ; you are carried away. Then you find the defects and excesses in it, which I will not stop now to describe. Then perhaps long after you take it up again to find that it is what Keats wanted it to be. " Do not the Lovers of Poetry like to have a little Region to wander in, where they may pick and choose, and in which the images are so numerous that many are forgotten and found new in a second Reading : which may be food for a week's stroll in the summer ? " *Endymion*, with its revival of the old English heroic couplet, its invention of new melody, has made for itself a place where it need not fear, though it cannot refute, all the censures that have fallen on it. It is not probably now the most favourite poem of anyone ; but it has come through the worst ; and it contains the *Hymn to Pan* which is in *Endymion* what the sonnet on

Fair youth, beneath the trees, thou canst not leave
  Thy song, nor ever can those trees be bare ;
    Bold lover, never, never canst thou kiss,
Though winning near the goal—yet, do not grieve ;
    She cannot fade, though thou hast not thy bliss,
  For ever wilt thou love, and she be fair !

Ah, happy, happy boughs ! that cannot shed
  Your leaves, nor ever bid the Spring adieu ;
And, happy melodist, unwearied,
  For ever piping songs for ever new ;
More happy love ! more happy, happy love !
  For ever warm and still to be enjoyed,
    For ever panting, and for ever young ;
All breathing human passion far above,
  That leaves a heart high-sorrowful and cloy'd,
    A burning forehead, and a parching tongue.

Who are these coming to the sacrifice ?
  To what green altar, O mysterious priest,
Lead'st thou that heifer lowing at the skies,
  And all her silken flanks with garlands drest ?
What little town by river or sea-shore,
  Or mountain-built with peaceful citadel,
    Is emptied of its folk, this pious morn ?
And, little town, thy streets for evermore
  Will silent be ; and not a soul to tell
    Why thou art desolate, can e'er return.

O Attic shape ! Fair attitude ! with brede
  Of marble men and maidens overwrought,
With forest branches and the trodden weed ;
  Thou, silent form, dost tease us out of thought
As doth eternity : Cold Pastoral !
  When old age shall this generation waste,
    Thou shalt remain, in midst of other woe
  Than ours, a friend to man, to whom thou say'st,
" Beauty is truth, truth beauty,"—that is all
  Ye know on earth, and all ye need to know.

Is there any difficulty about the meaning of this ?
Perhaps there is. At any rate we may imagine some
not incurably dull reader thinking it too fanciful and

conceited. " For ever shalt thou love and she be fair "
—is not this like the romantic conceit of Hans Andersen
putting life into the Dresden Shepherdess on the
mantelpiece ? No : it is not to be misunderstood as a
pathetic fallacy. The meaning is, the eternal world of
Art, including Poetry, is a living world :

> What little town by river or sea-shore,
> Or mountain-built with peaceful citadel,
> Is emptied of its folk this pious morn ?

That is life through poetic vision, and the poet means
you to see the same life in the other art of the Urn :
the art of the marble as you look into it turns to the
other art of poetical words and thoughts, and you
enter into it and are made free of it.

Hyperion, though a fragment and followed by another
fragmentary attempt at a new beginning, is for all that
the greatest of all Keats's poems. We return to it not
as to " a little Region to wander in, to pick and choose,"
but in surrender to the spirit of an heroic poem, to the
majesty that made Byron repent of his jeering, that
drew the generous-hearted wonder of Shelley.

In one sense *Hyperion* is a failure : it is a fragment.
Keats found that it was not going as he wanted it : it
is printed as a fragment : and before it was printed he
had gone back and made a new beginning with a
different plan. This is the second *Hyperion*, printed
first by Lord Houghton in his life of Keats and taken
by him as a first version of the poem. So it is taken
also by Swinburne in his essay on Keats ; but it is not
so. It is a rethinking of the poem. Why did Keats
try back like this ? What did he gain by the new
opening, the dream in which the dreamer is led by the
prophetess, the interpreter, Moneta, who is Mnemosyne,

who is the memory of the world, to see the story of
Saturn acted before his eyes ? What is the advantage
of this complication, this indirect way of presenting the
story ?

Keats had to try back because he could not end the
original *Hyperion* in the same style as he had begun.
He could not go further, because the story of the two
dynasties required more beauty for the Olympians than
even Keats could give. How could he do more when
he had put all his strength into the picture and story
of Saturn and his companions ? He stops at the point
where Apollo, the true god and hero of the new Olym-
pian age, is inspired with new life by Mnemosyne. To
go further required not less than the glory of Apollo
himself. Apollo with such resources of language as
Keats had would have seemed not much more than
equal to Hyperion. Keats had put an impossible task
on himself, to bring the very light of the sun into his
picture. There was only one way out of it : through
reflection. So he adopts the frame of the vision with
its interpreter. He dreams, and Moneta is to him
what Africanus is in the *Dream of Scipio*, and Dame
Philosophy in Boethius, and Virgil in the *Divine
Comedy*. What cannot be given directly might be
given by way of explanation and interpretation.
Moneta, if the poem had been continued, would have
interpreted the meaning of the new life of Apollo.

But this second *Hyperion* also was abandoned, and
we know now, since the publication of the Keats
Memorial Volume, that it was this second attempt of
which Keats was speaking when he says he has given
up *Hyperion* because there were too many Miltonic
inversions in it. His alleged motive does not seem to
explain either the one or the other fragmentary ending,

but if you do not press the term " inversions " I think you may understand that the explanation fits the second case much better than the first. It does not do for the first case at all well, and there is a sufficient explanation for the first in what I have said. The life of Apollo was more than Keats could render.

But with regard to the second fragment, the *Vision*, it is obviously true that there was an incongruity and incoherence between the speeches of Moneta and the epic of Saturn. Keats had to work the epic of Saturn into a frame of deep meditative poetry, and found it impossible. He uses the term " Miltonic inversions " because the style of his epic seems somehow forced and artificial when contrasted abruptly with the new passages of poetical instruction. There may have been something else that he does not say : the thoughts of Moneta mean a very intense ordeal of spirit. Keats had gone very far in his exploration of the dark passages, and in this deepening study of human life he was passing away from mythology : the story of Saturn, the speech of Oceanus, had no longer their old value for him ; he was going further, where there was possibly not much more for him to do within the limits of art. Had he come to the end of all his poetry ?

Here it may be of interest to remember that Keats, though you would hardly expect it, was a great admirer of Wordsworth's *Excursion*, which shows that he was not afraid of reflective poetry. Is there not some resemblance between Wordsworth at the stage of *The Excursion* and Keats at the *Vision of Hyperion* ? *The Excursion*, or one may say the whole intended poem of *The Recluse*, was to be a philosophical rendering of all the poetry in Wordsworth's mind. If Keats made a mistake in his philosophical second version of

Hyperion, was it not the same mistake as Wordsworth made when he thought he could gather up with heightened value in a philosophical poem the poetical ideas of all his earlier poems ? And is not *The Recluse* left a fragment for the same reason as the *Vision of Hyperion*, because the earlier poetry hindered it ?

It is strange to think of Keats disabled as a poet by too deep thinking. But that there was deep thinking there, in the second *Hyperion*, will be denied by no one.

In a sense Keats had come to the end of his course before his mortal sickness began to weaken him. There is something rather painful in the failure of his *Vision* : was there truly no way through ? The answer is that we must not make too much of logical progress in the lives of poets or other artists. Keats, with all his deep thinking, had not forgotten his own advice to let the mind be a thoroughfare for all thoughts. Thoughts and melodies came to him with no preparation. *La Belle Dame sans Merci*—where did that song come from ? Out of the air, as we say ; and it is the plainest truth about poetry that much of it is made through floating echoes and bodiless forms. Keats's ballad of the Fairy Queen and her deadly love is one that touches a world of real beliefs ranging from the North Cape to the South Sea Islands. And with nothing in Keats's reading or hearing to suggest it, his ballad tune agreed in cadence with an old Danish measure particularly associated with the fate of lovers. Few things are nearer the tone of Keats's ballad than the Icelandic song of the death of Tristram and Iseult. I mention this not as a curiosity of literature, but to show that the Muse or Mnemosyne her mother has not lost the gift of inspiration. For that seems to be, after all, the right word for the miracles of poetry.

XIII

HAZLITT

HAZLITT had no special liking for the Scotch : why should he ? But no one ever read the *Waverley Novels* with more thorough enjoyment, or felt more truly the power of the poetry of Burns. The English Association in Glasgow might find a local reason for attending to him in the fact that his father was a Glasgow student in the time of Adam Smith. Glasgow College, as Lord Bryce reminded us lately at a dinner of the Glasgow University Club in London, was long the favourite University of Nonconformist students from England and Wales—a connection that lasted even after Thomas Campbell founded London University on our model, free from tests ; even after the foundation of the University College of Wales. William Hazlitt, the elder, a Presbyterian Unitarian minister, with his Glasgow education, gave his son, we may believe, a different bent from that of most English literary men, his contemporaries.

Hazlitt has suffered in an odd particular instance from his acquaintance with Scottish dialect. Late in his life he wrote a *Chapter on Editors*, published 1830, the year of his death, in the *New Monthly Magazine*, never reprinted by himself, but by his son included in *Sketches and Essays*, 1839. In the *Magazine* and his son's collection, and in every edition since, you may read the opening sentence, " Editors are a sort of tittle tattle, difficult to deal with, dangerous to discuss." Even the edition of Mr. A. R. Waller and Mr. Glover, for which Henley wrote the introductory essay, prints it so, only adding in a note the cautious opinion that Hazlitt probably wrote " kittle cattle." " Kittle cattle " is what he wrote, and " tittle tattle " is what English readers have been content to read, and English editors to pass upon the confiding public. English editors would have done better if they had been " kittle," and less like dumb driven cattle. We have not R. L. Stevenson's judgment on them. He spent much time on a life of Hazlitt which came to nothing. There is a legend, says his biographer, Sir Graham Balfour, that he offered to write on Hazlitt for a biographical series, and was told that neither he nor his subject was of sufficient importance. No details are given, but we may say that if the story has any foundation the editor of the series was on that occasion not sensibly responsive to stimulus (*i.e.* " kittle ").

We know from various passages what Stevenson thought of Hazlitt : we wish we knew more. There is provokingly little in the published letters. He tried to get something out of Mr. Pegfurth Bannatyne : " Hazlitt—he couldnae take his drink—a queer, queer fellow ! " he added. We can guess how the unwritten Life would have amplified on this theme. We know how much of Stevenson is amplification and reconsideration of Hazlitt *On Going a Journey*. For Hazlitt was one who, like Stevenson, and Swift in Leslie

Stephen's phrase, shared the passion of the wise and good for walking.

I chose my title and text, when your President invited me here, without much thinking. I had nothing ready written, and I have done little study since. My motive was partly laziness. Anyhow, I thought, if I fail to make out any story of my own, I can always fall back on Hazlitt himself, and save myself by reading quotations. It was Hazlitt's own way in lecturing. On Burns, he tells his audience that he will give them the beginning of *Tam o' Shanter*—but he is not sure that he will know where to stop. And the whole of *Tam o' Shanter* is there, in his lecture. The example requires caution, and is not to be followed indiscriminately. I have tried to put together some notes, preliminary, before I come to the *Indian Jugglers* and *My First Acquaintance with Poets*.

Hazlitt was a philosopher and a painter before he wrote the essays which gave him his rank among English men of letters. As a young man—very young —he thought hard and independently on problems of moral philosophy ; he seems never to have dealt with metaphysics. I have never read his *Principles of Human Action, an Argument in favour of the Natural Disinterestedness of the Human Mind*, first sketched when he was 18, published in 1805. But he returns frequently to this subject in his essays, and it makes a difference lasting through all his life. If ever you find Hazlitt dry or abstract in his moralising you may be sure at least that his reasoning is sincere and thoroughly founded on old and long-continued meditation. His moralisings are not casual suggestions or mere talk, and the ascetic discipline he chose for himself in his youth is recognisable in the seemingly

capricious and random flings of his freer style, not
less than in his deliberate judgment on *Hamlet*, *Othello*,
and *King Lear*.

Likewise his training as a painter gives him an
advantage, or, indeed, puts him in a different class,
over the literary critics who venture at analogies
between poetry and painting. *Gusto*, a favourite term
with Hazlitt, is originally a term of art criticism, and
he uses it with more intimate sense of its value, we feel,
than those literary men who borrowed it from the schools
of painting. His painting terms may not mean for us
what they meant for him, who knew the pleasures and
the difficulties of painting, but it is something for us to
feel that the writer is speaking what he knows when he
says, *e.g.* about Burke, " his execution, like that of all
good prose, savours of the texture of what he describes,
and his pen slides or drags over the ground of his subject
like the painter's pencil." " Texture, ground, slide or
drag," any literary man can " have them all ready,"
like the people in Shakespeare who kept note-books for
effective words ; but Hazlitt uses them because he
knows as a painter from experience what they really
mean ; and we, reading, feel that we are listening to no
rhetorical pretender.

As a critic Hazlitt is open to many objections. He
saw no good in Shelley :

No one (that I know of) is the happier, better or wiser
for reading Mr. Shelley's *Prometheus Unbound*. One thing
is that nobody reads it. And the reason for one or both is
the same, that he is not a poet, but a sophist, or theorist,
a controversial writer in verse. He gives us, for representa-
tions of things, rhapsodies of words. He does not lend the
colours of imagination and the ornaments of style to the
objects of nature, but paints, flimsy allegorical pictures on
gauze, on the cobwebs of his own brain, " Gorgons and

Hydras, and Chimeras dire." He assumes certain doubtful speculative notions and proceeds to prove their truth by describing them in detail as matters of fact. This mixture of fanatic zeal with poetical licentiousness is not quite the thing. . . . The poet describes vividly and individually, so that any general results from what he writes must be from the aggregate of well-founded particulars : to embody an abstract theory, as if it were a given part of actual nature, is an impertinence and indecorum. (*On People of Sense.*)

Here, even if Hazlitt be wrong, as many of us think he is about *Prometheus Bound*, still it would 'be a mistake not to see what he means when he talks of " the aggregate of well-founded particulars "—he means imagination as distinct from allegory.

On the other hand, in a quite opposite way, he is surely wrong about Crabbe, when he takes his work for nothing but an aggregate of ill-founded and perversely chosen particulars ; as if there were nothing in Crabbe but crude realities. He quotes as an example the tidal river in *Peter Grimes*, where, not to speak of the admirable, lively effect of the passage as " mere description," he leaves out of account altogether the dramatic value of the scene, its place in the soul of Peter, its accompaniment to Peter's remorse and Nemesis. Even in his unstinted praise of the *Waverley Novels* there is this drawback, that he makes the author too much a mere transcriber of Nature—as if Scott's memory had nothing to do but remember. His painting experience might have taught him better— to find the shaping touch of imagination, even in the right suggestion of mere memory at the right time, in the idiom of Cuddie Headrigg, " Mither, will you renunce the covenant o' works ? " or Dandie Dinmont, " It's a' ane to Dandie."

For a diversion here, let me read Hazlitt's account of his father's portrait. Was there nothing but mere transcription, copying of reality, in this portrait?

One of my first attempts was a picture of my father, who was then in a green old age, with strong-marked features, and scarred with the small-pox. I drew it out with a broad light crossing the face, looking down, with spectacles on, reading. The book was *Shaftesbury's Characteristics*, in a fine old binding with Gribelin's etchings. My father would as lieve it had been any other book ; but for him to read was to be content, was " riches fineless." The sketch promised well ; and I set to work to finish it, determined to spare no time nor pains. My father was willing to sit as long as I pleased ; for there is a natural desire in the mind of man to sit for one's picture, to be the object of continued attention, to have one's likeness multiplied ; and besides his satisfaction in the picture, he had some pride in the artist, though he would rather I should have written a sermon than painted like Rembrandt or like Raphael. Those winter days, with the gleams of sunshine coming through the chapel windows, and cheered by the notes of the robin-redbreast in our garden (that " ever in the haunch of winter sings ")—as my afternoon's work drew to a close—were among the happiest of my life. When I gave the effect I intended to any part of the picture for which I had prepared my colours ; when I imitated the roughness of the skin by a lucky stroke of the pencil ; when I hit the clear pearly tone of a vein ; when I gave the ruddy complexion of health, the blood circulating under the broad shadows of one side of the face, I thought my fortune made ; or rather it was already more than made, in my fancying that I might one day be able to say with Correggio, " I also am a painter ! " It was an idle thought, a boy's conceit ; but it did not make me the less happy at the time. (*On the Pleasure of Painting.*)

Is there nothing but mere recollection in the story of it ? Indeed, there is much : there is the whole soul of the writer, and his *gusto* in writing : and nothing less than this makes us read Hazlitt. What he has to tell is his own life. " I have had a happy life," he said at the end of it, and surprised many who knew how unhappy in various respects it had been. But his essays prove that he was right ; even his lamentations prove it, even the letter to Gifford, " Sir, you have an ugly trick of saying what is not true about any one you do not like ; and it will be the object of this letter to cure you of it." Even in the outburst of rage against the reformers turned Tories :

Twice has the iron entered my soul. Twice have the dastard, vaunting, venal crew gone over it ; once as they went forth conquering and to conquer, with reason by their side, glittering like a faulchion, trampling on prejudices and marching fearlessly on in the work of regeneration ; once again, when they returned with retrograde steps, like Cacus's oxen dragged backward by the heels, to the den of Legitimacy, " rout on rout, confusion worse confounded," with places and pensions and the *Quarterly Review* dangling from their pockets, and shouting "Deliverance for mankind," for " the worst, the second fall of man." Yet I have endured all this marching and countermarching of poets, philosophers, and politicians over my head, "like the camomoil that thrives, the more 'tis trod upon." By Heavens, I think I'll endure it no longer ! (*On Paradox and Common-Place.*)

Where his shrewd wit tells most it is always with this sort of *gusto* :

Charles Fox is not to be blamed for having written an indifferent history of James II., but for having written a history at all. It was not his business to write a history— *his business was not to have made any more Coalitions !* (*On the Difference between Writing and Speaking.*)

On Cavanagh, the fives player :

He was a fine, sensible, manly player, who did what he could, but that was more than any else could even affect to do. His blows were not undecided and ineffectual—lumbering like Mr. Wordsworth's epic poetry, not wavering like Mr. Coleridge's lyric prose, nor short of the mark like Mr. Brougham's speeches, nor wide of it like Mr. Canning's wit, nor foul like the *Quarterly*, not *let* balls like the *Edinburgh Review*.

He could not have shown himself in any ground in England but he would have been immediately surrounded with inquisitive gazers, trying to find out in what part of his frame his unrivalled skill lay, as politicians wonder to see the balance of Europe suspended in Lord Castlereagh's face, and admire the trophies of the British Navy lurking under Mr. Croker's hanging brow. Now Cavanagh was as good-looking a man as the Noble Lord, and much better looking than the Right Hon. Secretary. He had a clear, open countenance, and did not look sideways or down, like Mr. Murray the bookseller. (*The Indian Jugglers*.)

Hazlitt, like Goldsmith, Charles Lamb, and Stevenson, lives very much in the memories of his youth ; more intensely and continuously than any one of them. His pleasure in writing of favourite authors, Burke or Rousseau, is in great part the pleasure of remembering what he was when he first read them, though he can defend and explain his authors, Burke, *e.g.*, on impersonal grounds. His generous admiration for Bonaparte runs through all his early reminiscences and touches his father's portrait, and his story of the persons that Charles Lamb would wish to have seen :

Those days are over! An event, the name of which I wish never to mention, broke up our party, like a bombshell thrown into the room : and now we seldom meet,

Like angels' visits, short and far between.

There is no longer the same set of persons nor associations. (*On the Conversation of Authors: Lamb's Thursday evening parties*.)

The event is the defeat of Napoleon, and you will find the event repeated in different essays of Hazlitt, while the sun of Austerlitz represents the earlier glory of Hazlitt and his hero.

For the happiness of his early life, which was his later happiness also, Hazlitt goes back to the year 1798 : the year of *My First Acquaintance with Poets* :

It was on the 10th of April, 1798, that I sat down to a volume of the *New Eloise*, at the inn at Llangollen, over a bottle of sherry and a cold chicken. The letter I chose was that in which St. Preux describes his feelings as he first caught a glimpse from the heights of the Jura of the Pays de Vaud, which I had brought with me as a *bon bouche* to crown the evening with. It was my birthday, and I had for the first time come from a place in the neighbourhood to visit this delightful spot. The road to Llangollen turns off between Chirk and Wrexham ; and on passing a certain point, you come all at once upon the valley, which opens like an amphitheatre, broad, barren hills rising in majestic state on either side, with " green upland swells that echo to the bleat of flocks " below, and the river Dee babbling over its stony bed in the midst of them. The valley at this time " glittered green with sunny showers," and a budding ash-tree dipped its tender branches in the chiding stream. How proud, how glad I was to walk along the high road that overlooks the delicious prospect, repeating the lines which I have just quoted from Mr. Coleridge's poems ! But besides the prospect which opened beneath my feet, another also opened to my inward sight, a heavenly vision, on which were written, in letters large as Hope could make them, these four words, LIBERTY, GENIUS, LOVE, VIRTUE ; which have since faded into the light of common day, or mock my idle gaze.

The beautiful is vanished, and returns not.

Still I would return some time or other to this enchanted spot ; but I would return to it alone. What other self could I find to share that influx of thoughts, of regret, and delight, the fragments of which I could hardly conjure up to myself, so much have they been broken and defaced. I could stand on some tall rock, and overlook the precipice of years that separates me from what I then was. I was at that time going shortly to visit the poet whom I have above named. Where is he now ? Not only I myself have changed ; the world, which was then new to me, has become old and incorrigible. Yet will I turn to thee in thought, O sylvan Dee, in joy, in youth and gladness as thou then wert : and thou shalt always be to me the river of Paradise, where I will drink of the waters of life freely ! (*On Going a Journey : Table Talk.*)

He was on his way to visit Coleridge : the 10th of April at Llangollen comes between Coleridge's winter visit to Wem and Shrewsbury as a Unitarian preacher, and Hazlitt's visit to Nether Stowey, where he walked and conversed with Coleridge and Wordsworth, the poets of *Lyrical Ballads*. Let me read the beginning of the essay (*My First Acquaintance with Poets*), even though, like Hazlitt with *Tam o' Shanter*, I may not know when to leave off :

My father was a Dissenting Minister at W——m in Shropshire ; and in the year 1798 (the figures that compose that date are to me like the "dreaded name of Demogorgon") Mr. Coleridge came to Shrewsbury, to succeed Mr. Rowe in the spiritual charge of a Unitarian Congregation there. He did not come till late on the Saturday afternoon before he was to preach ; and Mr. Rowe, who himself went down to the coach in a state of anxiety and expectation, to look for the arrival of his successor, could find no one at all answering the description but a round-faced man in a short black coat (like a shooting jacket) which hardly seemed to have been made for him, but who seemed to be talking at a great rate to his fellow-passengers. Mr. Rowe had scarce returned to give an account of his disappointment, when the round-faced man in black entered, and dissipated all doubts on the subject, by beginning to talk. He did not cease while he staid ; nor has he since that I know of. He held the good town of Shrewsbury in delightful suspense for three weeks that he remained there, " fluttering the proud Salopians like an eagle in a dove-cote " ; and the

Welch mountains that skirt the horizon with their tempes-
tuous confusion agree to have heard no such mystic sounds
since the days of

> High-born Hoel's harp or soft Llewelyn's lay !

As we passed along between W——m and Shrewsbury,
and I eyed their blue tops seen through the wintry branches,
or the red rustling leaves of the sturdy oak-trees by the
roadsides, a sound was in my ears of a Siren's song ; I was
stunned, startled with it, as from deep sleep ; but I had
no notion then that I should ever be able to express my
admiration to others in motley imagery or quaint allusion,
till the light of his genius shone into my soul, like the sun's
rays glittering in the puddles of the road. I was at that
time dumb, inarticulate, helpless, like a worm by the way-
side, crushed, bleeding, lifeless ; but now bursting from
the deadly bands that

> bound them,
> With Styx nine times round them,

my ideas float on winged words, and as they expand their
plumes, catch the golden light of other years. My soul
has indeed remained in its original bondage, dark obscure,
with longings infinite and unsatisfied ; my heart, shut up
in the prison-house of this rude clay, has never found, nor
will it ever find, a heart to speak to ; but that my understanding also did not remain dumb and brutish, or at
length found a language to express itself, I owe to Coleridge.
But this is not to my purpose.

Hazlitt is never grudging in his regard for the masters
who gave him freedom, Coleridge and Wordsworth.
He had seemed to himself to have no power of expression in words. Here is a passage, like many others :
speaking of Burke, he says :

If such is still my admiration of this man's misapplied
powers, what must it have been at a time when I myself
was in vain trying, year after year, to write a single Essay,
nay, a single page or sentence ; when I regarded the
wonders of his pen with the longing eyes of one who was
dumb, and a changeling ; and when to be able to convey

the slightest conception of my meaning to others in words
was the height of an almost hopeless ambition ! (*On
Reading Old Books : Plain Speaker.*)

Coleridge's talk gave him spirit and encouragement.
Lyrical Ballads, he says, gave him insight into the
mysteries of poetry. Both poets disappointed him
afterwards ; he resented Wordsworth's absorption in
his own poetry, not to speak of the change in his
political sentiments. But he never allowed his own
sense of poetry (or prose either) to be thwarted by
politics or personal considerations. One of the most
thrilling of all his utterances is a quotation, when after
some of his usual severities on Wordsworth, he breaks
out :

> Yet I'll remember thee, Glencairn,
> And all that thou hast done for me !
>   (*On Genius and Common Sense : Table Talk.*)

As for Coleridge, he was perpetually in Hazlitt's
mind, a grievance and a fascination from which he
could not escape. Hazlitt's malignity (or whatever
it is called), his shrewish carping, is like Swift's misanthropy (which Hazlitt understood)—the result of a
tragic contradiction, a torturing contrast between the
unseen Reality (*e.g.* the genius of Coleridge) and the
obvious phenomenal incompetence of genius when
required to work :

The man of perhaps the greatest ability now living is
the one who has not only done the least, but who is actually
incapable of ever doing anything worthy of him—unless he
had a hundred hands to write with, and a hundred mouths
to utter all that it hath entered into his heart to conceive,
and centuries before him to embody the endless volume of
his waking dreams. Cloud rolls over cloud ; one train of
thought suggests and is driven away by another ; theory

after theory is spun out of the bowels of his brain, not like the spider's web compact and round, a citadel and a snare, built for mischief and for use ; but like the gossamer, stretched out and entangled without end, clinging to every casual object, flitting in the idle air, and glittering only in the ray of fancy. No subject can come amiss to him, and he is alike attracted and alike indifferent to all—he is not tied down to any one in particular—but floats from one to another, his mind everywhere finding its level, and feeling no limit but that of thought—now soaring with its head above the stars, now treading with fairy feet among flowers, now winnowing the air with winged words—passing from Duns Scotus to Jacob Behmen, from the Kantean philosophy to a conundrum, and from the Apocalypse to an acrostic—taking in the whole range of poetry, painting, wit, history, metaphysics, criticism, and private scandal— every question giving birth to some new thought, and every thought "discoursed in eloquent music," that lives only in the ear of fools, or in the report of absent friends. Set him to write a book, and he belies all that has been ever said about him—

Ten thousand great ideas filled his mind,
But with the clouds they fled, and left no trace behind

(*On the Qualifications necessary for Success in Life : Plain Speaker.*)

A last quotation may be allowed here, Hazlitt's parody of Coleridge's talk—invented as a substitute for Hazlitt's regular piece of dramatic criticism— seemingly as true as the imaginary talk of Renan in the version of M. Maurice Barrès :

So we, for once, will invoke Mr. Coleridge's better genius, and thus we hear him talk, diverting our attention from the players and the play.

"The French, my dear Hazlitt," would he begin, "are not a people of imagination. They have so little, that you cannot persuade them to conceive it possible that they have none. They have no poetry, no such thing as genius, from the age of Louis XIV. It was that, their boasted Augustan age, which stamped them French, which put the seal upon their character, and from that time nothing has grown up original, or luxuriant, or spontaneous among them ; the whole has been cast in a mould, and that a bad one. . . . His (Racine's) tragedies are not poetry, are not passion, are not imagination : they are a parcel of set speeches, of epigrammatic conceits, of declamatory phrases, without any of the glow, and glancing rapidity, and principle of fusion in the mind of the poet, to agglomerate them into grandeur, or blend them into harmony. The principle of imagination resembles the emblem of the serpent, by which the ancients typified wisdom and the universe, with un-dulating folds for ever varying and for ever flowing into itself,—circular, and without beginning or end. The definite, the fixed, is death : the principle of life is the indefinite, the growing, the moving, the continuous. But everything in French poetry is cut up, into shreds and patches, little flowers of poetry, with tickets and labels to them, as when the daughters of Jason minced and hacked their old father into collops—we have the *disjecta membra poetae*—not the entire and living man. The spirit of genuine poetry should inform the whole work, should breathe through, and move, and agitate the complete mass, as the soul informs and moves the limbs of a man, or as the vital principle (whatever it be) permeates the veins of the loftiest trees, building up the trunk, and extending the branches to the sun and winds of heaven, and shooting out into fruit and flowers. This is the progress of nature and of genius. This is the true poetic faculty, or that which the Greeks literally call ποίησις. But a French play (I think it is Schlegel who somewhere makes the comparison, though I had myself, before I ever read Schlegel, made the same remark) is like a child's garden set with slips of branches and flowers, stuck in the ground, not growing in it. We may weave a gaudy garland in this manner, but it withers in an hour : while the products of genius and nature give out their odours to the gale, and spread their tints in the sun's eye, age after age—

> Outlast a thousand storms, a thousand winters,
> Free from the Sirian star and thunder stroke,

and flourish in immortal youth and beauty. Everything French is frittered into parts : everything is therefore dead and ineffective. French poetry is just like chopped logic ; nothing comes of it. There is no life of mind : neither the birth nor generation of knowledge. It is all patchwork, all sharp points and angles, all superficial. They receive and give out sensation too readily for it ever to amount to a sentiment. They cannot even dance, as you may see. There is, I am sure you will agree, no expression, no grace in their dancing. Littleness, point, is what damns them in all they do. With all their vivacity and animal spirits, they dance not like men and women under the impression of certain emotions, but like puppets ; they twirl round like *tourniquets*. Not to feel, and not to think, is all they know of this art or of any other. You might swear that a nation that danced in that manner would never produce a true poet or philosopher. They have it not in them. There is not the principle of cause and effect. They make a sudden turn because there is no reason for it : they stop short, or move fast, only because you expect something else. Their style of dancing is difficult ; would it were impossible.'' (By this time several persons in the pit turned round to listen to this uninterrupted discourse, and our eloquent friend went on, rather raising his voice with a *Paulo majora canamus*.) '' Look at that Mademoiselle Milanie with the ' foot of fire,' as she is called. You might contrive a pasteboard figure, with the help of strings or wires, to do all, and more than she does—to point the toe, to raise the leg, to jerk the body, to run like wild-fire. Antics are not grace : to dance is not to move against time. My dear Hazlitt, if you could have seen a dance by some Italian peasant-girls in the Campagna of Rome, as I have, I am sure your good taste and good sense would have approved it. They came forward slow and smiling, but as if their limbs were steeped in luxury, and every motion seemed an echo of the music, and the heavens looked on serener as they trod.'' (*London Magazine*, No. XII., December, 1820.)

If there is room at this time, a hundred years after, for a fresh study of the prose works of Coleridge, Hazlitt will claim a place in the record, a witness unexcelled by any in his evidence of Coleridge's power, more deeply than any other sensible of his failure. The story is worth remembering, if it were only to do justice to an English man of letters whose reputation has suffered, like himself when living, through casual freaks and faults which were really no more than the sparks and sputterings of an intense devotion, a fiery heart.

XIV

TENNYSON

An invitation to give this lecture before the University of Cambridge is an honour too great for any conventional words of acknowledgment ; but I may be permitted at the outset to offer my thanks to the University, and further to say that even if it had been possible to decline an invitation which comes with more than the force of a command, the name of Leslie Stephen would have been enough to drive away all craven scruples, and to put spirit, as he has done so often, into the hesitating wits and will.

No one standing in this place with a task so serious before him could ask for better auspices ; and I think it a fortunate thing that I am able to remember Leslie Stephen here to-day as in a sort of way his vassal and one of his company. I have sat by his side at College tables ; I heard him speak, in December, 1894, his noble commemoration of Stevenson, and although unhappily he had given up his occupation as Chief Guide before I was sworn in as one of the Sunday Tramps, yet my name is there in the list, and it will be a pleasure, I hope, to one or two others, as it is to myself, to find that one of the Sunday Tramps, though the latest and the least worthy, has been asked to give this lecture. But apart from these personal and private matters—which still I am bold to think are not irrelevant nor unworthy of this audience—the name of Stephen brings with it the thought of everything that is honest and sincere ; it gives the best encouragement that anyone could wish, though it does not make the task, in itself, less difficult.

In the Lives of the Poets, as of other men, we have all our favourite passages to which we turn by preference, and which we make into symbols or examples, standing for all the rest ; or which perhaps we remember for some trivial reason or unreason, because they touch on some associations of our own. Out of the Life of Tennyson I take one thing which is not altogether trifling, and which seems to me to be characteristic and memorable, though it is not part of the common tradition, the things that are generally repeated about the poet. It is the misunderstanding between himself and his friend Monckton Milnes over the poem which Tennyson refused at first to send to the album—*The Tribute*—which Milnes was editing.

Milnes was offended and wrote an angry letter. Tennyson's reply (given in the two biographies, Lord Houghton's and his own) brings out the character, temper and humour of a very remarkable man dealing with a very severe trial of his patience. His friend had lost his head, but kept his talent for language, and in some of his carefully chosen phrases (like " piscatory vanity ") had shown that he meant not only to quarrel but to wound. Tennyson's answer is a proof of the virtue of imagination in dealing with practical affairs. Milnes's sharpened phrases have their full effect, and Tennyson suffers the pain that was intended. Anger comes also, not mere resentment, but the passion that would have destroyed all vestiges of friendship. That can be made out from Tennyson's words: "I put down my pipe and stared at the fire for ten minutes till the stranger vanished up the chimney."

Milnes, the smaller man, had been only able to think of one thing; his friend in those ten minutes staring at the fire had taken in the case in all its bearings; had felt the injury, had understood the irritation of his friend, and been bitterly amused by his vanity and dumbfounded by his want of sense. Staring at the fire, he had seen all this as a poor wretched thing which *the Stranger*, the Accuser, was doing his worst to make into a lasting enmity. He stares the stranger out of countenance and up the chimney; the friendship remains unbroken, because Tennyson is magnanimous; and one need not require any more convincing proof of the largeness and generosity of his nature and his mind; of his intellectual virtue, if I may use the term freely and in no restricted or scholastic sense.

For many years past the Devil's Advocate has been busy, and it is impossible to ignore him. It is not on the ground of the biography but on the poems themselves that he must be met; nevertheless I take this passage from the biography to begin with, to show what sort of a man Tennyson might be in a problem and ordeal of personal conduct. The Lives of the Poets are often useful to correct false impressions; the Lives of Wordsworth and Keats do not prove that they were good poets, but they show that their adversaries were mistaken about them. Wordsworth among the Girondists, taking a share in the French Revolution, and Keats on his long walking-tour, travelling to the Ross of Mull, are very different from the tame soft creatures which some of their reviewers imagined

them to be. Tennyson's character was often misjudged
in a similar way ; the Life of Tennyson makes it
impossible to repeat the old false opinions.

The Devil's Advocate is always worth listening to,
and not always easy to refute. It may be true that
Homer could not draw the maps of a campaign nor the
plan of a country-house ; that Dante was too reckless
in his punishments and too careful about the spots in
the moon ; that Milton went wrong, if not as Bentley
thought yet in the way Pope has described him. It is
easy to collect instances of this kind, and of a much
severer kind, about these and other great poets. But
the plain man (though his authority would hardly be
allowed either by Milton or Tennyson) is generally
right, even if he may not be right in all particulars as
to this sort of argument. The plain man feels simply
that the good things are not touched ; that even
though the faults and errors may detract from one's
estimate of the poet's work as a whole, they do not
spoil the good things. Let us suppose that the *Lady
of Shalott* and the *Lotos Eaters* and *Tithonus* are
absolutely good ; then they are not less good because
other less good things were written by the author of
them. The plain man looks to those peaks and summits
of poetry and finds them beyond all comparison with
the lower levels where the historical critic is working
out his survey. The critic will go wrong unless he
recognises this other point of view and the fact that a
good poem has a value of its own which nothing can
spoil, as nothing in the world can take the place of it.
The essence of a poem is that it should be remembered
for what it is, not that it should be catalogued in an
historical series in relation with what it is not. This
is not meant to depreciate criticism or the history of

literature, but to show their necessary limitations; which perhaps are sufficiently obvious.

It is not enough for a poem that it should be what is called " touching "; one remembers Goethe's deadly saying about the hearts of sensibility: " any bungler can touch them." But it remains true that if a poem is not wonderful it is nothing; here as in philosophy wonder is the beginning of wisdom, and the end too, when the wonder of novelty has turned into the deeper wonder at the well-known, the familiar, the unfathomable beauty.

Where did the new music of Tennyson come from? It is the sort of question that the critic is always asking, and it is not as foolish as it looks. It is true that a good poem is a singular and miraculous thing; it is also true that most good poems have ancestors. Here we come to the other side of the matter. The plain man is justified in saying, as against the critic, that the *Lady of Shalott* and the *Lotos Eaters* are not spoilt by anything the critic may have to say about other things. But he is not justified if he says that the critic has no business to meddle with the ancestry of these poems; that it is irrelevant to look for the old story of Shalott, and impertinent to compare the *Lotos Eaters* with *The Castle of Indolence*. Here the weakness of the plain man is apt to show itself. He thinks too idolatrously of what he worships; he thinks that the more you know about the poem the less you will admire it. It may be so sometimes, but the poem that is damaged in this way is not worth troubling about. The Commentator of course needs to be carefully watched. He must not here debate the question whether Astolat is Guildford, as Malory says, or Dumbarton, as another author has surmised. But he will gain something if he follows out Mr. Palgrave's note to the *Golden Treasury* and finds the old Italian story in the *Cento novelle antiche*, which was read by Tennyson and from which he took the matter of his poem. This original story is not the same thing as Malory. It is taken from the same source as Malory, " the French book " of *Lancelot*. But it has quite a different effect, and the effect is nearly related to the English poem. The Italian story, like the English poem, is detached from its context ; it is not like the Idyll of *Elaine*, part of a large and complicated history. The Italian story has no ties and dependencies ; it is a thing by itself, in the old clear language, one of the beautiful small things of medieval art. It does not trouble itself with the story of the maid of Astolat as it is given in detail in the French book and in Malory ; it takes hardly anything from the French book but the death of the Lady of Shalott ; the voyage in the boat without a steersman ; and the marvel in the Court of King Arthur at Camelot.

Great part of the beauty of Tennyson's poem comes from the mystery of its story. It is a lyrical romance, and its setting is in a visionary land ; there is no burden of historical substance in it as there is in the *Idylls of the King*. This strange isolation of the story, making its own world, is part of the old Italian *novella* ; and it is this quality which makes the greatest distinction in the new order of romantic poetry to which Tennyson's poem belongs. It is this which is found in *La Belle Dame sans Merci* and in the most magical poems of William Morris's first volume. It makes these poems, and *The Lady of Shalott* along with them, very different from the older romantic school which went often to the Middle Ages for material, but (generally speaking) was rather dull regarding the medieval form. Neither *La Belle Dame sans Merci* nor *The Lady of Shalott* nor *Golden Wings* is a close imitation of medieval art ; but they all have that strange homeless quality which is found in some of the finest (not the most ambitious) medieval poems.

The verse of a poet shows his poetical ancestry better than anything else. Everywhere in the older poets one comes on the elements of Tennyson's verse. He knew all the different modes, from the least regular to the most exact. Coleridge's complaint (as recorded in his *Table Talk*, April 24, 1833) that Mr. Tennyson " has begun to write verses without very well understanding what metre is " is partly explained by the many poems in irregular verse in the early volumes. But these volumes show also—and show in perfection— Tennyson's command of the familiar forms and his skill in using them. In the verse of *Mariana* there is no technical innovation ; only the common elementary forms are employed in a new way :

> With blackest moss the flower-plots
>   Were thickly crusted, one and all :
> The rusted nails fell from the knots
>   That held the peach to the garden-wall.
> The broken sheds looked sad and strange ;
>   Unlifted was the clinking latch ;
>   Weeded and worn the ancient thatch
> Upon the lonely moated grange.

For one thing, the short line is here made weighty and solemn, nearly the equal of the heroic line. This in itself is no new effect, but it is used here in a new pattern ; and the change from the alternate rhymes of the first quatrain to the *In Memoriam* stanza in the second is poetical invention.

There are two great families of verse (not two only) in modern poetry, which can be traced back to the beginnings of modern poetry in Provence about the year 1100. One is used for long-sustained passages, and the heroic line is its chief instrument, as in the *Faerie Queene* or in *Paradise Lost*: the other has a shorter length of wave and rings more clearly; its base is generally the octosyllable. The poets may sometimes be divided into the one class or the other; thus Spenser, with the great Italian poets, belongs almost entirely to the first order; Burns, with Villon, to the second. Tennyson is of both parties; he uses the fuller measure, the larger period, in *The Lotos Eaters*, not to speak of his blank verse; but *In Memoriam* is in the shorter line, and from the first, from the "Chorus in an unpublished drama written early," he used the shorter line in its full strength:

> Each sun which from the centre flings
> Grand music and redundant fire,
> The burning belts, the mighty rings,
> The murmurous planets' rolling choir.

Gray had the same equal skill in both kinds. The Pindaric odes belong to the first; while for the second we may quote *The Long Story*:

> Full oft within the spacious walls,
> When he had fifty winters o'er him,
> My grave Lord-Keeper led the brawls;
> The seals and maces danc'd before him.

Which might easily be taken for Tennyson's own.

Burns's verse was imitated by Tennyson, as it had been by Praed, and it is possible to find in Burns some lines that agree, not only in metre, but in mode of speech, in poetic energy, in resonant phrase, with the

manner of Tennyson. I mean particularly the motto
of *The Holy Fair* (" Hypocrisy *à la mode* ") :

> A robe of seeming truth and trust
>   Hid crafty observation,
> And secret hung with poison'd crust
>   The dirk of defamation ;
> A mask that like the gorget show'd
>   Dye-varying on the pigeon,
> While for a mantle large and broad
>   He wrapt him in religion.

Tennyson uses this form in *Will Waterproof* and
Amphion, and fills it in the same way with compressed
significant language ; making, in *Will Waterproof*, a
small technical change (feminine rhyme in the second
quatrain only), but otherwise keeping the old measure.
There is no better example than the stanza into which
he has put Will Waterproof's vision of the whole world,
the verses where the ancient quarrel between philosophy
and poetry seems to be reconciled by the influence of
the Muse and the help of her Lusitanian servant :

> This earth is rich in man and maid ;
>   With fair horizons bound :
> This whole wide earth of light and shade
>   Comes out a perfect round.
> High over roaring Temple-bar,
>   And set in Heaven's third story,
> I look at all things as they are,
>   But thro' a kind of glory.

The new varieties of rhyme invented for *The Daisy*
and the poem addressed *to F. D. Maurice* are among the
most delightful things of this sort in the language, and
the beauty of Tennyson's art would suffer wrong if
these were not remembered :

> I climb'd the roofs at break of day,
> Sun-smitten Alps before me lay ;
>   I stood among the silent statues
> And statued pinnacles, mute as they.

> How faintly-flush'd, how phantom-fair,
> Was Monte Rosa, hanging there
>   A thousand shadowy-pencill'd valleys
> And snowy dells in a golden air.

In these and in a host of other rhymes Tennyson has done what Sidney has given as the work of the poet : " to make the too much loved earth more lovely." They dwell in the memory, like

> The rich Virgilian rustic measure
> Of Lari Maxume, all the way.

Tennyson's blank verse is of many different kinds, almost as various as Wordsworth's. Here again it is possible to find anticipations, in older poets, of some of Tennyson's effects ; in Landor's *Gebir* for example :

> And the long moonbeam on the hard wet sand
> Lay like a jasper column half upreared.

What strikes one first, and at first with pleasure, is the ingenuity of Tennyson's variations. He uses his blank verse according to Pope's rules in the *Essay on Criticism* ; he is fond of rendering Ajax and Camilla in the movement of his line. This is Ajax :

> He felt were she the prize of bodily force
> Himself beyond the rest pushing could move
> The chair of Idris.

This is Camilla, a little retarded :

> But while the sun yet beat a dewy blade
> The sound of many a heavily galloping hoof
> Smote on her ear, and turning round she saw
> Dust, and the points of lances bicker in it.

These passages are both taken from *Enid*, and there are many more in the same Idyll. There may be too much of this device ; yet it cannot be fairly said that these conceits of verse break up the solidity of the poem. Many different motives and graces are combined in the Idyll :

> as one
> That listens near a torrent mountain brook
> All through the crash of the near cataract hears
> The drumming thunder of the huger fall.

The likeness of Tennyson to Pope in some things is undeniable. There is the same clearness, the same regard for elegance of verse. Even in the noting of particulars, though Pope is not near Tennyson in fineness of perception, and though the fashion of his age discouraged such things, there are some resemblances. We all know the result of Tennyson's poetry in *Cranford* : " This young man comes and tells me that ash buds are black ; and I look, and they *are* black." In like manner many people who had played cards all their lives must have read the *Rape of the Lock* and been told for the first time by that other young poet that the King of Diamonds is always seen in profile, and must have looked and verified the statement that the only King who carries the globe is the King of Clubs. Tennyson's *Princess* is full of things that make it a modern counterpart to the *Rape of the Lock*. A poet's quality may be proved in his least substantial work, and this that follows is Tennyson's poetry, not at its highest, but no less authentic than the highest :

> —and then we turn'd, we wound
> About the cliffs, the copses, out and in,
> Hammering and clinking, chattering stony names
> Of shale and hornblende, rag and trap and tuff,
> Amygdaloid and trachyte, till the sun
> Grew broader toward his death and fell, and all
> The rosy heights came out above the lawns.

Blank verse can do anything ; among other things it may be lyrical. Wordsworth knew this when he

put a note to *Tintern Abbey* to say that he would not
call it an Ode, which means, of course, that he had
thought of it as an Ode and wished it to be so thought
of. *Oenone* is a lyrical poem following the example of
the Greek Idylls with their lyrical refrain ; but the
chief poem of this kind is *Tithonus*, which has no
refrain, and so escapes from the touch of artificiality
which might possibly be charged against the imitation
of Theocritus. And in *Tithonus* there are none of
those curiosities of verse, those " Ajax " and " Camilla "
passages, which are so common in the *Idylls of the King*.
The verse is all of the pure classical tradition—there
are no variations beyond what are commonly recognised
and known to every beginner. Yet the life in the poem
is infinite and infinitely varied :

> Whispering I knew not what of wild and sweet
> Like that strange song I heard Apollo sing
> While Ilion like a mist rose into towers.

The Devil's Advocate is very ready to discuss
Tennyson's " thought." An instance is given by Mr.
Gladstone in his essay on *Locksley Hall* (*Nineteenth
Century*, January, 1887). He quotes an article " of
singular talent " in the *Pall Mall Gazette*, December 14,
1886. This " states rather dogmatically that any
criticism which accepts Lord Tennyson as a thinker is
out of date," and Mr. Gladstone proceeds : " I venture
to demur to this proposition and to contend that the
author of *In Memoriam* (for example) shows a capacity
which entitles him to a high place among the thinkers
of the day."

Now it may be asked whether this demurrer does
not concede too much to the Devil's Advocate of the
Pall Mall Gazette. " Thinker " is taken as if it were
a simple unequivocal term. What it meant exactly

as used by those two parties would be hard to say ; but the Index to that volume of the *Nineteenth Century*, which contains articles by Professor Huxley, Mr. John Morley and the Duke of Argyll, suggests some of the names, " the thinkers of the day," with whom Tennyson is to be ranked or not to be ranked, according to one or the other opinion. Thought is here discursive thought, philosophical or moral argument. Tennyson as a thinker is compared with thinkers who use prose. There need not be any unfairness in this. There certainly are poems, like the *Essay on Man*, which enter into competition with the prose thinkers, and whose arguments are fairly judged by the same standards. There is nothing unfair that I can see in Mr. Gladstone's discussion of *Locksley Hall*. Whether his arguments are really valid is another question. Is the contention of *Locksley Hall sixty years after* really met by Mr. Gladstone's references to the penny post, cheap newspapers, and Mr. Thomas Cook's tourist agency ? It may be doubted. A Canadian critic at the time (with perhaps a little too much emphasis) said it was almost as if someone had answered John the Baptist " by pointing out that there had been great improvements in the Roman Law, that the system of imperial roads had been successfully developed, that the harbour accommodation at Ravenna had been increased, and that there had been a gratifying activity during a recent period in the building trade at Caesarea Philippi." But however that may be, there can be no doubt of Mr. Gladstone's good faith in the argument, nor of his right to take it up. Both the earlier and the later *Locksley Hall* are full of debatable matter. Both are criticisms of life, and what is criticism if it may not be challenged and canvassed ?

But there are other kinds of poetic thought besides that which can be discussed in prose. The poets, like other men, can play with all sorts of debatable commonplaces, and sometimes it is pleasant enough to follow them, to trace for instance Shakespeare on the human will and destiny, " the fated sky," " the inward quality,"—to compare the reflections of Hamlet or Brutus with the dogmatic certainty of Lysander, waking up under the spell of Puck and Oberon, and beginning at once :

> The will of man is by his reason sway'd.

But the poetical mode of thought is not shown best in the poet's moralising sentences. The noblest poetic thought has often very little that can be debated. The poetic discourse of *Obermann* cannot hold its own, for poetic wisdom, against the conclusion of *Sohrab and Rustum*, and if we were to choose, in Mr. Arnold's own way, a passage of deep seriousness from his books, it might well be *Cadmus and Harmonia* rather than the song of Empedocles.

> And there they say two bright and aged snakes
> Who once were Cadmus and Harmonia
> Bask in the glens or on the warm sea-shore
> In breathless quiet, after all their ills ;
> Nor do they see their country, nor the place
> Where the Sphinx lived among the frowning hills,
> Nor the unhappy palace of their race,
> Nor Thebes, nor the Ismenus any more.

Two of the most solemn passages in all poetry are the argument of true Fame in *Lycidas* and the speech over the death of Samson :

> Nothing is here for tears, nothing to wail
> Or knock the breast, no weakness, no contempt,
> Dispraise or blame, nothing but well and fair,
> And what may quiet us in a death so noble.

These meditations of the poet are wronged if any word is said about them in discussion of their substance ; one may argue with Milton about " the ruin of our corrupted clergy then at their height," but not about his poetical doctrine of true Fame :

> That strain we heard was of a higher mood.

So we may hold that the thought of Tennyson is not so well bestowed in the argumentative poems (like that which Mr. Gladstone refuted in the *Nineteenth Century*) as in some of those where he uses mythology, the legends of *Tithonus* or the *Holy Grail*, to convey his reading of the world. The difference between the two kinds of thought is very great ; and the nobler kind is not discourse but vision. It does not lend itself to discussion ; if it is once apprehended there is no more to be said, or no more than the words of Sir Bors in the *Holy Grail* :

> Ask me not, for I may not speak of it,
> I saw it.

One need not be afraid to defend the " thought " of Tennyson on the lower ground either. But there is not much to be gained for his poetry in this way. Much of his reasoning is opinion, as good as that of other thinkers, but not founded as most of Wordsworth's is on certain and irrefragable knowledge. It is generally far above the range of ordinary didactic poetry, but much of it has suffered through lapse of time and the change of fashions, and has become antiquated like the *Essay on Man*. What is least injured in this way, what best retains its value as philosophy, is the poem of the *Ancient Sage*, which is based on experience like that of Wordsworth's ; and the wisdom of the *Ancient Sage* is summed up in the

sentence that " nothing worthy proving can be proven."
Noble as this is, one feels that it is less excellent than
the mythological poems, where the thought is inextri-
cable from the bodily form, as in *Tithonus* :

> Upon thy glimmering thresholds, when the steam
> Floats up from those dim fields about the homes
> Of happy men that have the power to die,
> And grassy barrows of the happier dead.
> Release me, and restore me to the ground ;
> Thou seëst all things, thou wilt see my grave :
> Thou wilt renew thy beauty morn by morn ;
> I earth in earth forget these empty courts,
> And thee returning on thy silver wheels.

It is contended by some of the critics, and among
them by some of the greatest admirers of Tennyson's
poetry, that he indulges his genius too much in
curiosities of detail, in decorations that break the
structure. Besides the turns of his verse, there are
devices of fancy, it is said, which are too minute and
exquisite for great poetry. The illustrations are too
much for the main fabric. Certainly Tennyson makes
a liberal use of the Homeric simile ; and the Homeric
simile, no doubt, may be overdone. It has often been
satirised in many mock heroic works. But it survives ;
it is one of the great beauties of *Hyperion* ; there is as
much of it in *Sohrab and Rustum* as in the *Idylls of the
King*, and in neither is it untrue to its origin :

> So the sweet voice of Enid moved Geraint ;
> And made him like a man abroad at morn
> When first the liquid note beloved of men
> Comes flying over many a windy wave
> To Britain, and in April suddenly
> Breaks from a coppice gemm'd with green and red,
> And he suspends his converse with a friend,
> Or it may be the labour of his hands,
> To think or say " There is the nightingale."

An answer to the critics on this point has been given by Dr. Warren in his comparison of Tennyson and Dante, and I am content to follow the President of Magdalen and find in the similes of Tennyson the same proportions as in Dante, the same transgression, if such it be, from the main theme to the incidental, the same exorbitant delight in all the details of the simile. The faults in the construction and imagination of the Idylls are great and indefensible, and Sir Gawain and Sir Tristram have suffered heavy wrong. But the blame of this is not to be put upon the Homeric similes. It may be observed that some of the best and most elaborate come in the Idyll of *Enid* from which I have quoted more than once, and that the story of Enid will stand any fair test of criticism with regard to its plot, its characters, its unity of narrative. It is a poem which atones for a great neglect in English poetry. Enid, who is more like Nausicaa than any other earl's daughter of Romance, had been honoured by all Christendom, except in England, till Tennyson took up the story from Lady Charlotte Guest's *Mabinogion* and made good the failure of the older English minstrelsy. The story in its older forms, Welsh or French or German or Norse, is unlike most of the romances; it is romantic, with not a little of the higher comedy; romantic without the extravagance or affectation of the books of chivalry. The form of *The Lady of Shalott* or *Sir Galahad* would be quite unfit for this story. It can be treated in the fullest dramatic way; Geraint and Enid are modern characters, in every age that takes any thought about them, in the nineteenth century with Tennyson as in the twelfth with Chrestien de Troyes.

Tennyson perhaps never wrote any story with better success. The form of the dramatic monologue much more than the narrative Idyll gave Tennyson what he wanted ; for him as for Browning the dramatic mono-logue served better than either narrative or regular drama. His various imaginative studies are turned to more profit in this way than in any other—not only in *Oenone*, *Ulysses*, *Tithonus*, and *Lucretius*, but in *St. Simeon Stylites*, and the *Northern Farmer*, and many more, where Tennyson plays something like Browning's game, the humorous sophistry of different characters making out a case for themselves. It is in the dramatic Idylls that the intellectual strength of Tennyson is proved, though some of them may have little value for " thinkers " in the *Nineteenth Century* meaning of the word. It was not as a " thinker " of this sort that Tennyson made those early conquests, so well described by so many witnesses, best perhaps by Canon Dixon, as quoted in the *Life of William Morris*, or perhaps in that well-known chapter which describes the perplexities of Colonel Newcome over the taste of the younger generation :

" He heard opinions that amazed and bewildered him : he heard that Byron was no great poet though a very clever man ; he heard that there had been a wicked persecution against Mr. Pope's memory and fame, and that it was time to reinstate him ; that his favourite Dr. Johnson talked admirably, but did not write English ; that young Keats was a genius to be estimated in future days with young Raphael, and that a young gentleman of Cambridge, who had lately published two volumes of verses, might take rank with the greatest poets of all." The friends of Clive New-come were probably wiser in their admiration than in

XV

BROWNING

I begin with some of the difficulties ; it might be more prudent to suppress them. But it would be unjust and unlucky if I were to come here promising to say anything marvellously new or anything thoroughly satisfactory about the poetry of Browning. In the art of criticism, as in other dangerous trades, there are workmen's diseases, and one of the commonest is for the speaker to believe that he can " do " a subject in an essay of thirty-two pages, or a discourse not longer than two ordinary sermons. This illusion is sometimes pleasant in the young ; it is pleasantly described by Stevenson in the preface to his *Familiar Studies* : " So, by insensible degrees, a young man of our generation acquires, in his own eyes, a kind of roving judicial commission through the ages." But this happy confidence should not be allowed to settle down into a mere steady, secure opinion, a fixed belief that the speaker, living in the cool element of prose, can interpret all the translunary spheres of poetry, and put all the tears of the universe into his bottle. It is well to know the limits, and to understand that poetry is its own interpretation. The best one can do, and it is no dishonourable office, is to get the right point of view, to *praise* in the right way.

Here is another difficulty, or at any rate, a scruple. I never met Mr. Browning to speak to, yet I cannot help thinking of him as I saw him when he was still on this side of the picture, when he might be passed, any day, in London, walking in the crowd, perhaps quicker and more observant than most, yet one of the crowd of mortal men. Somehow, this makes him different from the poets one has never seen. It is easier and less invidious to talk about a row of volumes than a living man. I think of Mr. Browning as one who has stopped to speak to many of my friends, and I am more doubtful than ever about the beginning of this essay. I remember with sympathy Coleridge at Birmingham, when he was wakened up suddenly by the question whether he had seen a newspaper that day : " ' Sir,' I replied, rubbing my eyes, ' I am far from convinced that a Christian is permitted to read newspapers ' "— though he had come to the place to push the sale of his own paper, the *Watchman* : his remark, as he says, was incongruous with that purpose, but still, it may have expressed his true mind.

On the other hand, it is very pleasant to think of Mr. Browning " as he strikes a contemporary." I remember a gathering at Balliol, now about thirty years since, and the guests of the college as they met there, and Browning talking to Matthew Arnold at the foot of the steps of the hall ; and, before that, an autumn evening in the Island of Arran, the year that *Pacchiarotto* was published, when Browning met us on the Lamlash Road going home, and I provoked some scepticism in my companions by saying that he was the greatest man in the world.

That was a long time ago, and I am reminded, thinking of the dates, what a difference there is in the perspective of the history of poetry between the eighteenth and the nineteenth century. Browning, who died in 1889, is at nearly the same distance from us in 1910 as Dr. Johnson from the generation that read *Marmion*. But the interval seems much less. The nineteenth century is much nearer to us than the eighteenth century to our ancestors a hundred years ago. We think of Fielding and Gray as very far back in time, far separated from the age of Scott and Byron. Yet they are as near that time, in dates, as Thackeray to us, and nearer than the early poems of Tennyson and Browning, which are still read by many young people, without compulsion or any sense of duty, or any uncomfortable feeling that the poems are antiquated now. For poetry, we have still to live in the nineteenth century. A hundred years ago things were otherwise. In Miss Austen's time people read Cowper still. But Cowper is already coming to be old-fashioned in the literary conversations at Lyme between Anne Elliot and Captain Benwick—" having talked of poetry, the richness of the present age, and gone through a brief comparison of opinion as to the first-rate poets, trying to ascertain whether *Marmion* or *The Lady of the Lake* were to be preferred, and how ranked the *Giaour* and *The Bride of Abydos*, and, moreover, how the *Giaour* was to be pronounced. . . ." Cowper is old-fashioned, though his poems appeared in the eighties, and would correspond in date more nearly to *Departmental Ditties* than to *Men and Women*. The dates of Stevenson may be compared with the dates of Burns. When we read Scott's account of his meeting with Burns we think of Burns as a poet of a different age and world. Yet if you "apply" the nineteenth century dates to the eighteenth century, in the manner recommended by Euclid for triangles, " so that the line AB may be upon the line DE," it will appear that Stevenson was born nine years earlier than Burns, and died before him. And we are surprised to find that Burns is so far left behind in 1810, that Stevenson is so near to us now.

The fact is plain, that there has been no such poetic revolution in this century as there was in the last ; and though we may complain of some injustices in the way that things are shared by the Muses, the stewards of Helicon, there is compensation in the longer life and more enduring value of the older authors, more particularly of Tennyson and Browning.

Possibly the lapse of time may have made Browning easier; perhaps the poetry of George Meredith may have made Browning's verse less difficult in comparison. One does not hear so much of the protests against Browning's obscurity, of grievances like those of Gilead Beck in the *Golden Butterfly*. *Sordello* may be spoken of without a groan, and *Paracelsus* can be read at a sitting. Yet the difficulties are there—difficulties which are not the same thing as obscurity. The charge of obscurity has been repelled by Mr. Swinburne in his essay on *George Chapman*. Obscurity is not the right word. " He is something too much the reverse of obscure ; he is too brilliant and subtle for the ready reader of a ready writer to follow with any certainty the track of an intelligence which moves with such incessant rapidity." And later he speaks of the " faculty of spiritual illumination rapid and intense and subtle as lightning, which brings to bear upon its central object by way of direct and vivid

illustration every symbol and every detail on which
its light is flashed in passing."

Obscurity is not the word, but the difficulties remain.
Browning recognised this himself, in the revision of
Sordello, and the care he took to make the poem more
easily intelligible by means of the head-lines, which
give a summary of the argument. Why has this key
been left out of the recent editions ? It is an injustice,
and it calls for remedy. The publishers do not reprint
The Rose and the Ring without Thackeray's head-lines ;
why should they have retrenched the commentary on
Sordello, the poet's own marginal gloss ? The want of
it, for one thing, leaves a passage unexplained where
the acutest reader may require to be " edified by the
margent " :

> —stay—thou, spirit, come not near
> Now—not this time desert thy cloudy place
> To scare me, thus employed, with that pure face !
> I need not fear this audience, I make free
> With them, but then this is no place for thee !
> The thunder-phrase of the Athenian, grown
> Up out of memories of Marathon,
> Would echo like his own sword's griding screech
> Braying a Persian shield—the silver speech
> Of Sidney's self, the starry paladin,
> Turn intense as a trumpet sounding in
> The knights to tilt—wert thou to hear ! What heart
> Have I to play my puppets, bear my part
> Before these worthies ?

Shelley is meant here, but it is only from the head-
line on the next page—" Shelley departing, Verona
appears "—that one can learn this.

The poet's gloss to *Sordello* may be taken as a justification of the work of commentators, an acknowledgment that the matter of poetry can be partly translated

into prose. A book like Mr. Henry Jones's, on the Philosophy of Browning, if it needed an apology, might find one in this advice of the author, where he provides an analysis of the story. There is nothing in sound poetry that need be afraid of the prose interpreter. The example of Dante, too, might be alleged if it were necessary to prove that poetry and criticism may go together and be used in turn by one and the same author. The analysis of *Sordello* is less minute than that which Dante gives for his lyrical poems in the *Vita Nuova* and *Convivio*.

Nevertheless, it is sometimes dangerous to extract the prose sense of a poem ; dangerous, if the prose interpretation be taken in place of the poetry, or supposed to represent it fully. This is a dangerous incident to the most thoughtful poets, or rather to some of their readers. The poet comes to be valued for the amount of his work that can be translated, *i.e.* for that which is not poetry. This is blind and unreasonable ; but it is not uncommon with serious-minded students. On the other hand, the readers who have no liking for analysis are often disgusted with the commentary or the paraphrase. While their objections are sometimes due to laziness and want of thought, they may also come from a true sense of what makes the life of a poem, the indissoluble harmony of elements which no commentary can replace. They do not want merely what Wordsworth called " an extremely valuable chain of thoughts."

In Browning it is possible to find a much more articulate theory of human nature and the universe than in Wordsworth ; it submits more readily to be expressed in prose. It is found in *Paracelsus* and *Sordello*, in *Old Pictures at Florence*, and in the *Gram-*

marian's Funeral. It is a theory of progress ; not of
an endless advance merely, from point to point " in
unlimited series," but of the infinite Universe drawing
the human adventurer to work out, in his own life, in
knowledge and in power, everything that the universal
world contains. There is a superficial likeness in
Browning's theory to the " Perfectibility " of some
eighteenth-century philosophers ; the difference is
that Browning thinks of perfection as real, so that the
imperfect human pilgrim is not a mere wanderer on
from one stage to another, nor merely an instrument
along with other finite things in building up the fabric
of the Universe ; he is thought of as one compelled by
the Universe to put into his own small being all that
the whole world means. This is the tragic absurdity
of human life. Either it ventures the impossible, like
Sordello, " thrusting in time Eternity's concern," or
it cuts its ideals to fit the short human life allowed it,
the ship's cabin of Bishop Blougram's allegory—an
inglorious compromise. This theory as Browning held
it may (I believe) be stated in prose as a philosophical
argument. If this be so, there is in Browning a strong
element of purely intellectual as distinct from poetical
or purely imaginative thought, and this which is intellectual may perhaps be extricated or " disentwined "
(to use a word of Browning's own) from his poetry,
without disgrace either to his poetry or to the philosophical analyst. With Wordsworth this is impossible.
Wordsworth's knowledge, in which he is eminent above
all other thinkers in the world, is so essentially part of
his own life, so close to reality, that it will not bear
translation into any language but his own. Nothing
can take its place. Abana and Pharphar will not do
instead of the waters of Israel.

Theories something like Wordsworth's have been expressed in prose, and sometimes in phrases that seem well fitted for large advertisements : *e.g.* " Cosmic Consciousness," " In Tune with the Infinite." It looks as if Wordsworth's knowledge might be shared in part with people who not only have no poetic utterance, but no decent language at all to say what they mean. Wordsworth himself in his unfinished philosophical poem sought to give as argument what he knew as vision. But what is only known in vision can only be conveyed to other minds by some different art from logic ; by language like that of the stars, in momentary points of light ; by the language of poetry, where poetry comes nearest to music and is furthest from prose. Which does not mean that Wordsworth's knowledge is simply feeling, but that it is different from the intelligence which argues and explains. Browning, on the other hand, was openly and by his own confession given to analysis. One might quote from *Sordello* the head-line " Analyst who turns in due course synthetist," or compare that extraordinary poem *Pacchiarotto*, which was written as a travesty of *Sordello*, and flung in the face of the reviewers : " harsh analytics," is Browning's phrase there for the kind of minute work which many reviewers condemn in Browning.

The analytical mind is the critical mind, and its work is commonly thought to be the opposite of creation, of imaginative art, of poetry. One variety of it is the satire. The satirist, the analyst, expounds his subject instead of making the characters live and speak in drama. Browning knew as well as anyone the difference between the two processes, but he had something in him that made him unafraid of the dangers and hindrances of the analytic method. He knew (like Balzac, may we say ?) that it was senseless to refuse the analytic method when it was part of his own mind. Browning's policy is disclosed in the headline " Analyst who turns in due course synthetist." Let analysis do its best or its worst ; if the mind be made to prose the results of analysis will be prose ; if there be poetry in the mind the analysis may end in poetry. This is Browning's hope, and his *Sordello* note on the analyst-synthetist might serve as a label for *The Ring and the Book*, and for much else.

He begins often with an abstract instance, a case, a problem, instead of a character. But the poetic end need not be abstract or merely intellectual. *Mr. Sludge the Medium* may begin, abstractly, as a case : " How understand the self-justification of a humbug ? " And this problem is partly thought out in general terms. But the result is not abstract, and the proof is that it is amusing. The character embodies itself, like Chaucer's *Pardoner*, whose monologue or dramatic idyll (and the *Wife of Bath's* also) is in method very near Browning. Not far from Tennyson, either, we may say, remembering the *Northern Farmer* and the *Village Wife*, and others. But neither Chaucer nor Tennyson has the passion of a collector, like Browning ; he goes far further than they in his chase after the varieties. No corner is left untried, no problem is too old or too modern for him. Ixion is for him a character, not an ornament out of the mythology. The Queen of Sheba is there, and Queen Christina by her side ; Jochanan Hakkadosh, and Bubb Dodington. In the year after Sedan there appeared the revelation of Prince Hohenstiel-Schwangau, Saviour of Society.

The form of those studies is generally the same ; the monologue in blank verse. Some readers have been inclined to take this (as Browning himself no doubt very often did), simply for a convenient instrument, not too poetical, not very different from prose, a thing to be accepted as part of the author's humour. If this be the right view to take, then all Browning's value is in his matter, and there is nothing in his poetic form ; which would mean that he is not a poet at all. And so we may be led to consider his form and some of the interests of it ; and when we say poetic form what we mean is poetry.

Browning himself admitted that he was difficult. He tried in *The Ring and the Book* to write easier for the British public :

> O British Public, you who like me not.

In *Pacchiarotto*, not without dust and heat, he met his critics and told them his mind—gave them " nettle-broth," as he says in the *Epilogue* to the same volume. He sees the critics as a band of chimney-sweeps, dressed up for May Day, coming under his window with music of knuckle-bones and cleavers :

> Us critics as sweeps out your chimbly.

They have a grievance against his obscurity :

> The neighbours complain it's no joke, sir,
> You ought to consume your own smoke, sir !

In the *Epilogue*, in his parable of the vintage, he seems to admit a good deal of the charges against him. The critics say that his wine is rough ; that the true poetic wine has both body and bouquet. In his answer he does not maintain that his poetry has all the qualities. His answer is that he does not believe they really like good wine ; they talk about Shakespeare, but do they read him ? As for his own vintage, he does not deny that it may be rough ; he does not contend that it is both strong and mellow. What he is sure of is that it is strong and sound.

That volume of *Pacchiarotto* is very interesting for the history of Browning's own poetical life and his fortunes as an author. But it is not altogether pleasant. He does not " make the malefactor die sweetly," in Dryden's phrase. " A man may be capable, as Jack Ketch's wife said of his servant, of a plain hanging, but to make a malefactor die sweetly was only belonging to her husband." Browning's satire is a little old-fashioned, and has too much of the railing, " flyting " as the Scots have it, which recalls the savage origin of the Old Comedy. And the worst of it (for no one need give much concern or pity to the dunces in this contro-versy)—the worst of it is that Browning does not seem to know what his own poetry is really like. It is not enough to say that his poetry is rough but honest (for that is what his *Epilogue* comes to)—those who have lived on his poetry know that there is more in it than strength, and that the critical depreciation of Browning's verse is as futile as the rejection of Words-worth's, or the older condemnation of Donne. As to this last, it should be remembered that Ben Johnson's sentence to Drummond : " that Done for not keeping of accent deserved hanging," was spoken by the man who best understood and most valued Donne : " He esteemeth John Done the first poet in the world in some things." Lovers of Wordsworth and Browning might be allowed the same sort of freedom without impairing their regard for these poets' melodies. Wordsworth's verse is not to be judged by *Andrew Jones* or *Ellen Irwin*. There is ground enough in Browning for the *Heptalogia* parody :

> Melt down loadstars for magnets, use women for whetstones,
> Learn to bear with dead calms by remembering cyclones,
> Snap strings short with sharp thumbnails, till silence begets tones.

But it is wrong to take harsh colliding consonants as a true sample of Browning's art. It is well to remember the music that he has added to the store of English poetry—poetical music in which he is not the opponent but the partner of Tennyson.

Many people doubtless have amused themselves with thinking of the great rival authors—Tennyson and Browning, Thackeray and Dickens, Macaulay and Carlyle—who seem, in that age, to represent in pairs the two opposite kinds of literature. For these two orders various names may be found—the obedient and the exorbitant, law and impulse, angels and devils, in Blake's meaning of these words, which is not on the side of the angels. But if you look closer at the great champions, though you will not find their differences less interesting, you will find that these are not so epigrammatically neat as they might at first appear. There is more likeness of Macaulay to Carlyle, and of Carlyle to Macaulay, than one thought ; Tennyson is not so angelic nor Browning so rebellious as he should be for the purpose of a rhetorical explosive contrast. Between Tennyson and Browning there are strong affinities, the same sort of power, largely the same ideas, the same policy. Compare *Joannes Agricola* and

St. Simeon Stylites ; consider again the way both poets took the dramatic monologue as vehicle for much of their most original thought, and the way the thought of Ulysses corresponds to the ruling passion of Browning. If *Fra Lippo Lippi* and *Bishop Blougram's Apology*, and still more *Prince Hohenstiel-Schwangau*, are diffuse beyond the limit of Tennyson's idyllic form, remember the other poems, so richly compact : *Artemis Prologises* and *The Bishop orders his tomb in St. Praxed's.*

The resemblance goes far deeper than this choice of a frame or these coincidences of thought. The poetic invention of Tennyson and Browning alike is shown in their rhyming forms. Their new melodies carry on the life that had been recovered by the poets before them ; they are the successors of Wordsworth and Coleridge, of Shelley and Keats, in the freedom and variety of their verse. Let no one think that this is merely an affair of prosody ; or rather, let no one think that prosody is merely a science of patterns. Some people may see nothing more in the stanza than a figure on the printed page, like the figures of those old-fashioned metrical toys, the poems composed in the shape of an altar or a pair of wings. But the difference between the verse of *Abt Vogler* and *Rabbi Ben Ezra* is much more than this. The poetic measure, the stave or stanza, has a soul in it, a movement which is not only the utterance of life but the poetic life itself. It is not (except in mechanical work like some of the old Pindarics) a mere shape given to words and sentences. As it comes to the poet, before the poem is made, it is part of his inspiration, an unbodied melody with the life of the poem in it.

Browning's blank verse in its ordinary fashion is

truly represented in Calverley's burlesque.   The trick
of it may be found—a sort of prophetic parody—in
Elvira, or the worst not always true, a drama by a Person
of Quality (the Earl of Bristol) in 1667 :

> Prythee, if thou lov'st me
> Hold me no longer in suspense, Chichon.
>   *Chi.* Why then, for fear—the devil a bit for love—
> I'll tell you, sir, that luckily I met
> The drab Francisca at the Capuchin's,
> Lodging behind her lady, I think on purpose ;
> For I perceived her eager sparrow-hawk's eye,
> With her veil down (ne'er stirs a twinkling-while
> From its sly peeping-hole), had found me straight.
> I took my time i' the nick, but she outnicked me.

Both Browning and Tennyson are fond of licence
and variations and resolution of feet in their blank
verse.   But Browning, like Tennyson, will have none
of these variations in his most solemn passages.

> O lyric love, half angel and half bird,
> And all a wonder and a wild desire !

Nor is there any such licence admitted when he is
thinking of pure beauty—the Greek islands and their
sweetness and light :

> Cleon, the poet from the sprinkled isles,
> Lily on lily that o'erlace the sea.

His art is shown as truly in irregular verse as in the
more formal measures.   But the irregular verse suggests
a difficulty that may be found by many readers ; it is
worth considering.

They are told that Browning is one of the greatest
poets ; they come on something that reminds them of

the *Ingoldsby Legends*, the Tipton Slasher, Rarey drum-
ming on Cruiser, Jane Lamb that we danced with at
Vichy—comic rhymes : ranunculus, " Tommy make
room for your uncle us," and hundreds more of such
offences. Even when there is a less outrageous style,
there still remains a great heap of comic poetry, which
to many sober and worthy readers is a violent and
painful thing. " Comic poetry," they think, is the
next thing to profanity ; one does not speak of a comic
prophet. Possibly it is people of that sort who are
intended in *How it strikes a contemporary* ; the boy's
mistake about the poet whom his father called " Cor-
regidor " :

> My father like the man of sense he was,
> Would point him out to me a dozen times ;
> " St—St," he'd whisper, " the Corregidor."
> I had been used to think that personage
> Was one with lacquered breeches, lustrous belt,
> And feathers like a forest in his hat,
> Who blew a trumpet and proclaimed the news,
> Announced the bull-fights, gave each church its turn,
> And memorized the miracle in vogue.
> He had great observance from us boys ;
> We were in error ; that was not the man.

It is strange, and it is one of the great disappointments in Browning, that he should have made so poor
a case for Aristophanes and his Comic Muse, in the
book devoted to their *Apology*. But his own lyrical
freedom is that Muse's gift abundantly.

> To solder close impossibilities
> And make them kiss.

If we must choose, the poem shall be Waring, a poem
more personal than many of Browning's springing from
a suggestion in his own life like those that set Words-

worth on his poetical inventions.   The friend has gone,
and the brooding memory, in a sort of dream, mingles
the true nature of the friend with all sorts of possibilities,
fancies—the play of the mind, which seems arbitrary
and casual in this poem, being really an accompaniment of the main thought, which is of Waring and his
genius.   The passage that brings out the music is
where Iphigenia comes to the poet's mind.   He is
thinking of Russia—Russia makes him think of the
Crimea, the Tauric Chersonese—then of Iphigenia in
Tauris—and the verse changes from its loose variety
into the sounding " square " verse—the old heroic
measure :

> Or who in Moscow, toward the Czar,
> With the demurest of footfalls
> Over the Kremlin's pavement, bright
> With serpentine and syenite,
> Steps with five other Generals
> That simultaneously take snuff,
> For each to have pretext enough,
> And kerchief-wise unfold his sash,
> Which, softness' self, is yet the stuff
> To hold fast when a steel chain snaps,
> And leave the grand white neck no gash.
> Waring in Moscow, to those rough
> Cold northern natures borne perhaps,
> Like the lamb-white maiden dear
> From the circle of mute kings
> Unable to repress the tear,
> Each as his sceptre down he flings,
> To Dian's fane at Taurica,
> Where now a captive priestess, she alway
> Mingles her tender grave Hellenic speech
> With theirs, tuned to the hailstone-beaten beach,
> As pours some pigeon, from the myrrhy lands
> Rapt by the whirlblast to fierce Scythian strands
> Where breed swallows, her melodious cry
> Amid their barbarous twitter.

It would be pleasant to go on, to quote from *Rudel*, to repeat again the songs *In a Gondola* :

> Which were best, to roam or rest,
> The land's lap, or the water's breast !

But that means that the poet himself is growing impatient of his prose commentator, and is taking the business into his own hands. It is time to stop. The poet may be left to do his work ; to prove, even against his own argument in *Pacchiarotto*, that what he has to give is not knowledge only, nor strength only, but beauty. The simplest and most satisfactory name for it is poetry.

XVI

ESSAYS IN ROMANTIC LITERATURE

WHEN all these essays [1] had been written, at intervals and on various occasions in the course of nearly twenty years, George Wyndham found that he had completed a large part of a book with a continuous theme. It had been in his mind long before to write the history of romantic literature from the Middle Ages onward ; and, " without knowing it," there he had in his prefaces to Ronsard, Shakespeare, and North's *Plutarch*, with his rectorial address at Edinburgh on the Springs of Romance, his Charles d'Orléans and Villon (" the poetry of the Prison "), his Elizabethan Adventurers, and his speech in honour of Sir Walter Scott, so many chapters of his book ready to take their places along with those that were still to be written, on the Chroniclers and the Crusades, on Chaucer, on the new French Romantics.

This sudden thought was not vanity, nor the delusive phantom of a *magnum opus* never to be realised. It was a sensible review of what he had actually completed, and no candid reader of these essays can fail to see that this instinctive and unconscious design has

---

[1] *Essays in Romantic Literature*, by George Wyndham (Macmillan, 12s. net).

given them a character of their own. They are more than pleasant reminiscences of a lover of books, or the confessions of a discursive reader amusing himself in libraries while his material interests are elsewhere. George Wyndham was deeply engaged in politics when he wrote on Ronsard and Shakespeare, Amyot and North ; still he wrote, not for a distraction, to unbend his mind, like Mr. Fox reading Homer or Ariosto, but because his mind was for the time fully taken up with the study of poetry and " the other harmony of prose " (as Dryden calls it), with character and adventure and the impression of past ages.   He had always something to say, and he knew that to say things well more was needed than a gift of phrases.   Mr. Charles Whibley has described him truly : " His enthusiasm kept pace with his passion of discovery.   He combined with what Hazlitt called ' gusto ' a marvellous patience.   If he wrote with excitement, he deemed that no labour in the collecting of facts went unrewarded."   The reward is that his most laborious study and his longest discourse, the introduction to North's *Plutarch*, is also the most varied and most expressive.   The patience of the student turns to fervour of thought and security of style, and his largest piece is at the same time his finest.

In a note at the end he acknowledges his debt to Mr. W. E. Henley, the editor of the *Tudor Translations*, in which series North was reprinted.   The friendship of Henley and George Wyndham will not be forgotten by their friends surviving ; it is recorded in Henley's dedication of Hoby's *Courtyer*, in the same series, to the " soldier, courtier, scholar," and Mr. Whibley describes, from his own acquaintance with both, the part taken by Henley in advising and training the younger man.

An occasional mannerism—as " there you shall find "
—remains in these essays ; the dullest literary detec-
tive, when he comes on it, is justified in his crowing :
" Ha ! the usual trick of the *National Observer*." But
many talk of Robin Hood that cannot shoot with his
bow. Henley's art of prose was a good deal more than
mannerism, and his pupil brought no small strength
and skill of his own to take counsel with Henley's
experience and judgment. He was in danger, always,
of too much eloquence, " always for altisonancy and
colour." So Henley is quoted in Mr. Whibley's introduction, giving wholesome advice : " But—! you
forget to jine your flats." This favourite traditional
formula may be used as a test for the whole of this
book. Though some of the arguments are less firmly
explained than others, there will be found in all of
them that devotion to the matter in hand which is the
foundation of good writing :

> cui lecta potenter erit res
> Nec facundia deseret hunc, nec lucidus ordo.

Is this sentence of Horace, this motto of Corneille's,
too much of a commonplace for quotation here ? We
have ventured it, for *lecta potenter* is the right phrase
for Wyndham's themes and his way of taking them.
Not all of his acquaintances understood the concentration of his mind on the things that really interested
him, and for those who did not he passed as a florid
and ornamental rhetorician. He need not complain :
he is in the same boat with Dr. Johnson (another
adventurer), whom every Mr. Brisk could censure for
his long words and large periods. Such lively wits
(who have been known to laugh at a Victorian gentleman saying his prayers) may be amused at the per-

oration on Ronsard here : the hope that France and
England may share in a " yet larger traffic between
their several possessions in the realms of gold." " Then
the poets of the two lands endowed with the most
ancient and glorious traditions of song, may raise again
their Hymns to Divine Beauty in conscious antiphonies
from either shore." This might be thought rather
diffuse and opulent (Tennyson's words about a peroration of his own) ; but Wyndham's belief in the Idea
of Beauty was too sincere to be afraid of the judgment
of this world, too enthusiastic for expression in tame
language.

He was at home in the sixteenth century, and that
makes the real substance of his book, though it begins
with the medieval tales of Troy and Thebes and King
Arthur, and ends with the praise of Sir Walter Scott.
The fifteenth-century French poets, Charles d'Orléans
and Villon, are an introduction to Ronsard and the
Pléiade, and all the rest belongs to the great age of
the Renaissance. How could the author escape from
the rule and worship of Urania? The heavenly Beauty,
though it was profaned by a thousand hypocritical
preachers and sonneteers, none the less informed the
spirit of some of the greatest artists. Michael Angelo
was not ashamed, writing poetry, to make confession
of his faith in the Platonic Idea of the Good ; innumerable formalists in prose and verse might make a living
out of the Platonic philosophy ; but that did not spoil
or degrade the Ideas for the artist who knew their
meaning and had proved it through his own work.
Wyndham, who had found it true in his own reading
and understanding of poetry, spoke out and used the
old language of the *Pléiade* and of Spenser where it
suited him. No more than Ronsard or Shakespeare

does he make noble abstract phrases stand in stead of definite individual figures and melodies.

Mr. Whibley, who refers to Pater's essay on Joachim du Bellay, might have named an earlier book quoted by Pater—Andrew Lang's *Ballads and Lyrics of Old France*. It is nearly half a century since this little white book appeared, and it is not yet antiquated, nor should it be forgotten. There are things in it not to be found in English elsewhere. Andrew Lang, with his strange uncertain power of divination, took Jacques Tahureau for one of his favourite poets out of that generation in France, a poet seldom named ; as he chose Gérard de Nerval later, and never gave him up. Andrew Lang carried his readers away, and there is none of them but will look for praise of Jacques Tahureau, and be disappointed not finding him along with the more famous of that company.

One defect may be noted in his Ronsard ; there are not enough quotations. There is no want of quotations in his essay on Shakespeare. It was a preface, not to a selection, but to all the poems complete (1898) ; and quotations were wanted to prove points in his criticism. It would appear that many writers have spoken of *Venus and Adonis* and *The Rape of Lucrece* without reading them. No one has read them or enjoyed them more thoroughly than Wyndham ; he took them simply, to begin with, as he always did all his authors ; then he set himself to clear away the fallacies which had stood in their light. Shakespeare's two heroic idylls appear to have suffered through unfair competition and comparison with the *Canterbury Tales* on the one hand and the *Earthly Paradise* on the other. Stories in verse may be easier

than great tragedies ; but good narrative poets are as
rare as any, and readers who look for poetical stories
find that Shakespeare's policy is not for them. Chaucer
in his most elaborate work, which is *Troilus and
Criseyde*, never lets the ornament impede the story ;
the passion and the fortunes of those two tragic come-
dians are continually in the mind of the reader, who
tells the story to himself in his own way all the time
he is following the poet. That is the secret and the
triumph of the artist in narrative, whether epic poet
or novelist. But a reader used to this mode will be
apt to complain of Shakespeare, and perhaps even to
speak disrespectfully of the Renaissance, for overload-
ing and forgetting the course of the story. The answer
to any such complaint is to read the author who is
accused of wrongdoing. George Wyndham's reading
of Shakespeare's poems is thus partly on the defensive.
But his argumentative and critical defence is unimportant when compared with the positive, direct and
unscrupulous praise which makes the defence complete.
Cavils are silenced when you see that the author means
something, in his own way, and that he has carried out
his intention. Wyndham reads Shakespeare's two
poems with intelligence, and enjoys them ; it is as
simple as that. It would be hardly worth while saying
so, only, as it happens, many good judges have not
read the poems clearly and have tried them by wrong
standards. Wyndham's criticism is almost always
praise ; ridicule and rejection may be amusing, but
the real task of criticism is to find out the good and
praise it rightly. This is what he does with *Venus and
Adonis* and *The Rape of Lucrece*. " Is not this good ? "
he asks. And if good, is it not what the poet intended ?
Then why demand from him something else ? It is not

a new problem, nor a difficult solution ; only, it had never been so clearly put with regard to Shakespeare's poems. It would give a wrong impression here if it were thought that Wyndham's preface is all mere eulogy. There is, perhaps, only too much patience bestowed on the details of the life of Shakespeare, and some want of proportion, some falling away from the masterly *ordonnance* of the *Plutarch*. But even if this be so, it is compensated by the reading of Shakespeare. The remarks on Titus Andronicus, the comparison of Ovid's alliteration and his conceits with Shakespeare's, take up very little room, but they throw light upon large tracts of poetry. As for the examination of the Sonnets, those who look for manifest subtilty and paradox will go away and say there is nothing in it. There is only the reflection of Shakespeare's poetry, only the melody of Shakespeare's most liquid verse explained by repeating it. The interpreter lets his clients hear what he himself has heard in it. The miracle of it is not impaired. Shakespeare in his poems and sonnets comes out as a master of most varied arts —sometimes with a richness of figure and decoration that almost hides the thought and argument, and again with that transparent diction, and melody which flows and eddies in utter clearness, like the wells of Thames in the Cotswolds :

> Shall I compare thee to a summer's day ?
> Thou art more lovely and more temperate—

in style the very opposite of the overloaded Renaissance ornament. They had this skill of language—not Shakespeare only, but his compeers : this also, along with fancy, conceit, hyperbole and rich language, " armoury of the invincible knights of old," belongs to Drayton and Daniel, though Shakespeare is best of all.

George Wyndham thought that his essays on Shakespeare and Plutarch might be pruned and shortened, if they were to be published as chapters in a book. But his Plutarch is better designed than his Shakespeare, and there is nothing in it that any reader (except Polonius and his friends) would wish left out when once he sees what the author is driving at. This is, first of all, a refutation of common prejudices against Plutarch, and particularly of the view that Plutarch is an eminent moralist, and therefore not good at politics on the one hand, or portraiture on the other. Wyndham, on the contrary, finds in him political sense, a coherent plan of Greek and Roman history in which the several lives take their place. Further, it is proved by examples and quotations that Plutarch is a moralist with imagination, who understands individual character and is not misled by abstractions of virtue or vice. In Plutarch's stories the personages move independently, "every man in his humour." The philosopher may know how far they are from real freedom : but as a biographer Plutarch does not reduce his heroes to moral illustrations.

Then Amyot is taken up, then North ; and Wyndham revels in the languages that he loves best, in the century that brought France and England to full mastery of prose. It is easy enough, with sufficient leisure, to compare authors and translators. Any sentence will give something to take hold of and show up. Wyndham, however diligent he may have been in this sort of study, has more to offer than curious specimens of old language, quaint travesties of the original. He admires both Amyot and North as masters of style, and it is to bring out their beauties that he compares them. The " literature of the subject " here finds little room. The much canvassed problem of North's share in the origins of Euphuism is not mentioned here—a hobby horse that " suffers not thinking on." It might have come on and done no harm. Wyndham was not the man to neglect anything that bore on his immediate subject. Most probably the trivial rhetoric of Euphues seemed unimportant and uninteresting beside the more subtle art of prose here explained. One may imagine how Mr. Henley enjoyed the whole of this discussion, thinking, no doubt, of his own great enterprise (never carried through) on the language of the English Bible. Then, to complete the argument, a reading of Shakespeare's *Roman Plays* along with North's *Lives*. Naturally this has not the scope of Mr. MacCallum's complete examination of all the ground. Perhaps, at this point, it may be remarked that in three of these essays George Wyndham took up subjects which still were waiting for fuller treatment. What he wrote is not disqualified either by Mr. MacCallum's large book on Shakespeare's *Roman Plays*, or, in the other two cases, by Gaston Paris on Villon, or by M. Jusserand on Ronsard.

The Lord Rector in his address at Edinburgh paid his audience a compliment which possibly not all of them appreciated at the time, as there was no one to tell them that he had taken more thought and given more care to the composition of his speech than any Lord Rector since Disraeli's oration at Glasgow. Disraeli on the Spirit of the Age made a more popular choice of a text, and, although he quoted Sophocles in the original Greek, made less demand on the intelli-

gence of his hearers. George Wyndham spoke about
the results of his reading, and gave his Edinburgh con-
stituents a careful description of what he had found
for himself in the Middle Ages. Mr. Whibley puts
some considerations very fairly traversing his friend's
argument. Romance did not first begin with the
French poets of Gawain and Lancelot in the twelfth
century : the *Odyssey* and the *Æneid* are full of it,
and the romantic schools of the Middle Ages drew as
much from Virgil, Ovid, and Statius as from the legend
of King Arthur. The essay on Plutarch in this volume
finds romance in the world of Greek and Roman history.
Pretty certainly, if *The Springs of Romance* had been
revised for a larger history many things would have
been expressed in a different way. As it stands, the
essay, venturous, hazardous, as the author knew it to
be, is like the rest of the book, right in what it praises,
and right in the chief historical point which it urges,
namely the difference made in the whole life of Christendom by the French romantic school of the twelfth
century. Romance is everywhere, latent or expressed,
in all ages, but there never was such a general agreement
in the Western world, such community of ideas as in
the twelfth century, through the vogue and influence
of the French authors of romance. They changed the
fashion of the world, and so thoroughly that much of
it came safe through the next great revolutions, Renaissance and Reformation. The romance of the twelfth
century survives and is strong in Ariosto and Spenser,
and though Ascham reviled the Morte d'Arthur,
Joachim du Bellay, with no less pride of Greek and
Latin learning, told the young ambitious poets of his
day not to neglect the story of Tristan.

It was a good deed to collect these chapters of

XVII

DIVINA COMMEDIA

OTHER poets have been critics, but no poet, no great artist, that ever lived has come near Dante in equal powers of imagination and analysis. There is a common opinion that the artist who shows himself acute in criticism, in explanation of technique, is probably too clever to invent and create. The skill of analysis and dissection is so different from the ways of imagination that we are apt to think them incompatible. The microscopic eye of the critic is at the other extreme from the power of the artist who sees things and shapes them in a new original way with a kind of habitual readiness like instinct in its freedom. But Dante, whatever the processes of his art may have been, shows never any disinclination to speak about them. The poems of the *Vita Nuova* are none the worse (he thinks) for the notes appended in which he describes and divides the argument, and tells where all the changes and transitions come, where a new section begins, and so on.

In the *Divina Commedia* the exact arrangement, the fine ingenious work, the minute particulars, sometimes as conceited as anything in Cowley, have given scope for commentators from Boccaccio to Tozer, none of them too precise for the poet's own mind, none too

philological for the author of the *De Vulgari Eloquentia*,
none too astronomical or too deep in physics for the
poet who spends his first hour in Heaven with Beatrice
listening to her discussion and conclusive theory of the
spots in the moon. Dante provides so much entertainment of various sorts for astronomers, historians, and
divines, that we have to be warned sometimes not to
forget he was a poet: at the same time we may be
sure that he would have valued lightly any foolish face
of praise which should neglect his science or try to
apologise for Beatrice on the moon. No one who makes
much of inspiration at the expense of knowledge,
judgment, and calculated art, need hope for any success
with Dante. While his inventive genius, the triumph
of his poetry in vision, music, and story, is as safe
beyond challenge as Homer's, yet in every line you can
trace him taking thought and making sure of every
syllable. He is as large as Homer, in every sense of
large, of *largesse*, and with all that, no device in the
art of words is too minute for him.

Dante is the first modern poet to understand the
progress of poetry, the succession of schools, the changes
of fashion in art, in painting as well as poetry. Once
Cimabue was the master, now Giotto has the cry:

> Credette Cimabue nella pintura
> Tener lo campo, ed ora ha Giotto il grido,
> Sì che la fama di colui oscura.
>   Così ha tolto l' uno all' altro Guido
> La gloria della lingua : e forse è nato
> Chi l' uno e l' altro caccerà di nido [1]—

even so Guido Cavalcanti has taken the glory of verse
from Guido Guinicelli, and who knows but another is
coming who will displace them both. Dante is aware

[1] *Purg.* xi. 94-99.

of his own place and rightful claim in the succession of poets, and none the less because he brings it forward here in the *Purgatorio* in an argument on the vanity of fame :

> Non è il mondan romore altro che un fiato
> Di vento, che or vien quinci ed or vien quindi,
> E muta nome, perchè muta lato [1]—

" the world's rumour is no more than the breath of wind that blows now this way and now that, and changes name as it changes sides."

There are two other passages in the *Purgatorio* where Dante comes back to the ancestry of Italian poetry, and his own place in the succession. Bonagiunta da Lucca, a poet of the older fashion, recognises in Dante the new poet of the sweet new style—

> " Ma di' s' io veggio qui colui che fuore
> Trasse le nuove rime, cominciando :
> *Donne, ch' avete intelletto d' Amore ?* "
> Ed io a lui : " Io mi son un che, quando
> Amor mi spira, noto, ed a quel modo
> Che ditta dentro, vo significando."
> " O frate, issa veggio," desse, " il nodo
> Che il Notaro, e Guittone, e me ritenne
> Di qua dal dolce stil nuovo ch' i' odo.
> Lo veggio ben come le vostre penne
> Diretro al dittator sen vanno strette,
> Che delle nostre certo non avvenne.
> E qual più a guardar oltre si mette,
> Non vede più dall' uno all' altro stilo " [2]—

" Art thou not he that brought out the new rhymes, beginning : Ladies who have of love intelligence " ? And I replied : " I am one who when Love inspires find melody, and as he dictates to my mind so do I give utterance." " Brother," he said, " here I see what

---

[1] *Purg.* xi. 100-102.　　[2] *Purg.* xxiv. 49-62.

hindered the Notary of Lentino, and Guittone, and me from the sweet new style that I now hear. Our pens did not like yours follow close the dictation of the Master : this is the difference between the one and the other style, and it is waste of time for a poet to seek to please otherwise than thus."

The meaning of this is that Bonagiunta with the other poets he names, Jacopo da Lentino (the Notary) and Guittone d'Arezzo, belongs to an older school less deep and true. Dante's " dolce stil nuovo " is won through sincerity and faith in the power that inspires him. I do not intend to take up again the problem of the " dolce stil nuovo " ; only to mention here Dante's sketch of the history of poetry ; an earlier, lighter, less imaginative school is followed by another order, more intent on loftier ideas. Dante is not alone in the new style, and in *Purgatorio* xxvi. he pays reverence to the father of the new poetry, Guido Guinicelli :

> il padre
> Mio, e degli altri miei miglior, che mai
> Rime d' amore usar dolci e leggiadre.[1]

Though Guido Guinicelli had been mentioned before as a poet of a bygone day whose place had been taken by a younger poet, Guido Cavalcanti, yet Dante does not think him antiquated as Bonagiunta and the Notary are. There are different ways in which poetry may grow old : the school of Bonagiunta is refuted and disqualified, so Dante would have us think, but not the poetry of Guido Guinicelli. That poet who began the right way suffers no loss from the lapse of time. Dante is free from the pedantry of those who think that the good things of past years are regularly

---

[1] *Purg.* xxvi. 97-9.

and as a matter of course disabled through the march of intellect, the discoveries of the new generation. He distinguishes ; sometimes the earlier stage of art is proved to be defective. Bonagiunta's poetry is too weak to last. Sometimes, as with Guido Guinicelli, no advance made by the younger Guido, and not the achievements of Dante himself, can take away the glory of the discoverer.

We may think perhaps that Dante was a little hard on Bonagiunta and on the Notary. He is proud of his own new style, his deeper devotion to the Master Power of poetry. He is of the same mind towards the lighter poets as Ronsard to Clément Marot. But Marot is not killed by the Pléiade ; Boileau recognises Marot's good qualities, and Bonagiunta and Jacopo da Lentino are found by Rossetti worth translating, though his own poetic mind is more akin to Guido Guinicelli and to Dante. It is not my intention, however, to go fully into the merits of these cases : what I wish to infer from Dante's expressed opinions about poetry, both in those passages of the *Purgatorio*, and in the *De Vulgari Eloquentia*, his Latin prose essay on Italian form and style, is that he was not far from the point where poetical study turns into theoretical classicism, the classical ideal in its purity and its intolerance. The pride of poetic art was no new thing ; the Provençal poets had elaborate theories of the difference between plain and fancy work in poetry ; the *trobar clus*, poetry closed, encased, hidden in difficult phrasing, was well known to Dante and he admired it : of all the Provençal poets he praises most the most difficult ; and in the *Purgatorio* it is Guido Guinicelli who points out Arnaut Daniel, him who surpassed all others as the poet of love.[1]

[1] *Purg.* xxvi. 115 ff.

If Dante admires, as he does, a poet whom most modern readers find difficult, too fond of unusual language and of artifice in verse, we may take this as a sign that he himself is capable of similar modes of art. The miracle of Dante is that with all these temptations to the most extreme sorts of learned poetry, and with no principles to restrain him, but on the contrary, all his theories leading him into the danger of over reflection, his Comedy should be more like Homer than anything else we know in the verse of Christendom.

Dante's likeness to Homer is noted by Tasso, a critic almost as curious as Dante himself in his combination of erudite regular theory and original impressions. Dante was the first modern poet to use with full consciousness of its value the epic simile, and his similes are Homeric in their fulness, clearness, and security. Clearness, *chiarezza*, is Tasso's word to translate the Greek ἐνάργεια, which in Latin he says is *evidentia*—a quality of imagination in which he finds Homer and Dante excelling other poets. A comparison of similes in Homer and Dante is a pleasant occupation. Let me quote from *Inferno* ix. and from *Iliad* xxi. and ask if they are not like minded :

> E già venia su per le torbide onde
> Un fracasso d' un suon pien di spavento,
> Per cui tremavano ambedue le sponde ;
>   Non altrimenti fatto che d' un vento
> Impetuoso per gli avversi ardori,
> Che fier la selva, e senza alcun rattento
>   Li rami schianta, abbatte, e porta fuori.
> Dinanzi polveroso va superbo,
> E fa fuggir le fiere e li pastori.
>   Gli occhi mi sciolse e disse : " Or drizza il nerbo
> Del viso su per quella schiuma antica,
> Per indi ove quel fummo è più acerbo."

Come le rane innanzi alla nimica
Biscia per l' acqua si dileguan tutte,
Fin che alla terra ciascuna s' abbica ;
   Vid 'io più di mille anime distrutte
Fuggir così dinanzi ad un che al passo
Passava Stige colle piante asciutte [1]—

" And now there came over the wan waves a crashing sound full of terror, whereat both the banks trembled : not otherwise than when a wind tearing from the cold to the heat smites upon the forest, and stays not, but breaks and beats the branches and sweeps them away : passing on with its dust exultant, driving the wild beasts and the shepherds before it. And Virgil bade me look [he had been keeping Dante's eyes shut for fear of the Gorgon], and said : ' Turn the nerve of sight over that ancient foam, there where the smoke is bitterest.' As frogs before their enemy the snake scatter all through the water till they find each a nook in the earth, even so I beheld one who came walking over the Stygian flood dryshod, and more than a thousand souls of the lost fleeing before him."

Now Homer, *Iliad* xxi. :

" As locusts before the onset of fire rise and flee to the river : the fire burns unwearied, rushing on with speed : and they skulk in the water ; so before Achilles was the flood of eddying Xanthus filled with the mingled rout of chariots and men. . . . And as before a dolphin of the sea the other fishes escape, and crowd the corners of the fair haven in fear : for verily he eats if he catches them ; so the Trojans along the course of the great river skulked under its banks." [2]

Mr. Arthur Platt some years ago in the *Journal of Philology* took the similes of Homer to see what might be made out of them with regard to the life of the poet.

[1] *Inf.* ix. 64-81.   Lines 12-16, 22-26.

One of them proves that the author lived by a tideless midland sea ; the child on the shore in Homer knocks down the castle he has built : the child who plays on the shore of the Ocean stream does nothing of the sort : he waits for the tide to swallow his building. Dante, of course, is entirely different from Homer in all his personal history, and in the crowd of local allusions,— which do not begin before the ninth canto of the *Inferno* ("Sì come ad Arli, etc.," vv. 112 ff.). But it might be amusing to take the impersonal similes, like that which I have quoted, and treat them as Mr. Platt does Homer's. For an example I might take Dante's goatherd standing propped on his staff, watching his flock as they lie ruminant in the shadow during the heat of the day in *Purgatorio* xxvii. This, like Homer's child, does not belong to the coasts of the Ocean stream, and though there is no name of an Italian hillside we can tell where to look for the goatherd. The quaintness of Homer, occasionally, is like Dante. Take for instance the man cooking a sausage in the *Odyssey* (xx. 24) : "But he, Ulysses, tossed about, like a man holding a pudding stuffed with blood and fat to a strong clear fire, who turns it to this side and that, keenly wishing to get it done (μάλα δ'ὦκα λιλαίεται ὀπτηθῆναι) ; so to this side and that Ulysses tossed, and wondered how he should lay hands on the bold suitors, one alone against so many." In disregard for conventional dignity Dante can equal this, when the thousand blessed souls in the second Heaven coming to see Dante are compared to the fish in a fishpond when they think they are to be fed, all shooting to the place :

> Come in peschiera, ch' è tranquilla e pura
> Traggon i pesci a ciò che vien di fuori
> Per modo che lo stimin lor pastura ;

Sì' vid'io ben più di mille splendori
Trarsi ver noi ; ed in ciasun s' udia :
" Ecco chi crescerà li nostri amori." [1]

Along with the similes go other sorts of description :
it does not matter how they come in. Both poets,
Homer and Dante, know equally well the life of the
two voices, mountains and the sea ; both are happy
and pitiless when they think of floods in a mountain
river. The Scottish spate in the *Brigs of Ayr*
would have pleased them both. It is nearer Dante
than Homer in its local names :

> While crashing ice, borne on the roaring speat,
> Sweeps dams, an' mills, an' brigs, a' to the gate ;
> And from Glenbuck, down to the Ratton-key,
> Auld Ayr is just one lengthen'd tumbling sea.

We think of the Archiano and the Arno in flood carrying down the body of Buonconte da Montefeltro.[2]

It is in similes and descriptions that Dante comes
nearest to the fashion of the heroic poem, as followed
by modern authors in imitation of the ancients,
Camoens, Tasso, Milton. He does not attempt the
regular epic in twelve books; that was left for Boccaccio.
Dante escaped the danger of the heroic poem, and he
has suffered some depreciation in consequence. Bembo
in the *Asolani* compares Dante's poem to a rank
unpruned vine, to a rich wheatfield infested with wild
oats and cockle. The most crushing sentence comes
from Sir William D'Avenant in his letter to Mr. Hobs
which is the preface to his *Gondibert* :

For I will not admit Ariosto, no not Du Bartas, to the
rank of heroicks, lest by so doing I should seem to make
room for Dante, Marino and others.

Salvatore Rosa in his satire on poetry is not quite as

---

[1] *Par.* v. 100-5.   [2] *Purg.* v. 115 ff.

harsh as this, but not very different in meaning when
he speaks of the world applauding Bavius and Maevius,
great asses, "arciasinoni," who have read nothing but
Dante, and yet wish to play Solomon in judging Tasso,
and put the *Morgante* higher than his *Jerusalem*—

> Applaude ai Bavi e Mevi arciasinoni,
> Che, non avendo letto altro che Dante,
> Voglion far sopra i Tassi i Salamoni,
> E con censura sciocca ed arrogante
> Al poema immortal del gran Torquato
> Di contraporre ardiscono il Morgante.

From which it would seem that the *Divina Commedia*,
like *Don Quixote*, was for some time held by superior
persons to be a vulgar book, thumbed and admired by
people incapable of the finer shades. But Dante we
know has the very highest standard of poetical style :
he explains it in the *De Vulgari Eloquentia*, and his
description in that essay of the loftiest lyrical poetry
makes no concession to vulgar taste. If some things
in the *Divina Commedia* are low, judged by the standard
of the finer shades, are we to suppose that they are
lapses, involuntary, right-hand backslidings and left-
hand fallings off from poetical true faith and righteous-
ness ? It does not seem likely : it is more probable
that Dante knew what he was about when he speaks
in the highest Heaven of cutting the coat according to
the cloth ; [1] when Beatrice uses a vulgar byword for
which Sancho would have been rebuked by his master :
" Let them scratch where the blains are " (which is a
temperate rendering of " Lascia pur grattar dov' è la
rogna " [2]—nearly the same phrase is used where it
seems more at home by the man from Navarre, the
" barattiere," in Malebolge [3]) ; and it is not a sufficient

---

[1] *Par.* xxxii. 140-1. [2] *Par.* xvii. 129. [3] *Inf.* xxii. 93.

explanation to say that Dante interpreted Comedy as a less exacting form of art, allowing freedom of language. In his poem there are no concessions to human weakness; he means it to be, and knows that it is, a divine poem, " sacro poema " [1] ; it has exacted from him the uttermost in thought and skill ; for many years it has made him lean, his whole mind has been bent to it, it is himself in the fire of all his strength, in the light of all his science ; in vision, devotion, music, never anything less than the full expression of his power. It is so great a work of art that much of it failed to touch the perception of the learned artists who followed. Michael Angelo read it truly, and he speaks of Dante as misunderstood by the unworthy ; he himself, Michael Angelo, would go with Dante into exile, equal with him in fate, might he be equal with him in such achievement:

> Di Dante dico, che mal conosciute
> Fur l' opre sue da quel popolo ingrato,
> Che solo a' iusti manca di' salute.
> Fuss' io pur lui ! c' a tal fortuna nato,
> Per l' aspro esilio suo, con la virtute,
> Dare' del mondo il più felice stato.

The depreciation and misunderstanding of which Michael Angelo speaks is what Dante has to pay for his great success and good fortune in coming too early for the common fashion of the Renaissance, and particularly too early for the regular epic poem. He might have fallen into that danger ; he was not out of the danger of critical formalism. His admiration for the very formal poet Arnaut Daniel is proof of this, if, as I think, he admired that author chiefly for his invention of the *sestina*. The *sestina* is a poetical form which there are very few to love. The merit of it

[1] *Par.* xxv. 1.

for Dante is that it is absolute, self enclosed, leaving no possibility of enlargement. The *canzone*, the solemn ode, is more elaborate with infinitely more variety; but the *canzone* has no fixed number of stanzas. The sonnet is complete in itself, but the sonnet may take in a *coda*, like one or two of Michael Angelo's, like Milton's satirical sonnet on the Forcers of Conscience. The *sestina* when complete allows nothing beyond itself: a poem of six stanzas, six lines each, six identical rhyme words repeated in each stanza so that each word in turn fills each of the six places, an epilogue of three lines, containing the six words again, two in each line. This pleased Dante because it was a microcosm, absolute like the Universe, and like the Universe returning upon itself.

The world, as Dante's mind comprehends it, is known at first as centred in the globe of earth, the heavenly spheres of the planets, the fixed stars, the primum mobile, moving round it; the highest heaven, the heaven of quiet, embracing all. But the highest heaven is not infinite space, with circumference nowhere. The circumference is the true centre, because it is the mind of God; and there, when Dante comes to it, the centre of the earth is seen to be no centre, but circumference: the external limit of reality. What we call outermost, the highest sphere, is innermost to the Beatific Vision; our earth, with its centre so called, is truly the outer region of the absolute world.

The *sestina*, a trifling monotonous poetical toy, was overvalued by Dante, because it seemed to him an image of the Universe in its completeness, a perfect round. This opinion may be challenged and disputed; if it is right, and it seems to me plausible, it shows that Dante was not free from the sort of idolatry which later, with different idols, made Renaissance literature often so sterile, so immune from freedom and originality. But Dante was happily free to invent as he thought best ; his heroic poem is not an epic according to receipt; his grand style is not prescribed in an academy; and the result is something more Homeric than any deliberate imitation of the *Iliad*.

One proof of this statement may be offered in addition to what has been said about the similes of Homer and Dante. Homer differs from his imitators in never seeming to doubt the truth of his story. Virgil cannot in the same way persuade us that he believes what he repeats, that he knows all about each one of his characters. Homer gives the impression that he could tell much more about every one ; there are pedigrees and family histories at the back of all the *Iliad*, as there are in the great Icelandic sagas. In the *Aeneid* we cannot help thinking that the author knows no more than he tells, and we do not ask for information about Gyas and Cloanthus. The Italian romances are without disguise openly, humorously, often content with names : the paladins of Charlemagne, " Avino, Avolio, Ottone e Berlingiero," [1] so often repeated are at last a familiar joke shared by the story-teller with his audience : no one thinks of taking them seriously, and " Avino Avolio " becomes a sort of nickname for a romantic puppet show. Dante of course dealing in his heroic satire with his own life, and largely with his own acquaintance, is more particular and has more credence for what he tells than any epic poet. But the fulness and definiteness of his particular references go far beyond what he has to tell about the Lapi and Bindi of Florence. This mythology is as definite as his

---

[1] *Orlando Furioso*, c. xvi. st. 17.

Italian history ; the strength of his belief is not restricted to his personal reminiscences, no touch from
Ovid's *Metamorphoses* is merely ornamental ; no matter
of fact in all his poem is given with greater force, with
more intense reality, than his vision of Fortune,[1] which
might be taken for the merest allegory if we did not
know it for the mind of Dante breaking through all his
formulas.

Allegory, mythology, what can words like these do
to explain this fresh discovery, this unchartered
reverence for a daughter of the voice of God, unknown
to the Scriptures, the Fathers, and the Schools ?
Allegory and mythology of course there is in plenty,
and any amount of recollections from books : it is here
perhaps that the ways of Milton and Dante are nearest
one another. Milton is weak in many places where
Dante is strongest : Milton in *Paradise Lost* does not
believe his own story ; his world would have seemed to
Dante as crazy as his chaos, and more uncomfortable
from its pretence of reason and religion. But when it
comes to be a matter of old stories, old poems and
romances, there is not much difference in sincerity
between Dante and Milton. Milton indeed is hampered
by his conventional duty of disbelief in false gods.
Dante has never any scruple about the Divinity of
Apollo or Minerva. But Milton sometimes forgets that
he ought to cry " Pagan ! " And in *Lycidas* old stories
come true, as they do perpetually in Dante. The
common objection to the mythology of *Lycidas* might
be urged with much greater force against the incongruous
beliefs of Dante : and all the force of objection vanishes
when a reader enters into the mind of the poet. The
absurdity of pastoral, which provoked Dr. Johnson,

[1] *Inf.* vii.

becomes truth when it is known and felt how much the Sicilian Muses meant to the two young Cambridge men : the Nymphs, Orpheus, Aeolus, and Proteus, and Panope, the river of Cambridge, the vision of the guarded mount, are all equally in the mind of Milton, equally true in imagination, and Phoebus speaks the musical words in which Milton said what he meant in the higher mood more fully than ever afterwards till he found the right words for his tragedy of *Samson*. And in *Paradise Lost* and *Paradise Regained*, however different the fashion of the story from Dante's, there is equal sincerity in the similes and illustrations ; for example, Dante and Milton both are fond of romances, and so Arthur and Charlemain find their way into the sacred poems, English and Italian, because the authors will have it so. There is nothing conventional, nothing of Gyas and Cloanthus, or " Avino Avolio " in Dante's memory of the horn of Roland and the dolorous rout,[1] now in Milton :

> Lancelot, or Pelleas, or Pellenore.[2]

They are there because the mind of the poet is there. In this mode of poetical reminiscence and allusion the *Divina Commedia* has a great advantage at the start over Milton's epics ; because it is from beginning to end the story of the author's mind and soul, and nothing that belongs to his life is irrelevant. " Mens cuiusque is est quisque," says the interpreter in Cicero's Dream, which is a forerunner of Dante's progress. Dante made his divine poem very simply with all its elaborate learning and philosophy : it is the story of what he had in his mind,

> brave translunary things,

[1] *Inf*. xxxi. 16-18.   [2] *Par. Regained*, ii. 361.

XVIII

ITALIAN ROMANCE: BOIARDO

A HUNDRED years ago Mr. William Stewart Rose published a prose summary of the *Orlando Innamorato* (Blackwood, 1823); in the same year he dedicated his translation of Ariosto (Mr. John Murray, publisher) to Sir Walter Scott of Abbotsford, Bart., " who persuaded me to resume the present work, which had been thrown aside, on the ground that such labour was its own reward."

" There is a great deal of it," said Diana Vernon, looking at Mr. Francis Osbaldistone's MS. of an earlier translation. But for Scott himself there was none too much of the stories of Orlando. Scott of course had a welcome always for anything in the shape of romance, in prose or rhyme; but his liking for the Italian poets was nothing exceptional in his day. It was not only sentimental young men like Edward Waverley and Francis Osbaldistone, but also Mr. Fox took up Italian epic and romance, Ariosto, Tasso, for amusement, as readily as he unbent his mind over Homer, Virgil, and Apollonius Rhodius; and Byron's study of the *Morgante Maggiore* went far beyond the immediate return that he got from Pulci in the way of hints and models for his comic stanzas. The old fashion of Italian reading in England has passed away ; the elegancies of Italian scholarship have given place to Dante, who makes heavier demands in some ways on his students, but leaves them no time for the lighter accomplishments of verse and prose.   The example of Milton and Mathias is seldom followed, in their writing of Italian verse ; the name of Louisa Grace is not to be found in the *Dictionary of National Biography*, though Carducci has written the praise of Luisa Grace Bartolini.   Here in the College of All Souls we may fairly claim a share in the study of Italian romance through the edition of *l'Avventuroso Ciciliano*, by Busone da Gubbio, an early historical novel in prose, edited at Florence in 1832 by Giorgio Federico Nott—the Rev. George Frederick Nott, sometime Fellow of All Souls and Prebendary of Winchester, Bampton Lecturer 1802 ; editor also of Wyatt and Surrey ; to be distinguished from his uncle, Charles Lamb's " negative Nott," a gentleman of similar likings in literature.   Italy and England were working well together about that time for right appreciation of old Italian poetry.   Ugo Foscolo wrote in the *Quarterly Review*, vol. xxi., an essay on Italian romance, taking his occasion from Whistlecraft, *The Monks and the Giants*—Frere's mock-heroic poem in the Italian style.   In 1830 Antonio Panizzi began the publication of his Boiardo and Ariosto (London, Pickering, 1830-1834), with an essay on the romantic narrative poetry of the Italians.

Matteo Maria Boiardo, Count of Scandiano, was one of the " rich men furnished with ability, living peaceably in their habitations," who have left behind them a good memorial : we may add from the context in the book of the Son of Sirach, called *Ecclesiasticus*, " such as found out musical tunes and recited verses in

writing " : which the commentary interprets as dis-
tinguishing lyric and epic verse. He was indeed of an
open and free nature. Everyone speaks well of him.
He was a country gentleman, a reading man, fond of
hunting. The picture of a stag-hunt in our University
gallery, attributed to Paolo Uccello, might do very well
as an illustration of Boiardo :

> I correnti cavalli e i cani arditi
> Che mi solean donar tanto diletto.

He was a man of business ; for the last seven years of
his life Governor of Reggio (for a year or two, in the
same period, of Modena also) under the Duke of
Ferrara. Letters of his, written earlier, show him in
correspondence with the Council of Reggio, defending
their water-supply against encroachment from the
profiteers of those days, and at the same time watchful
of his own rights. An honest man, as good as his
word.

In literature he is distinguished, with a character of
his own. His Italian poems are various : sonnets,
madrigals, *canzoni*, eclogues ; a comedy of Timon of
Athens, translated from Lucian in *terza rima* ; he wrote
Latin verse also. He translated Herodotus, Apuleius,
the Latin lives of famous men, then attributed to
Probus, now generally known as Cornelius Nepos, the
Cyropaedia of Xenophon. It is uncertain whether he
knew Greek.

The Italian scholar who discusses " Boiardo tra-
duttore " in the volume of *Studi su Matteo Maria
Boiardo*, published at Bologna in 1894, finds no proof
that he had used Laurentius Valla's Latin translation
of Herodotus. Whatever faults may be found in his
translations they cannot want interest, if it were only

as part of the life of a Lombard gentleman in the fifteenth century. There is no need to elaborate the obvious remark that his translations show how far Italy was ahead of other countries. Compare him with Lord Berners, another great translator who had tastes in common with Boiardo. Lord Berners translates Froissart and the French prose romances of Huon of Bordeaux and Arthur of Little Britain. A hundred years later than Boiardo you find the Elizabethan translation of Apuleius, and the beginning, no more than two books, of Herodotus.

Boiardo's large original poem, the *Orlando Innamorato*, was slightly damaged in popular favour when Ariosto appeared ; and much worse by the revised version of Berni, which practically cut off his original work from the libraries till Panizzi republished it. Yet the name of Boiardo was not forgotten ; where few would expect it you find, in Sorel's history of the Eastern Question, the dilettante trifler Frederick of Prussia quoting Boiardo's excellent advice to take Fortune, or Fata Morgana, by the forelock ; and applying this to opportunity in Poland. A little later in *Orlando* the moralist may have read Boiardo's illustration of the text *magna regna, magna latrocinia* ; the episode of the robber who is asked to explain himself, and answers that he only does what the great lords do :

> Rispose il malandrin : questo ch' io faccio
> Fàllo anche al mondo ciascun gran signore.

Boiardo's fame was not eclipsed by the *Orlando Furioso*. Spenser, who owes so much to Ariosto and Tasso, quotes Boiardo in the verse of the *Faerie Queene* (iv. 3. 45) : the " famous Tuscane penne " is Boiardo, not Ariosto :

Nepenthe is a drinck of soverayne grace

. . . . .

Of much more price and of more gratious powre
Is this, then that same water of Ardenne
The which Rinaldo drunck in happie howre
Described by that famous Tuscane penne.

And it is Boiardo's Angelica, not Ariosto's, who comes
so suddenly into *Paradise Regained*, reminding us where
the poet's younger feet had wandered " among those
lofty fables and romances which recount in solemn
cantos the deeds of knighthood founded by our victorious kings, and from hence held in renown over all
Christendom."   Milton in a prose essay places Ariosto
of Ferrara as high as Dante and Petrarch, " after both
these in time but equal in fame " : but it is Boiardo he
remembers in his epic verse :

> Such forces met not, nor so wide a camp,
> When Agrican with all his Northern powers
> Besieg'd Albracca, as romances tell,
> The city of Gallaphrone, from thence to win
> The fairest of her sex, Angelica,
> His daughter, sought by many prowest knights,
> Both Paynim and the peers of Charlemain.

Boiardo is not named by Spenser or Milton.   A feeble
version of three cantos was printed at London in 1598 :
" Orlando Inamorato, the three first books of that
famous noble gentleman and learned poet Mathew
Maria Boiardo, Earl of Scandiano in Lombardie.
Done into English Heroicall verse by R. T. gent."

   The name of " Matthew Bojardo " appears in Shel-
ton's *Don Quixote* (1612) in the chapter on the curate
and the barber in the library : a few pages further on
Milton may have read Don Quixote making the same
comparison as himself, and taking the same measure of
great armies : " Thou dost deceive thyself saying so,

said Don Quixote, for we shall not haunt these wayes two houres before we shall see more armed knights then were at the siege of Albraca, to conquer Angelica the faire." Gines de Pasamonte, we are told in the second part, stole Sancho's ass from under him by means of the device which Brunello used, the master thief in Boiardo, when he stole the horse of Sacripante at Albracca. It is done by propping up the saddle, loosening the girths, and withdrawing the animal while the rider keeps his seat : this trick of course requires absence or distraction of the owner's mind : Sancho was asleep, and Sacripante was thinking.

After Spenser and Milton, Peacock is the English author who has spoken with most respect of Boiardo ; many readers of *Gryll Grange* must have owed to him their first acquaintance with the Italian romantic poet, as well as the Greek poet of Panopolis. Nonnus and Boiardo are pleasantly associated, and even those who go no further will have learned something fresh about poetry from Peacock's quotations.

It is hard to describe the labyrinth of Boiardo's invention, and it cannot be recommended indiscriminately to all readers. Few have time for it, and the fashion of books of chivalry is not what it was. There may be chances still open for an heroic poem in forty-eight books, but it is not yet in sight. The *Faerie Queene*, however, is not forgotten ; to many in different generations it has seemed an inexhaustible land of romance, a world to be lost in ; and the Italian romances of Orlando and Rinaldo, Ruggiero and Bradamante, generally come to our imaginations as something like the matter of the *Faerie Queene* or the *Morte D'Arthur* —an immense rambling fairy tale. The difference is that there is nothing in Italian romance like the pathos

of Malory and his French Book, or the richer music of
Spenser. On the other hand the Italians, even in the
greatest tangle and confusion of their plots, seem always
to keep their heads, to know what they are about :
their common sense secures for their work a kind of
practical value which Spenser wants. Spenser's sage
and serious moralising is sometimes incredibly unreal :
the Italian fictions are coherent and rational in tone
and aim, however monstrous their magic may be. It
is true that in all their enchantment there is not a touch
of mystery, nothing of the Northern twilight : their
Fata Morgana has no power or spell to compare with
La Belle Dame sans Merci. There is something to
make up for that in Boiardo's command of his subject
which is not far short of Ariosto's success in composition ; the perplexities of Orlando are all in a measure
controlled from the centre. There is too much monotonous fighting, and giants and witches are too frequent;
one has to allow for what the audience demanded, and
Boiardo wrote for a gentle audience which shared the
taste and the staying power of the simple folks in the
market-places, who would never complain of repetition.
It is impossible to tell the story effectively in any
abstract : Mr. Rose certainly did not, and no one is
likely to try again on his scale. The best we can do
is to quote, as Peacock does, or refer to some of the
places where Boiardo comes out strong. He is strong,
I should say, in the siege of Albracca and all its episodes,
particularly in the appearance and exploits of the
warrior Indian queen Marfisa ; strong in the mustering
of the African forces under Agramant, the council of
the chiefs, the character of Rodomont—much greater
and more terrible than with Ariosto, fearing neither
God nor man, trusting entirely in his own might and

main.   In the humours of Astolfo, in the romantic
youth of Ruggiero, Boiardo has won successes of his
own, making ready for Ariosto.   Through all the in-
tricacies of his story and the several beauties of his
similes and other ornamental passages there is the
triumph of his style and the perpetual free and easy
demeanour of the artist who comes just at the right
time in the progress of poetry, catches the popular
fashion, the common tradition, just when it is fit for
change into something better, without loss of its native
qualities.   Boiardo's romance is the romance of the
street minstrels, ennobled, but not disguised.

Changes of fashion in literature are a proper subject
for history, which is the record of change.   But this
history with its categories and labels, its periods,
species, evolution and all, is often a weariness to poets
and lovers of poetry, who find (to quote the language
of Johnson) " particular features and discriminations
compressed and anglobated into one gross and general
idea"—the individual beauties, which alone are living
things, sacrificed to an abstract notion of things in
general.   They object to the philosophical historians
as a dismal set of pedants to whom their theories of
evolution, their enumeration of groups and schools, are
more important than the beauty of any one poem—
dunces, who lump together in one compartment in-
ventors and imitators—from Marlowe to D'Avenant,
all the Elizabethan drama, treated as a movement, an
idea.

It can be overdone, the evolution of literary species.
One remembers Brunetière tracing lyric poetry in
France, and finding it in the seventeenth century
transformed into funeral orations.   The theory seems
to imply a single substance (lyric poetry) going through

this metamorphosis, a given quantity of energy to be thus transformed. It is not easy to see what is gained for lyrics or for sermons, or how they are better understood through this explanation of their essence and life-history.

But the reader who rightly refuses to accept any excellent substitute for poetry, or to be put off with general ideas in place of a living world, is not quite right if he denies the influence of fashion, and he loses something if he is not occasionally surprised at the ways of general ideas. The life of poetry is nothing without particular poems ; but no poems are merely individual, and ideas and general forms are part of their life ; the history of schools and periods is not all pedantry.

One great occupation of scholars in medieval poetry is to make out the relation of popular minstrelsy to the art of " courtly makers," as the old language named them. The difference is found everywhere, and is everywhere consciously recognised. That is the meaning of the *Tale of Sir Thopas* : the style of the common minstrels is not good enough for the gentleman who reads the best French and Italian poetry. Here, in the *Canterbury Tales*, there is a clear-cut distinction between popular verse and accomplished art. Sometimes it is not so easy to distinguish ; and in Italy, unlike England, Germany, and France, a perfect accommodation was made between gentle and simple, through the means of the octave stanza, which came to be used invariably as the one proper sort of stave for epic and romance. Anyone in England could tell at once the difference between the Rime of Sir Thopas, or Sir Degrevant, or the good knight Sir Percyvelle, and the verse of Chaucer's *Troilus*. The verse of Sir Thopas belonged to the travelling minstrels ; the verse of

Troilus was rhyme royal, fit for the King's Quair. The verse of Sir Thopas never " throve to earl-right " till it was taken up and re-fashioned, long afterwards, for Drayton's *Nymphidia*, for Tennyson's *Lancelot and Guinevere* :

> All in the blue unclouded weather.

But in Italy things were otherwise : there was no obvious outward difference of stanza : Boccaccio the ambitious poet writing an epic in twelve books, adopted the common eight-line stanza which the public entertainers used for their rhapsodies of Aspromont and Montalban. It was originally a lyric verse of eight lines, the first four rhyming alternate, the last four in couplets. That is the scheme of the Tuscan *rispetti* which is used in popular lyric over various regions of Italy. It is itself (like the epic themes in the market-place) of noble origin : its base is the line of eleven syllables, and its movement is often as graceful as the finest art. It may possibly have a special charm for Northern readers ; one may guess this from Turgenieff's story of the *Three Meetings*, with its burden from Valdichiana :

> Passa que' colli e vieni allegramente
> Non ti curar di tanta compagnia.

The Northern fancy is easily caught by any song of over the hills. But making allowance for that, we will believe that the Tuscan *rispetti* are nearer Dante and Petrarch, in gait and style, than the best of the English ballads are to Shakespeare. The great poets do not scorn them ; when they meet these wandering songs they say " We are pilgrims too ! "

> Ma noi siam peregrin come voi siete :

which I quote from the *Purgatorio*, partly because it is very near the mode of the popular lyric.

The common stave of the *rispetti*, *strambotti*, or whatever their right name may be, is not exactly the same as *ottava rima* : the first, the *rispetto*, is a quatrain followed by two couplets ; the *ottava rima* is six lines, alternate rhyme, with a couplet following. But in early Italian octaves you often hear the echo of the original lyric verse ; the second half of the stanza is a part by itself, and it often repeats a phrase, just as the lyric *rispetti* do. This is Tuscan popular lyric :

> Ti mando a salutare per gli uccelli
> Giacchè non ho altri servi da mandare.
> Si posano sugli alberi e su i cerri,
> Non han più forza da tanto volare :
> Si posano sugli alberi di Pisa ;
> Ti mando a salutar, rosa fiorita ;
> Si posano sugli alber di Livorno ;
> Ti mando a salutar, bel viso adorno.[1]

And this is early narrative in *ottava rima* :

> Or chi potrebe contar l' alegreza
> Che fanno a Carduino in su quel' ora ?
> Se tutto il mondo fusse in gran tristeza
> Non si ricorderebe in tanta glora.
> Sentendo il nano di ciò la certeza,
> Nella città n' andò sanza dimora
> Colla donzella c' avea in conpangnia ;
> Nella città gran festa si facia.

I quote from the very pleasant old romance of *Carduino* (ed. Pio Rajna, 1873), which is an Italian variant of *Sir Libeaus*, Li Beaus Desconnus, the Fair Knight Unknown—Guinglain, son of Gawain. The relations of the different versions were explained by Gaston Paris long ago, with his usual unfailing skill. *Carduino* may be recommended to anyone who wishes to compare French, English, and Italian romance in

[1] Tigri, *Canti popolari italiani*, 1856, p. 39.

the Middle Ages—particularly as *Sir Libeaus* is one of
the neatest and most intelligible of all the books of
chivalry.

The octave became the only available verse, not only
for epic and romance, but for the popular religious
drama in Italy. Instead of the ingenious varied
measures of the English miracle plays, the Italian
Sacre Rappresentazioni use the octave stanza. This
universal reign of the octave made easy the passage
from popular to learned and ambitious poetry. The
shape and measure of the stanza have their origin in
court poetry ; Boccaccio had no reason to be ashamed
of it ; there was nothing in it to be despised or ridiculed,
as Chaucer thought there was in the minstrel's verse of
Sir Thopas. So, after Boccaccio, Luigi Pulci in Florence
composes his *Morgante* between jest and earnest, following closely the work of older minstrels ; so Boiardo
in Lombardy, a follower of Petrarch in his lyric verse,
takes the matter of popular minstrelsy, the popular
themes of Roland and the Four Sons of Aymon, and
spins his yarn according to the demands of the market-
place, yet with no derogation from his poetical art.
And so there came about the curious result that in Italy,
the first home of the Renaissance and the pride of the
new learning, there was no such sharp division between
the Middle Ages and the new style of poetry as there
was in England between popular romance and the
studied art of Chaucer. The rhymes of Roland and
the Sons of Aymon grew and throve into heroic poetry ;
not only the *Orlando Furioso* but the deliberately
classic epic of Tasso is founded on popular romance :
Tasso's first poem is an epic of *Rinaldo*, Renaud de
Montauban, son of Aymon.

In England the imagination of the Middle Ages was

not lost, but it survives in a different way. Chaucer's verse is carefully studied from foreign models ; Spenser too has to find his own verse ; while Ariosto and Tasso simply take the old tune as it comes to them. It is amusing to find in Portugal and Spain the *ottava rima*, the verse of the Italian street minstrelsy, becoming the property of ambitious poets, with the air of a superior person, putting the older native fashions on their defence against the intruder.

In France the most remarkable feature of poetry in the fifteenth century is the independent genius of Villon. Villon and Boiardo make a strange contrast. The Middle Ages were exhausted in France before the time of Villon ; the old tradition of romance had failed ; he was left to himself, with nothing to fill his mind. French epic had migrated to Italy, all for the benefit of Italian poetry.

One may be led far, in following those legends : it is not irrelevant to mention that while Boiardo was making what he could out of Roland and Reynold, in England Caxton was printing the *Life of Charles the Great*, and the right pleasant and goodly history of the *Four Sons of Aymon*. The chapbook of the *Quatre Fils Aymon* is said to be still good merchandise in France : in Italy its place is taken on the bookstalls by a less interesting romance of chivalry, *I Reali di Francia :* containing among other matters the life of Sir Bevis of Hampton, and ending with the childhood of Roland (Orlandino). It is pleasant to find, in this prose chapbook, the old heroic names, even though the old heroic verse be wanting, and the prose style not equal to Malory. The Sons of Aymon is a much better story, originally one of the best of the *chansons de geste*, and its plot not much disfigured in the prose, even of the chapbook.   The end is curious : the Italian poets (I think) have neglected it ; their Rinaldo does not end as a saint and martyr.   It is not very relevant to Boiardo, but I ask leave to mention the death of Reynold of Montauban, as told in the romance.   At the end of his days Reynold left Montauban alone in poor clothes, and walked to Cologne on the Rhine. There the great church was building, and he got work as a labourer helping the masons.   He did ten times as much as the other hodmen, and took much less in wages. This of course provoked their envy and (to speak their villainous language) he was done in as a blackleg, and his body thrown into the river.   But there the fish joined to bear him up and hold him floating against the stream ; so it was known that he was a saint, and he was enshrined as St. Reynold.

I would not leave Boiardo, " that famous noble gentleman and learned poet," without a salute to his lyric poetry : poetry which I will not now attempt to explain.   It may be read with pleasure, though it is in a convention which did not seem to promise much for lovers of novelty.   But there is never any certainty that conventions will not be renewed and made young, when the right sort of poet takes them up.   Michael Angelo in his sonnets and madrigals repeats many old devices—the Platonic Idea of the one Eternal Beauty revealed and worshipped in many forms : with Art for its servant.   We all know how dull this may be made, repeated by brisk or gloomy hypocrites ; in Michael Angelo's verse it comes as if he had discovered it for himself at the creation of the world.   Boiardo's cast of mind is not the same, but he too makes things fresh in the old forms.   It would take too long to explain, but it can easily be proved by anyone who will try.

The beauties of his lyric verse are simple and unaffected;
recollections of things seen, woven into musical tunes;
the stars of night, the morning star, the glittering of
the sea at dawn, which he takes from Dante :

> il vago tremolar de la marina
> al sol nascente lucida e tranquilla.

Boiardo's lyric poetry reminds one of Sir Philip Sidney,
who is like him in other ways, as a scholar and an
author of romance.   There is the same sort of intensity
and sincerity, the same lively pictorial effects, the same
professed scorn of rhetoric :

> Ben ho più volte nel pensier stampite
>   Parole dotte e note sì suave
>   Che assai presso giungeano a sua bellezza :
> Ma poi che l' ho leggiadramente ordite
>   Par che a ritrarle el mio parlar se inchiave
>   E la voce mi manche per dolcezza.

But all this needs time and another occasion to explain
and prove.

Boiardo made no end of the *Orlando Innamorato* ;
he broke off with Italy all fire and flame, and the
foreign invaders breaking in :

> Mentre che io canto, o Dio redentore,
> Vedo l' Italia tutta a fiamma e foco,
> Per questi Galli che con gran valore
> Vengon per disertar non so che loco :
> Però vi lascio in questo vano amore
> Di Fiordispina ardente a poco a poco ;
> Un' altra fiata, se mi fia concesso,
> Racconterovvi il tutto per espress..

His own last stanza is the best conclusion to any talk
about him : still light of heart and hopeful :

> No public and no private cares
> The free-born mind enthralling.

XIX

TASSO

I HAVE been asked to speak about something Italian,
and I gladly accept the invitation, because I have
always been fond of the language and have lately been
grieved to see it so much neglected in comparison with
its former reputation in England. It is true that
Dante is studied in England in all sorts of ways from
the minutest scholarship to the widest University
extension ; but the study of Dante is rather a different
thing from the love of Italian poetry, and we may
believe that it is sometimes taken up by those who
find in it a philosophy or a religion ; Browning has
suffered in the same way.

It was the Germans that drove out the Italian poets,
Petrarch and Tasso, from their place in the homes of
England. The encounter of the two opposing forces
is reflected in Hogg's Life of Shelley, where he describes
his first meeting with Shelley at dinner in the College
Hall. The two freshmen fell to discussing the respec-
tive merits of German and Italian poetry ; they
discovered, after Hall, that neither party knew anything
definite about either literature, but the fact that this
could be chosen as a subject of debate is significant of
the times. Werther, the Robbers and Götz of the
Iron Hand, Faust and Wilhelm Meister, the harp of

Swabia, the prophetic vehemence of Carlyle and others,
made the Italian poets look feeble and old-fashioned—
for a time. Now they are avenged in a way ; for
though the German language has kept its imposing
place in schemes and theories of education, it is more
for its historians, philologists and chemists than its
poets or romancers that it is valued now ; the romantic
treasures of Musäus, Tieck and Hoffmann, even, to a
large extent, of the great Jean Paul himself, have
turned in the usual manner of fairy gold ; and Schiller
is not nearer to the mind of the present age than Tasso
is. But though the fame of the German schools of
romance and poetry has died away and given place to
stronger voices from France, from Norway or Russia,
the mischief, as far as Italian is concerned, has been done;
the great Italian authors have never recovered the
position they held for centuries in England and lost,
or began to lose, about a hundred years ago. From
the time of Wyatt and Surrey [Chaucer, as we know,
failed to set the fashion for Italian literature in England]
to the days of Scott and Byron, the Italian poets were
a source of amusement, instruction and inspiration in
different ways for all sorts of bookish people in this
country. Young men like Waverley and young men
like Charles James Fox read Tasso and Ariosto. There
are few who have kept that taste, but since I began to
think of the subject of this discourse—in fact it was no
longer than last Sunday—I discovered that a friend of
mine had read *Gerusalemme Liberata* through in the
Christmas holidays and thought it was a good story
and in some things better than the *Aeneid*. I cannot
believe that there were many others at the same time
in the island of Britain engaged in a like pursuit : reading the *Orlando Furioso* or *Morgante* ; the fashion is

pathos—the hero fallen to rags and misery. At the same time there is much more in it than mere pathos ; if there is not heroism nor the sublimity of Dante's scorn and indignation in exile, there is at any rate the dignity of high thoughts and a fine ambition, of a " gentle spirit," to use the Italian phrase that naturally suggests itself, the " spirito gentil " of Petrarch's beautiful ode.

Torquato Tasso was the son of Bernardo, and seldom have father and son been more alike ; they had the same tastes in literature, the same simplicity of mind ; Bernardo the poet of *Amadigi* and Torquato his son the poet of the *Rinaldo* and the *Gerusalemme*, both of them thoroughly taken up with their work and their poetic ideals and the right principles of the heroic poem ; they are like two children with a toy theatre, moving about in the world of lessons and other duties, their heads full of problems about new scenery and the best way of working figures on their stage. There are few things more touching in the lives of the poets than Torquato's belief in his father and his father's epics. There is one story in particular which gives in a few lines the character of both men :

" Know therefore that my father, being at the Camp of Spain in the service of the Prince of Salerno his master, was persuaded by the chief persons of that court to make a poem out of the Romance of Amadis which in the judgment of many, and I agree with them, is the most beautiful and perhaps the most edifying of its kind. . . . Having therefore taken this advice and being thoroughly acquainted with Poetics and particularly with the doctrine of Aristotle, he studied to make a poem with unity of action, and formed his fable on the despair of Amadis through the jealousy of

Oriana, ending the poem with the battle between Lisuarte and Cildadan ; and many of the more important events before or after he told in episodes, or digressions, or what you will. This was the design, not to be bettered by any master of the art. But finally not to lose his reputation as a good courtier he surrendered that of best poet ; you shall hear how.

"He was reading some books of his poem to the Prince his master, and when he began to read the rooms were full of gentlemen listening to him ; but at the last there was none left ; from which thing he concluded that unity of action was nothing delightful in its nature, since in his art he had managed it so that nothing of the art was to blame ; wherein he was in no wise deceived. Perhaps he might have contented himself like Antimachus of Colophon who would rather have Plato on his side than all the world ; but when the Prince added his command to the common persuasion it behoved him to obey.

"But with sad heart and with a darken'd brow because he knew well that without the unity of the fable his poem lost its perfection."

Bernardo like his son had to prove the bitterness of the courtier's life ; he was a loyal servitor to the Prince of Salerno and was exiled along with him when the Prince offended the Emperor Charles V. His household was broken up ; and it had been a family that seemed made for happiness. They were unlike the people that are generally taken as representative Italians of the Renaissance, the panthers and the serpents in human form that figure in the Italian novels and the English dramas of that age. These were decent people, a true family ; there was a daughter Cornelia, older than Torquato, and it was to her that he made his way in his distempered wanderings, when he escaped from Ferrara. His mother died when he was twelve; and Tasso's first letter of those that have come down to us was written in that year to the noble lady Vittoria Colonna, asking for help and giving an account of the family fortunes: "Our father, poor old man, has nothing but us two, fortune has robbed him of his property and of the wife whom he loved like his soul." It is true to say that Tasso never forgot what was implied in these simple words.

He was at Padua with his father in 1560 when he was sixteen and there was put to study law, and like other famous poets didn't like it and wrote poetry instead. His father was easily persuaded to let him have his own way; Bernardo was himself scarcely older in taste and ideas than Torquato, and the *Rinaldo* published when Torquato was eighteen is a poem of the same class as the *Amadigi* of Bernardo Tasso. Bernardo died in 1569; Torquato by that time was well established in favour at the Court of Ferrara under the patronage of the Duke Alfonso with the friendship of the Duke's sisters Leonora and Lucrezia. The romance of Tasso's life, the story of his love for Leonora d'Este, is well known, but most probably untrue; few modern historians accept it and there is no evidence that the Duke was offended by the poet in this way; if he had it would have been easy and natural for him, as Mr. Symonds says, to remove Tasso altogether instead of taking the trouble to put him in confinement. But the evil days were still some distance ahead. After some travels to France and back again to different parts of Italy he returned to Ferrara, and there produced his pastoral drama the *Aminta* (*i.e. Amyntas*), favola boschereccia, " sylvan drama," as it is called.

This is one of the famous literary things whose fame is rather difficult for the twentieth century to appreciate. But about its reputation and its value for the whole of Europe in its own day and later there can be no doubt. The evidence is collected in the elaborate work of Ménage, one of the most learned men in France in the age of Corneille, who made a beautiful book out of the *Aminta*, with his own commentary written in Italian, part of which is made up from " authors' opinions " in which the English admirers are not represented.

The Pastoral idea has long ceased to have the influence and the inspiration that it once had, and there is no present need for Dr. Johnson's frequent charges against its vanity. But something is to be gained by trying to understand it, and that is the easier now that we have Mr. Greg's description of Pastoral Poetry and the Pastoral Drama, and it is not impossible to recover in imagination a little of the old charm of the Golden Age—O bella età dell' oro—as it appeared to the poets of the Renaissance. If the *Aminta* and the *Pastor Fido* its companion and rival are too far away and too foreign for us, we have much nearer to us the *Faithful Shepherdess* of Fletcher, which does not any longer need Beaumont's generous advocay to win applause for it. Not that either the *Faithful Shepherdess* or *Comus* can take the place of Tasso's *Aminta*. The English poems have their own beauties, but neither has the Italian melody of the lyrical passages ; to find anything like them in English one must go to the free verse of Milton *On Time* and *At a Solemn Music* where the rules of composition are purely Italian.

Tasso had been working at his epic poem ever since the completion of his *Rinaldo*, and it was finished not long after the *Aminta*. Then the troubles of its author began, with a vengeance. His sorrows came from his epic poem, and the story is one of the strangest, incomprehensible to anyone who does not know the literary manners of the revival of learning, inexhaustible by any research or historical knowledge in its mixture of pendantry and idealism, good faith and bad, a tragical absurdity.

Tasso sent out his poem in MS., asking for opinions, and he got them, all kinds of scruples, objections, advice of candid friends. He was an anxious-minded man, and melancholy in the old true sense of the word, Burton's and Ben Jonson's; and he was a learned critic, a theorist about his art. It is the plain fact in plain language, that he was worried out of his wits by the theoretical philosophy of the heroic poem. It may be questioned whether his friends or his enemies (the Florentine Academy) had most to do in bringing on his madness.

One has to try to understand the importance of literary theory in those days. It was as solemn as religion and religion was mixed up with it. We know something of it in England. Gibbon wrote an essay on the problem : Whether a catalogue of the forces sent into the field be a necessary part of an epic poem. Hume in his review of the *Epigoniad* treats the poetical work with a refreshing absence of scepticism ; in any uncertain universe the heroic poem appears to have been for him a substantial reality, to be accepted with reverence. Wilkie, the author of the *Epigoniad*, was, it is true, a fellow countryman, and we know from Dr. Johnson that the Scots are not a fair people. " Sir, the Irish are a fair people, no Irishman ever speaks well of another."

But the respect for the epic poem in England and

Scotland in the eighteenth century was nothing to its importance in the sixteenth, and Italy from the time of Dante had shown an extraordinary power of seriousness in dealing with literary questions. Tasso had shown this in his own prose writings. He began very early to discuss the doctrine of epic, and he was at it for thirty years.

Curiously, in spite of the revival of learning and the authority of the ancients there was in Italy even among the pedants a strong feeling for the national romantic poetry, and for the *Orlando Furioso*, the great, the perfect poem of that kind ; so that Tasso was hard buffeted on both sides, by the classical pedants on the one hand and the fanatics of Italian romance on the other. His epic, in theory and practice, was too romantic for the one faction and too classical for the other—who said in so many words that the only difference between epic and romance was that the romance was an amusing epic and the epic was a tiresome and unpleasant romance, and Tasso's *Gerusalemme* more tiresome than the rest. The war of ancients and moderns had begun.

There is a story of two Italian gentlemen fighting a duel about the merits of Tasso and Ariosto ; one of them was mortally wounded, and had time to confess, poor man, that he had never read the author for whose sake he was a martyr. It is like the case of Shelley and Hogg, though they were less thoroughgoing in their debate. Perhaps the story is not true, but Tasso's own story is proved in only too many pages of his own letters and essays, and his own life was lost in the controversy about the Epic Poem.

It was not all vanity, though there is much futile " expense of spirit " in the shadowy battle of the books.

It was complicated with religious troubles. Tasso, a pupil of the Jesuits, had to make his peace with those who found his epic a profane work ; he wrote with more politic irony than is customary with him, desperately sincere as he usually is, an allegory of the *Gerusalemme*, to stop the mouths of the rigid righteous. Allegories of this sort, known before to Petrarch and Boccaccio, became common hypocrisies with the epic poets, and even Pope conforms to the rule. Unfortunately (one may think) Tasso was not hypocrite enough for his own comfort or for the progress of his own poetry. The accusations went home to his heart, and poisoned him. His madness was partly religious mania, something like Cowper's ; he believed himself guilty of heresy, and spent his latest years in purifying his poem ; rewriting it without the offences in it, cutting out the beauties.

It was in the year 1577 that he first broke down in a fit of melancholy madness. He was much pitied and not unkindly treated at first, but he could not stay in Ferrara. He had the delusion that his life was threatened, that he was in danger of poison. So he went home : walking from Ferrara to Sorrento, where he came and took refuge with his sister Cornelia. But he could not stay, and for a year or two he wandered about Italy, like Bellerophon in that strange passage in the *Iliad* :

yea he wandered alone over the Aleian plain, eating his heart, shunning the track of man.

He went back to Ferrara, and there he was kept in the hospital of St. Anne from 1579 to 1585. His prison may have been described too gloomily by rhetoricians and poets, but Montaigne who came to see him there was made angry. It was worse, because the captive was more hopeless, than the prisons of Camoens and Cervantes in Portugal and Spain.

Tasso's literary intelligence, except for the religious fears that made him spoil his poem, was unaffected, and he wrote much, letters, dialogues, essays. He lived for ten years after his release. He died in Rome in the monastery of Sant' Onofrio on St. Mark's Day, 1595. He knew some time beforehand that he was near his end, and came to the monastery, as he wrote to his friend Costantini, that in the conversation of the good fathers there he might begin his conversation in heaven. In his lifetime he had met with some injustice and much unhappiness, but he does not seem to have been broken down, nor ever to have lost even in his worst days of mad suspicions and fears, the " gentle spirit " of honour. The story of Tasso is worth knowing, whatever may be the present value of the *Gerusalemme Liberata*.

Tasso's great poem has suffered in the course of time from the general depreciation of epic, from the competition of other studies. One need not try to make out that it is necessary now for everyone, though it may still be a book that no gentleman's library should be without. There is a great deal of pretence in literary monuments ; and the immortality of a poet often means not much more than a place in the library. And a foreign poet in a foreign language can never come really home in the same way as those of our own speech. But those considerations and obstacles need not prevent us from trying to understand ; there is many an author who at first seems strange, and yet afterwards by a little study can be known and understood. To understand Tasso rightly one needs first of

all leisure, and then some acquaintance with old
romances, some natural liking for the books of chivalry ;
and further a sense for the Italian rhymes and the
melody of Italian verse.

Tasso with all his learning and his literary conscience,
his reading in Aristotle and Homer, never set himself
up as a rival to Ariosto ; that was done by his enemies.
He himself, the son of Bernardo, in all his practice
before his unfortunate *inquistata* and in all his theory
to the very end made plain that he knew the beauty
of Italian romance, of the popular poetry which scholars
like Boccaccio and Ariosto had taken up before him.
He had his reward in the popular favour.

The *Gerusalemme Liberata* did not frighten people,
as many an epic poem has done, by solemn magnificence
and the authority of Aristotle ; it found its way where
the simpler romances had gone before, the rhymes of
Lancelot, and of Gawain's son, of Florio and Biancifiore,
of Morgante, of Buovo d'Antona. He was sung by
the gondoliers of Venice. (This is not a mere fable
for the tourist.)   It is one of the good things about the
Italian renaissance, that with so much absurd pomp,
so much formalism and empty verbiage, there always
remained possible an appeal to the people ; the vulgar
taste helped the Italian narrative poets, just as the
London audiences, the groundlings, the many-headed
bench, in spite of the gibes of superior persons like
Shakespeare, Ben Jonson and Beaumont, saved the
English drama from sterile magnificence, from the
classical blight.   That peril of narrow classical imitation
had threatened the Italians in the age before Tasso,
in the correct blank verse heroic poem of Trissino,
which was written on strict principles with few concessions to the vulgar. But Trissino's poem went under

like the English *Gorboduc,* and Ariosto and Tasso came out together not as competitors but allies in a triumph like that of the great Elizabethans. This at least is certain about Tasso's epic poem that with all its study and artifice and critical theory at the back of it the Italian genius is not defrauded, and the Italian audience gets its due, full measure of adventures told in musical verse.

Some critics appear to think it is spoilt by Tasso's learning. Of course it has not the freedom, the winning carelessness of Ariosto ; but Tasso knew that there could not be a second *Orlando,* he tried for something different, and he succeeded. It is a different kind of fairy story, and it gains something from its more definite plan ; the siege of Jerusalem is more important in the composition than the siege of Paris in Ariosto, and it does not in any serious way interfere with the divagations of the knights and ladies, Tancred and Rinaldo, Erminia and Clorinda. There is not in the poem the endless variety of the *Orlando Furioso,* but taking it merely as a story the reader must be hard to please who finds it too limited in its changes of scene and motive.

In thinking of Tasso's life and works together one cannot but be struck by his sincerity as an artist, and his thorough devotion to his proper business, when his temperament and his misfortunes might seem enough to distract him and to spoil his skill. He is like Petrarch in many ways, like Rousseau in many, sensitive, ill at ease in the world. But his poetical mind is kept at work independent of his own private griefs. In his poetry and a large part of his prose he is impersonal, not turning his sorrows into literature, but freely and frankly concerned with his poetical building, with problems of construction, proportion, ornament and so forth. He is taken out of himself by his romance of adventure, and though in his biography he may appear like a mere Man of Feeling, a Bel Tenebroso, his poetic work is on a large and generous scale ; in spite of the Jesuits and the Counter Reformation and the decline of Italy he has still the Italian gift of construction and invention, and his place as an artist is near the untroubled and lighthearted poets, Boccaccio and Ariosto. He is different from them, but far more different from the plaintive authors. Tasso complained in his letters, but when he turned to his poetical task he lost himself in the enchanted forest and in the golden age.

Shortly after Tasso's death Thomas Churchyard published his *Praise of Poetrie* and added a note in the margin : " Torquato Tasso an Italian knight and poet laureat who departed from oblivion to immortalitie this last Aprill 1595, whose memorie shall never vanish."

Whatever one may think of literary fame, it is surely something for a poet to be thus spoken of, and thus to make friends for himself, in countries not his own.

XX

MOLIÈRE

To begin with, let the Devil's Advocate have his say.
Molière's enemies provide him with arguments;
Molière's best friend among the poets, Boileau, admits
some of their charges, particularly that of clowning
and buffoonery :

> Etudiez la Cour et connoissez la Ville.
> L'une et l'autre est toujours en modèles fertile.
> C'est par là que Molière, illustrant ses écrits
> Peut-estre de son Art eust remporté le prix,
> Si moins ami du peuple en ses doctes peintures
> Il n'eust point fait souvent grimacer ses figures ;
> Quitté, pour le bouffon, l'agréable et le fin
> Et sans honte à Terence allié Tabarin.
> Dans ce sac ridicule où Scapin s'enveloppe
> Je ne reconnois plus l'Autheur du Misanthrope.

Could he have said much worse about Shakespeare ?
Sans honte ! It is not a charge that can be lightly
evaded, and it is not far-fetched or hypercritical. It
is there all the time, and the English reader need not
be primed with Meredith's Essay on Comedy in order
to see the difference between Scapin and the Misanthrope. Is it worth while, when Don Juan is on the
scene, to get a laugh out of the blow which is meant
for Pierrot and lands on Sganarelle ? Not even the

Misanthrope is safe : the scene with Alceste's stupid
servant at the end of the fourth act is noted by the
corrector as rather too elementary for the finest of all
comedies in the world.

The finest ? Yes ; and so fascinating that true believers, who of course are true lovers, will swear, as
they follow it, that it is the only play in the world—
here at last the quintessence, the eternal Idea, not in
abstraction, but full of the life and movement of pure
comedy, nothing omitted, nothing lost, nothing left
over for other comic poets to attempt. This frame of
mind, which is worship, may of course be misunderstood ; it is going too far, says the sober critic. After
all, there are other plays in the world, and Congreve's
Millamant is not discountenanced in comparison with
Molière's Célimène. But to the true believers this is
irrelevant : they have found in the Misanthrope the
end of their quest for the very essence of comedy ;
here they are at home, triumphant. And here, naturally, the noise of the adversary is silenced—his censures
and complaints not refuted, simply ignored. *Sans
honte* ! There are many possible answers to this reproach—*e.g.* Mrs. Carlyle's favourite story of the
Feckless Man's repartee to the pompous pitying Bailie,
" Be wae for yoursel' ! " But there is no need, though
good defence may be set up against the detractors of
Molière, and though we may think that Boileau, his
friend, is willing to concede too much to those who cry
" Farceur ! "

" Aux farces pour jamais le théâtre est reduit "—the
real answer is the presence of the Misanthrope : there
the detraction dies away.

Molière in his critical remarks on his challengers says
many things very quietly and shortly that sum up

and dispose of long, large, and tedious controversies. Thus on the dramatic unities (in the *Critique de l'Ecole des Femmes*) : " These are easy notes made by good sense to secure the pleasant effect of the play, and good sense is capable of the same at any time without recourse to Horace or Aristotle. *Je voudrois bien savoir si la grande règle de toutes les règles n'est pas de plaire.*" The result of this on the Abbé d'Aubignac and other patrons of the unities is like the simple speech in *The Emperor's New Clothes* : " The Emperor has nothing on." Hear what the innocent child says !

But there is another saying of Dorante in the same piece which is incalculably more significant. The unities, after all, never really troubled anyone worth protecting ; Corneille's policy towards them is not much different from the words of Dorante ; he treats them as respectable advice to working playwrights ; and no sensible reader of Racine ever found him suffering from constraint. It is another matter, a fresh discovery, when Dorante explains that comedy is more difficult than tragedy : " et c'est une étrange entreprise que celle de faire rire les honnêtes gens." Nothing more true had been said since the early morning hour after Plato's Symposium, when Socrates was heard explaining to Aristophanes and Agathon that tragedy and comedy were proper work for one and the same poet.

Matthew Arnold, it is true, in his essay on the French Play in London (when the Comédie-Française came here in 1879), thinks that Molière ought to have been a tragic poet, and that he was put off by the weakness of French tragic verse. ⸗ The critic, with his favourite device of quotation, has no difficulty in contrasting the effect of the French tragic Alexandrine with that of Shakespeare's blank verse, or in proving that the rhythms and rhymes of *Hernani* leave him cold. It may be admitted that Molière's verse in heroic drama—that is, in *Don Garcie de Navarre*—makes little attempt to do better than the ordinary conventional style, and does not scruple to repeat " vos divins appas " and similar customary phrases, which make one think of the notary's eloquence in a later most admirable French comedy : " Daignez, Mademoiselle, corroborer mes espoirs ! " But Matthew Arnold's objection to French verse leads him too far when he finds *Tartuffe* and the *Misanthrope* actually suffering from their burden of rhyme. " The freshness and power of Molière are best felt when he uses prose, in pieces such as the *Avare* or the *Fourberies de Scapin* or *George Dandin*." The freshness and power of Molière's prose who would deny ? But it is going too far to find his genius better expressed in *L'Avare* or in *George Dandin* than in the two great rhyming comedies ; to find in the verse of Alceste and Célimène constraint and artifice. M. Rigal is surely more plausible when he detects in Racine the pupil of Molière, using for tragedy the natural easy mode of dialogue which is the poetry of Molière. There is no need, for the present, to say more on this point : what is really important is that Molière did not think less highly of his dramas because they were not tragical ; that he saw and appraised truly the right task of the comic poet. He knew something about tragedy, and Racine's bad behaviour (taking his plays away from the company of the Palais Royal) did not prevent Molière from seeing the distinction of Racine. But success in tragedy is not so rare as in comedy ; he feels that, and says so ; it is what is felt, whether said or not, by every follower of the Comic Muse. Meredith's essay on Comedy is a proof of this. No essay on tragedy is compelled to go far and wide to hunt for tragedies ; they crowd before the mind. Comedy in Meredith's essay is an elusive goddess, an idea seldom caught, seldom realised or made obvious on the stage. This is not to be set down as Meredith's wilfulness or peculiar conceit : is it not universally felt how very singular and rare is the right sort of comedy ? When not even the fine art of Goldsmith is quite good enough (so they say) " producing an elegant farce for a comedy " ; when of Congreve's few plays only *The Way of the World* is allowed to be absolutely good. It is not that the lovers of comedy are hard to please : contrariwise, they find true comedy everywhere—in fragments and patches and medleys. What they do not find, or hardly, is the perfect work, where the Muse herself conducts the orchestra, and nothing is flat, superfluous, or grating. The *Misanthrope*—some would add *Tartuffe*, and some *Les Femmes Savantes*, but the *Misanthrope* surely—has this place. Here is what is meant by comedy.

The persons are few, but no one notices this as a defect or a lowering of vitality. There are enough for the whole world of good society to be represented there. It is the comedy of good manners, like not so very many : not like *Tartuffe*, or *L'Ecole des Femmes*, or *L'Avare*. One other play of Molière's, *Les Femmes Savantes*, keeps to the true world : without are *bourgeois* and peasants. But *Les Femmes Savantes* is the play of good manners in a different sense from the *Misanthrope* : it is narrower in scope, being more definitely satirical and depending on " humours " more occasional and transitory than the eternal contradiction, the immortal harmony of Alceste and Célimène. The scene of Trissotin and Vadius is all very well in its way, but it is rather mechanical and caricatural : it is not out of place in *Les Femmes Savantes*, though that play, in the main, is more subtle than this scene ; but there is no room in the *Misanthrope* for any such exhibition.   In the *Misanthrope*, it is true, the sonnet of Oronte belongs to the world of *Les Précieuses* and of *Les Femmes Savantes*, but it is not introduced to show up the faults of fashionable taste : that is a secondary thing ; its real purpose is to bring out Alceste's uncompromising sincerity.   We are gainers by the way in hearing the lovely old verse of Alceste's ballad :

> J'aime mieux ma mie, au gué !
> J'aime mieux ma mie.

But the theatrical value of this lies in Alceste's refusal to be conventionally polite, and in his disgust at Philinte's conventional compliments.

The characters in the *Misanthrope*, as usual in comedy (and not infrequently in real life also), fall into contrasting pairs—Alceste and Célimène, Alceste and Philinte, Célimène and Arsinoé.   Philinte, the good-natured, easy-going man of the world, has to argue with his friend's stubborn principles to prove that truth is not always convenient.   Arsinoé, a very valuable person, a prude in the old as well as the later sense of the word, well deserving her place in the comedy, puts out her cold malignity against the more lively and brighter mischief of the spirit of Célimène.   Part of the play, indeed most of it, is in the old fashion of debates and contentions—the mode from which, as Mr. Neil showed us in his edition of the *Knights*, all comedy is descended. Now contrasts and debates on the stage are dangerous ; they may look too much like got up things, not imaginative, but merely calculated contrasts.   The way to cure this is to use imagination to fill up the abstract outlines. And there is another way, well understood by Molière and nowhere more excellently employed than here, and that is to let the surrounding world, the fashion of life common to all the characters, have its right proportion in the story. Atmosphere counts for as much in the *Misanthrope* as in the "Meniñas" of Velasquez: the people on the stage are not, as many of the Elizabethan *dramatis personæ* are, hard-shelled individual atoms of humanity, moving in worlds unrealised, without any visible means of subsistence. The fashion of the age is one of the antagonists of Alceste, but it is much more than an object to be railed at for complacent and undiscriminating flattery. It is much more than that, and more than Alceste recognises. If he himself were not in that world, living as part of it along with Célimène, Philinte, Oronte, Arsinoé, and a few marquises, his proud soul would be nothing to us; and it is Molière's great success that he has kept this world alive, along with and through his characters.

Are the friends of Molière to be judged according as they judge Célimène? It is a very delicate question, and indeed it must not be pressed. The facts of the case are considerably against the lady; she is, if not perfidious, at any rate not scrupulously sincere, and she speaks with a cruel tongue. Are we to accept the obvious judgment, and congratulate Alceste on being well rid of her? Possibly not.

The historians of Molière tell us that the comedy of Alceste and Célimène followed the heroic comedy of *Don Garcie de Navarre*, and used over again some of the drama of jealousy that had failed to impress the public in its original shape. *Don Garcie* undoubtedly was a failure, and as a failure it is often allowed to

remain unnoticed. But there are some strong scenes
in it, and they have their bearing on the *Misanthrope*.
Don Garcie is not Alceste ; he is simply the humour of
jealousy dressed up for an heroic Spanish play ; with
just enough human life to serve for a contrast to the
noble lady Done Elvire. Elvire in the heroic comedy
is not a counterpart of Célimène, except that she has
a half reasonable man to deal with : Elvire is much
less amusing than Célimène, being no more than true
heart and good sense. But in her treatment of
Don Garcie, since the problem is not unlike what
Célimène has to face, we can to some extent make out
what Molière had at the back of his mind. He does not
tell us everything about Célimène, and the partisans of
that lady may be justified in believing that she is worth
fighting for. And it may be said here that generally
those who refuse to take the ordinary view of Beatrix
Esmond will be found, with as much wisdom or the
want of it, on the side of Célimène. Done Elvire gives
them some encouragement. She has to talk to a man,
Don Garcie, who is jealous perpetually and on all sorts
of occasions : she explains to him that it will not do,
most admirably ; and, contrary to the usual practice
of elegant females in drama, she does not take the first
opportunity of misunderstanding her lover, nor even
the last occasion, when she might have broken with
him for ever and incurred no blame. What would she
have said if Don Garcie had been of the same mind as
Alceste ? Clearly she would have told him a truth or
two, plainly but with no bitterness ; she would not
have let him go ; neither would she have accepted his
lodge in a wilderness as a feasible scheme of a happy
life. She would have seen the vanity of the creature,
have felt that his emulation of the noble savage was

really selfish, a touch of the egoist ; and since Alceste, though suffering from " the distempered devil of self," is a right sort of man, he would have come round. Molière, it is proved, had not forgotten Don Garcie when he wrote the *Misanthrope* ; if Célimène at the end does not talk like Done Elvire, it is not that Molière thinks she has no case to defend. What Alceste exacts from his wife to be is more than Done Elvire would have yielded, we are sure of ; and that being so, we refuse to think the worse of Célimène on account of Alceste's indignation.

The English (" tardy, apish nation " though they may be) need not be altogether discontented when they review their transactions with Molière. Not everything is in all respects to their credit : the " Dunciad " keeps " the frippery of crucified Molière " among the property of the Dunces, and Wycherley's intromissions with the *Ecole des Femmes* and the *Misanthrope* are held to be regrettable. But England, owing, it is said, a good deal to Saint-Evremond's conversation with his English friends during his long compulsory residence here, was quick to discover and enjoy Molière. Molière need not be ashamed of his strongest English advocate, though the name of him be John Dennis. John Dennis was one of the first Englishmen to see the Alps " with a delightful Horrour, a terrible Joy," and one of the first to praise Molière :

For *Molière's* Characters in his Tartuffe are Masterpieces, mark'd, distinguish'd, glowing, bold, touch'd with a fine yet daring Hand ; all of them stamp'd with a double Stamp, the one from Art and the other from Nature : No Phantoms, but Real Persons, such as Nature produces in all Ages, and Custom fashions in ours. His Dialogue, too, is lively, graceful, easie, strong, adapted to the Occasion, adapted to the Characters. In short 'tis by this Comedy and by the is not commonly understood in England that the French laws of drama, the unities and similar things, did not begin to be really important till twenty years after the death of Shakespeare, and that Molière, with his travelling company and his very varied stock of theatrical tricks—Johannes Baptista Factotum—was not very far removed from Thespis (or Lope de Rueda) and his cart; really nearer the elementary beginnings of drama than Shakespeare when he came to town. The " Roman Comique " of Scarron is contemporary evidence : it may not have been taken direct from Molière's story, but it shows what the life was like : very admirable it is, and one of the best of the vaga-bond romances, though this is not the place to pay Scarron his due. The series of Molière's published works begins towards the end of his wandering years with *L'Etourdi* (acted at Lyons) and *Le Dépit Amoureux* (Béziers) : then Molière is established in Paris (1658 ; at the Palais Royal, 1660), and one might expect him thenceforth to have at least as much freedom as Shakespeare had when once he was fairly started. Shakespeare occasionally works to order : let us accept the story of Queen Elizabeth and *The Merry Wives of Windsor*, and repeat the origin of *Henry VIII.* in the manager's demand for a spectacular play. But usually Shakespeare seems to have been left free to choose his subjects and vary his methods as he thought fit. Molière has very little freedom : he is hindered in *Tartuffe*, an invention of his own ; he is hindered in *Don Juan*, which was anyone's subject, as hackneyed as Punch and Judy. He is dependent on the Court, and is called on for *comédies-ballets* ; he has to please the parterre, and he gives them (not all grudging) the thumpings of Sganarelle and the mockery of Medicine.

Terence is translated to Tabarin (the zany of a mountebank), as Boileau complained ; the *Phormio* of Terence to the *Fourberies de Scapin*. And this near the end, close upon *Les Femmes Savantes*. To the last of his days, and he died in the *Malade Imaginaire*, he kept the old talent for all the fun of the fair, and with all his irritability and nervous ill-temper he never seems to have found anything wrong in it, anything degrading in a change from high to low comedy. He had his great disappointments : not to speak of the *tracasseries* about *Tartuffe* and the *Festin de Pierre*, he must have been hurt at the failure of *Don Garcie de Navarre*, at the poor success of the *Misanthrope*. But does he ever complain of anything that is required of him for the King's entertainment ? Never, except incidentally when he has not enough time to invent, compose, rehearse, and stage what is wanted. Nor is there want of spirit in the compulsory pieces. *Les Fâcheux* is not a play ; it is a hurried set of odd characters, satire rather than comedy. Nothing in Molière is livelier, though you may hesitate whether the greatest and therefore the most amusing bore is the hunting man or the gentleman who insists on your hearing his hand at piquet, all of it, to the end :

> Et par un six de cœur je me suis vu capot.

The French stage in the House of Molière has never discouraged the more obvious sort of comedy, and it is really part of the spirit of Molière that he should have agreed with the groundlings in their easy laughter, as well as with the quality in their finer shades.

" Courage, Molière ! voilà la bonne comédie ! " That was the voice of the people, they say, after *Les Précieuses Ridicules*. It was a good opinion, though